James Hinton

Philosophy and Religion

James Hinton

Philosophy and Religion

ISBN/EAN: 9783337068318

Printed in Europe, USA, Canada, Australia, Japan

Cover: Foto ©Thomas Meinert / pixelio.de

More available books at **www.hansebooks.com**

PHILOSOPHY AND RELIGION

SELECTIONS FROM THE MANUSCRIPTS

OF THE LATE

JAMES HINTON

EDITED BY

CAROLINE HADDON

LONDON
KEGAN PAUL, TRENCH & CO., 1, PATERNOSTER SQUARE
1881

[*The rights of translation and of reproduction are reserved.*]

EDITOR'S PREFACE.

THE anomalous literary form of this book requires a few words of explanation. Its contents can be classified neither under the head of Sermons, Essays, Diary nor Table Talk, although they partake by turns of the nature of all these.

The readers of James Hinton's *Life and Letters* will remember that from the time he began his career as a philosophical thinker he was accustomed to write down every day the ideas that presented themselves to him. Wherever he might be—in the street, in society, at a concert, in church—he would jot down memoranda of the thoughts that struck him, and these he would write out clearly in the evening. This habit was first begun as a necessity of his mental life; he could not, he said, push on to new discoveries unless he thus disencumbered his mind of its burden. Afterwards he pursued the practice with a more distinct conviction of the usefulness of such a record of the process of the intellectual life as was thus afforded. Owing to the peculiar nature of his thinking, no mind could furnish a more admirable field for such observations. For the more the mental operations resemble the unconscious animal functions, the more do they lend themselves to scientific observation. No doubt there is a thought life in humanity, whose laws, if we could trace them out, are as invariable as all other laws of nature, but it is not generally possible to observe this life in the individual, in whom self-consciousness, arbitrary determination, or a timid conventionality, interferes with the freedom of the mental operations. Still more rare is a mind that can register its own operations without disturbing their spontaneity, or can commit to writing the utterance of tender and passionate emotion without rendering the fountain of feeling turbid and impure. But it is this that James Hinton has done in four large volumes of printed MSS. and an equal mass of written pages.

It is a wealth which his executors feel as a burden of responsibility as long as it is practically locked up from the public. The printed volumes have been placed in the British Museum, and they may be purchased; but their voluminous nature prevents any, save the few, from exploring them, and many gems of thought and expression are thus hidden. At the request of numerous lovers of James Hinton's writings, I have attempted to extract some of these. As the MSS. follow no order except that of time, and are as promiscuous as the entries in a diary, the arrangement of them was not an easy task, and it was rendered still more difficult by the habitual parallelism of James Hinton's thinking. He always saw one thing in and through another. Regarding matter and mind as the phenomena of Spirit, how could he avoid speaking of the one in terms of the other? "Every man who tells us anything worth knowing tells us *one* thing," he says somewhere; and this is eminently true of himself. Passion controlled, or motion resisted, is the one thing he sees in the moral as in the material world: this is holiness; this, too, is physical life. How can they be kept apart? Everywhere, in the life of the individual body and mind, and in the larger life of humanity, he beholds this double process, nutrition and function, which constitutes the vibration of Life. It is by this that truth is evolved, and that the moral development of the race is effected. To one not familiar with these large generalizations, the symbolic language used for brevity by Mr. Hinton is sometimes enigmatical. He will condense into a single expression a whole series of analogies previously worked out and habitually present to his mind. This kind of shorthand wants deciphering, and in the Preface to the original volumes which follows this, will be found explanations of the chief terms used with special meanings.

It will be readily understood that this altruistic method of James Hinton's thinking made it difficult to classify a series of extracts under any one title. There are many passages which might be equally called metaphysical, physiological, ethical or religious. From his metaphysics the translation to ethics is easy and inevitable. The central idea of the former is that the "self" is a defect, a "not," or minus quantity: by this conception he transforms the whole field of experience; it becomes a key in his hand to unlock some of the most intricate mental problems. But removed from that abstract region into the sphere of practical ethics, this truth becomes the very principle of Love. For if the self be a deadness, a negation, self-sacrifice can be nothing but an entering into Life, and all pain, regarded as the instrument and means of sacrifice, changes its character and reveals itself as good. Evil to the self cannot but be good to that Being of which self is the negation. The bearing of this principle upon the conduct of life is obvious. Its application is the very "secret of Jesus," the easy yoke that makes the burden light, the conquest of ills by self-renunciation, humility, and trust. Thus the classification of these selections was rendered difficult by the very characteristic of Mr. Hinton's thinking which gives his work its chief value, that complete interpenetration of heart and intellect which harmonized all his conceptions, and made them converge, as it were, into one focus.

I must disclaim, on behalf of this book, any attempt to set forth a coherent or complete account of the author's metaphysical and ethical system. It may, rather, be looked upon as presenting a transcript of his table talk, bringing back the image of the man as he appeared to those who lived in daily converse with him. James Hinton was, too, by the nature of his genius, emphatically a *seer*, not a constructor of systems. He simply took the conception, to which he gave the name of Actualism, and flashing it like a torch upon the various dark problems of life and mind, revealed everywhere glimpses of order and beauty. He offers no other proof than this: "that which doth make manifest is light." That much remained still obscure no one was more aware than himself. "I have not seen that yet," he would frequently say; and it filled him with an amazement—not of admiration—to find most people ready with a "view" of every subject. He used to say that wherein he differed most from other men was in knowing the "feel" of ignorance.

I must call attention to the fact that these extracts are from the earlier series of MSS., and represent the growth of the writer's thoughts from 1856 to about 1861. This early date should be borne in mind, because many things in these papers may seem at variance with the later utterances of the writer. No man was ever more indifferent to the charge of inconsistency; not from any disregard of accuracy, still less of allegiance to principles, but because he viewed all thought as a life, the imperfect stages of which must seem to contradict one another until surveyed in their completeness. That a statement was true was no reason why it should not be denied; indeed that process was needful to its fuller re-affirmation. He was therefore most tolerant of "deniers," and held them to be eminently useful; whilst that anyone should rest contented in a negative stage indicated to him a curious sort of paralysis of the mental life. He had, he said, but one advice to learners in the art of thinking: Go on. This habit of his mind should be remembered in reading the religious passages, when his language is sometimes hardly to be distinguished from the crudities of pulpit theology. Those who are accustomed to his phraseology know that he often used theology as the allegorical presentation of philosophy. Illustrations of this will be found in the following pages.

I have not, therefore, altogether discarded such passages. To have done so would have been to lose something of the freshness and force with which these thoughts were originally presented, and also of the interest which attaches to them as anticipations of truths afterwards more completely attained. He himself called these anticipations "affirmations of the moral sense," and knew that they could not be held permanently in that form: other intellectual elements would come in and demand recognition, to the temporary exclusion of the truth first discerned. But it was his delight to trace how these suppressed affirmations were restored with fuller evidence at a subsequent stage; and it was this that induced him, on revising the MSS., to leave untouched some of those crude expressions.

It is for their suggestiveness that these "thoughts" will be chiefly valued. They must not be compared with the polished sentences of *pensée* writers such as Joubert or Novalis. They might rather be called "chips," fragments from the workshop of a great builder.

The important later series of MSS. have not been used in the preparation of this volume. They are chiefly concerned with working out the position which Mr. Hinton latterly adopted in regard to some questions in ethics. To selections from these writings, to which he himself attached greater value than to any other part of his work, I propose to devote a subsequent volume.

CAROLINE HADDON.

AUTHOR'S PREFACE.

THIS volume contains a transcript, unaltered, except by omissions and by verbal corrections, of papers written at various intervals, simply as a private record of my thoughts. They embrace subjects of many kinds, often having no special connection, save that they were regarded from a common point of view, and were felt to throw on each other a mutual light. To render them intelligible, a few things should be stated.

These papers are not to be assumed to represent my present opinions. They are not a statement of my thoughts, but a history of them, and present, not the results, but the process. Necessarily, therefore, they contain that which I now think erroneous or partial. Here and there I have indicated this by a brief remark, but on the whole I have treated the papers as documents merely, and not as subjects for criticism or statements for revision. I have, indeed, specially sought not to exclude my errors, wherever they seemed to me to have any vital connection with the progress of my ideas, because the chief value which I attach to the papers is that of being an exact transcript of a process that has taken place quite independently of any volition of mine, and the record of which may perhaps have the same interest that Science finds in every natural event, quite apart from its intrinsic importance.

I take, however, this opportunity to explain a few terms which occur in meanings other than their customary ones.

The terms *nutrition* and *function* I have adopted from physiology, and applied to the mental and moral life of man. They mean always the production of a *tension*, and its ceasing; with this idea also implied, that the tension is produced in an "organization," that is, under conditions whereby the ceasing of the tension produced definite results, or a "function." For example: the process of a *reductio ad absurdum*, with its impossible consequences enforced by sound logic, and ending in a correction of the premiss, is a mental "nutrition," ending in a "function;" the tension against reason is the nutrition. The change of basis, in which the tension ceases, is the function. So too in the cases in which a false thought of right enforces a false duty, making a "tension" against the moral reason, which ceases with a truer apprehension of the duty: here is a *moral* nutrition and a function.

The words *theory* and *interpretation* are used in a sense precisely corresponding. Theory means that which is imposed on us as true while there is an error in the basis of our thought; interpretation, the rectifying of the basis.

The word *polarity* has been used rather in unusual

Author's Preface.

connections than with unusual meaning. It denotes nothing more than an oppositeness in two things, which implies in them a special tendency to union. The positive and negative electricities are examples of polar opposites.

Continuous and *transitive vibrations* are sufficiently explained by the context. The motion of a pendulum is a continuous vibration, the upward motion being of the same form as the downward; a body falling into water, and making the water rise, is a transitive vibration; the upward motion, though equivalent to the downward, being changed in form.

One new word I have introduced, which I would prefer to have omitted if it had not been too much interwoven with the thoughts—the word *actualism*. This term I gave, for convenience, to the general conception I had formed: it is parallel to idealism, materialism, positiveism, &c., and was adopted to express the idea that all existence is truly active or spiritual, as opposed to inert or dead.

As I have been re-perusing these writings, I have grown more and more conscious how far my words have often been from conveying my whole meaning; how my very thought, indeed, has changed and grown beneath my hands, and from being what seemed like a clear perception, has become only a suggestion of far distant things. I have felt this especially in relation to God and Nature. To me, Nature means God's action towards me and towards man; and it is so much, and grows to me perpetually so much more, and so joins itself with

Revelation, and becomes one with all that I have most prized in that, that all seems to come into it, and I cannot draw a line; nor can I even try. But I know this is no end—my eyes are dazzled; others will judge for me.

To any reader who has felt interest enough to extend his glances at these papers even to their end, let me say that I hope he has felt this about them, that with whatever weaknesses and errors and waste of time and thought they are mixed, yet there is in them some sign of the opening of a road into farther truths. This is all they were wished to afford.

JAMES HINTON.

CONTENTS.

I.

METAPHYSICS.

THE nature of the world—The hypothesis of matter—The universe is God's action perceived as motion—Nature is action—Nature is one with man—Berkeley's error—The mind is not more real than the external world—The laws of Nature are given by man—The work of Science is to harmonise our perceptions with our conceptions—Can we know the fact of the world?—How come we to perceive a physical world?—Wherever sin is, matter is—The law of cause and effect is a form of thought—God's act is not the cause but the fact of the world—Granting illusion, all mysteries are removed—The error of regarding this as an imperfect physical world—The mental is physical—Things are forms of the spiritual—Science now is too abstract—The error of "inherent tendencies," etc.—Nature is a process felt as matter—Metaphysics is a Mathematics—The world is the symbol of an unknown quantity—Matter = x—Science, like Mathematics, exists for the sake of the unknown quantity—The point, that is, absence of matter, is the only infinite, and the symbol of God—The molecule is in reality a point—Chemistry and Physics correspond with Mathematics—Metaphysics and Science must be used together—What will make Philosophy popular?—The tendency of Positivism—The life of Metaphysics 1

II.

NATURE KNOWN BY THE MORAL EMOTIONS.

Man's response to right—The actual is known by the conjoint use of sense, intellect and moral being—Man fell by the conscience—Men really judge by their feelings—The evil of thinking that God acts for results—Mysticism is allied to Science—The Mystics are interpreters—The intellect attains freedom by subjection to the moral sense—The physical is the moral—Nature is Holiness—Nature is man's bride—Nature is "the hands of the living God"—We must recognise negation of Being—Love of God is the love of all things—The world as a work of genius—The organic is not the highest in Nature—The future Science—Nature's secrets are won by sympathy—Evil of the doctrine of special creations—"Design" is a necessary consequence of the assumption of matter—Science is done for love—To be natural is to love—Nature is perfectly beautiful, therefore ideal beauty is less perfect—Nature is God's ideal—All mental life is the representation of Nature—To account for error is to show it beautiful—Evil is nutrition—Painting recalls to us the spiritual fact of Nature—The function of Art is to reveal the holiness of Nature—Art will advance as Science has—The future of the world 52

III.

MENTAL PHYSIOLOGY.

Moral and emotional facts stand on the same basis as physical facts—False perceptions are the condition of mental life—Nature is always first misunderstood—There is no method for discovery—The relation of logic to imagination—The place of those who want logic—The significance of paradox—Sleep in mental life—Breathing in mental life—Genius and talent—Talent is nutrition, genius function—Man's mind is female, woman's male—How genius and talent are affected by paradox—Genius is common sense—Mental life arises from failure—Men are parts of a whole—May genius be found common?—In humanity, as in genius, there is no design—Nutrition and function are the life in thinking—Submission to the thought of others is disease—Saying is seeing—The mental life of humanity 100

IV.
THE ART OF THINKING.

How to think rightly—Truth is suppressed and comes back in higher form—All thought is necessary—Opinions are like institutions—Necessity of surrendering good opinions—Opinion is form only, and must change to preserve its value—We only know form; to know the fact is to love—That which must be thought must be distinguished from that which is true—Use of analogy—Thought is Nature, and therefore cannot be false—All opinions are true under their conditions—The danger of fear in thought—The value of logic—What are axioms?—Newton's work great by its incompleteness—Truth is the union of opposites—The minus in thinking—Necessity of sacrifice in thought—The nature of hypothesis—All advance in thought comes by right use of words—No ends in thinking—Thinking is an especial work—Parallel of thinking to art—Imagination the chief element in true thought—The Art element in true thought parallel to the Gentile element in Christianity 133

V.
THE SELF AND CONSCIOUSNESS.

Individuals are states of humanity—Individuals are separate because physical—Man as a parasite—The self is negation—Eternal life is deliverance from the self—Descartes perverted modern thought by starting from the self—The untrustworthiness of consciousness—True consciousness is the opposite of self-consciousness—Unsatisfactory nature of the doctrine of immortality—The desire for immortality is not man's highest aspiration—What absorption into God means—Love is not self-sacrifice—We want martyrs—To give love is to create—Men are sacrificed for man—How happiness is attained—Only love can satisfy—Happiness is a putting aside of consciousness—Pleasure comes from want—Personality is not highest—God is not personal—The Trinity—God is Being—No mind without body—God as light—The fact is love and is shown by Christ 163

VI.

THE BIBLE.

Nature interprets the Bible—The work of the Bible is to give man life—What death means—Inspiration—No need for inspiration—To have life is to be inspired—We must not be afraid of the Bible—The source of the Bible's power—We put the divine element away from the present—The difference between physical and spiritual is one of perception—Redemption cannot be partial—Religion must not appeal to the selfish emotions—The mistake of our Christianity—The supposition of a physical hell—Hell cannot be remorse—The world accounted for by God's act and man's death—Christ does not save from the punishment of sin—What God's hell is—Heaven is love—Christ's work will cease—"This is my body" shows the spiritual nature of all existence—Prayer changes, not the fact, but the phenomenon—Christianity is not a theology but a fact—Our Christianity is dead—How Christianity may be surpassed 189

VII.

HOLINESS.

Nature is self-control—The moral life is parallel to the mental—To be moral is to act—*Ago ergo ego*—Misery only removed by removing selfishness—No action but right action—There is no true arbitrary action or free-will—Arbitrary action is sin—Freedom because necessity—Man cannot fail because he is a part of Nature—The only mystery is man's death—The moral lesson of Science—Our moral life is passion controlled—The phenomenal nature of evil—Sin as inaction—The analogy of disease to sin—Evil to the individual is good to the race—Life comes only from death—We are redeemed, not tempted, by matter—Creation is self-control—God has no physical power—"Creation out of nothing"—The creature is one with the Creator—Self-sacrifice is not loss—A selfish world is the necessary phenomenon of an altruistic world—No nutrition without a final function—The resurrection of the dead comes by Man 216

VIII.

ETHICS.

The practical problem is to unite work for man with the devotion connected with work for God—How to keep up the enthusiasm of religion—Not imagination but faith—Stoicism and actualism—The world is altruistic—Man's business is with the present—The practical as existing for the sake of the reflective—The evil of exalting individual over general regards—The self as the devil—Genius is a sufferer, not a doer—Our Christianity cannot give the enthusiasm which only can raise men above selfishness—Self-sacrifice is extended politeness—Poverty does not involve loss of refinement—A return to Nature—Good manners in the sphere of morals—The child state of humanity—The value of good manners as showing the pattern for life—The world goes best by being let alone—Mill's argument for liberty—What martyrdom is—The eternal necessity of martyrdom—Sociology—Social evil is nutrition—The life of society—Trade should be made a profession—The world was never worse than now—The evil of our modern life of refinement—Good is determined by its relations—Woman, like religion, needs to be liberated—Egoism is not the true basis of man's life—To be heroic we must advance—Future times will owe to this age the culture of the heart 245

PHILOSOPHY AND RELIGION.

I.
METAPHYSICS.

THE nature of the world—The hypothesis of matter—The universe is God's action perceived as motion—Nature is action—Nature is one with man—Berkeley's error—The mind is not more real than the external world—The laws of Nature are given by man—The work of Science is to harmonise our perceptions with our conceptions—Can we know the fact of the world?—How come we to perceive a physical world?—Wherever sin is, matter is—The law of cause and effect is a form of thought—God's act is not the cause but the fact of the world—Granting illusion, all mysteries are removed—The error of regarding this as an imperfect physical world—The mental is physical—Things are forms of the spiritual—Science now is too abstract—The error of "inherent tendencies," etc.—Nature is a process felt as matter—Metaphysics is a Mathematics—The world is the symbol of an unknown quantity—Matter = x—Science, like Mathematics, exists for the sake of the unknown quantity—The point, that is, absence of matter, is the only infinite, and the symbol of God—The molecule is in reality a point—Chemistry and Physics correspond with Mathematics—Metaphysics and Science must be used together—What will make Philosophy popular?—The tendency of Positivism—The life of Metaphysics.

MEN may adopt three views concerning the nature of the world. (1) That there is a material and an actual (spiritual), both truly existing, and necessarily with a certain antagonism between them; this leads rightly to asceticism. (2) That there is only the material; this being the true existence (at least to us), and such as we perceive it. There is (to us) no actual. This is positivism, as it speaks. (3) That the sole true existence is the actual; and that this material, or real, is our way of perceiving it. This last is actualism (or positivism as it truly is), the practical inference being that we have to deal with the real, but on the principle that it is truly actual, if we could see it aright, getting at the true Being by leaving out the negation. Now which is the best?

Newton says, "the first cause is certainly not mechanical." This is just the point at which science stops: the conversion as it were of this first cause into mechanical cause, or motion. Or as the problem may be better put: what is that wherein consists the act of spirit becoming motion? This is the problem, to bridge the gulf which separates a spiritual act from motion—the mystery of creation is here. The hypothesis of matter or a substratum in which motion inheres as one of its properties is evidently simply a mode of solving the difficulty; the hypothesis was manifestly *invented* for that object. It appeared, I suppose, simpler that a spiritual being should create matter and put it in motion, which motion would then "naturally" continue, or continue by the laws of motion (whatever that means) than that a spirit's action should itself be motion. And indeed at first sight this solution does seem to have some advantages; to our minds it does seem natural that matter should move, there is a conformity between the nature of the two things: also it does not seem so hard to understand that a spirit should put matter in motion: not that the idea is at all simple or intelligible, but I suppose we readily accept the supposition because we are conscious of being able to do the same thing; by our spiritual act, our *will*, we move matter. The idea has that deceptive appearance of comprehensibility which arises from familiarity. Also by supposing a creation of matter *once* and putting it in motion, which continues as a matter of course, we throw back the difficulty if we do not diminish it: it does not press on us as a present mystery—the thing was very wonderful when it took place, but it was so very long ago that it does not concern us much, and besides it was altogether a different process from any that takes place now, so that it is no wonder if we find it mysterious. But upon this we may remark (1) That it does not really relieve the difficulty. (2) That it rather substitutes a greater difficulty for a less one. (3) That it is in point of fact utterly inadmissible. If a spiritual may become a physical action at any time, why not now? Why suppose two processes or orders of things when one, which must in any case be supposed, will suffice? And again, as has been said, we are conscious continually in ourselves of a spiritual act becoming a physical act; why should we exclude God from doing that which we do ourselves? If part of the motion which exists is our spiritual act, why is not the rest of it God's spiritual act? Why two different causes for like events. But the difficulty is, by the hypothesis of matter, really rendered greater. We cannot see how a spiritual act, either our own or God's, can produce or be (which is a better term) motion; but hard as this may be we do at least perceive it in our own experience, whereas the *creation* of matter is a thing at once much harder to conceive, and entirely beyond experience. It is not only inconceivable as a process but is illustrated by no analogies. That God creates the world by a spiritual act, as we by spiritual acts take a part in the production of the phenomena, appears by the side of this past and done creation of matter, a thing of course, so simple by comparison, that we almost forget that it too is an impassible mystery. But also this hypothesis of matter is inadmissible (as long seen) on scientific grounds. Useless and worse than useless as an explanation of the fact which it was invented to explain, it is positively shown to be false alike by metaphysics and by science. It fills the world with needless mysteries without helping in the least to remove a necessary one. But though the hypothesis of matter only makes bad worse, the problem may be attempted in other ways, and, as it seems to me, somewhat mitigated if not solved. Berkeley tried to do this by affirming the world to be God's action upon man's mind, which is at least better than the material hypothesis, although open on one side to fatal objections. I propose this view: That the universe is God's action *absolutely*, and quite independently of any percipient. But God being a spirit, His action, of course, is spiritual action. How then do we see it as physical, i.e. as motion, which is not a spiritual attribute? (I do not say as matter and motion, because the idea of matter is evidently derived from motion, viz., through resistance, which is only motion opposed to motion.) This is my solution. We perceive God's spiritual action as motion, because we ourselves, by our own finite nature, impose a limit on it; i.e. God's action being in itself unlimited, having relation neither to time nor space, we, by virtue of our finitude, perceive it in relation only to such boundaries: that is, we see it as motion, the material universe.

This is why the laws of Nature are truly the laws of our minds, why the conceptions by which material phenomena are bound into science are supplied from within, not gathered from without; why it is in truth

Metaphysics. 5

himself that man studies in the universe. Science is man's view of God's action. Doubtless each order of intelligent beings has a different science; according to the limit their nature compels them to put upon the divine action. Our perceptions themselves involve the ideas of space and time; they are only human "forms," not actualities; and we can conceive of force only as motion; whatever God might do, if we perceived it, it would be motion to us.

We must have *action*, getting rid of matter altogether. The one error of science is the considering action as substance; and so, in its advance, we get rid of substance continually, seeing nature more and more truly, till at last, giving up substance altogether, we get the true nature, the spiritual, the divine. And we take with shame, yet a shame that should be full of hope and joy, the "inertia" wholly to ourselves. Inertia is selfishness, the subjectness to passion, the not acting, the true or spiritual death.

Surely Nature is one because knowledge is one. To comprehend anything is to have it in us—one with our own central "thought." Surely we "comprehend" nothing but axioms: comprehension is of one fact, at once primary and ultimate. As I have said of life, it comprehends all and is comprehended in the least. Our comprehension is of life; our minds being life we comprehend life. This and this alone we understand or know. To understand a thing is for it to become one with us. The mere accumulation of ideas and theories —nutrition—is not truly knowledge, in fact it is error, which is opposed to it: it is a mere preparation for it. Knowledge is the result of interpretation or function, which is always one, however various the nutrition or assimilation or resulting organization; the functional process has ever an absolute oneness. In short we know a thing only when we see that it is merely a form of our own thought—our own thought being ever and necessarily one.

The conformity of all our senses, the constant impression produced, is due to the fact of organization, and our forming part of one universal organization.

To affirm of any thing or fact that it is "seen" or "perceived" is to assert that it is only phenomenal; but not therefore that it does not indicate a reality; that is the very thing it does do, by virtue of the principle of causation. Its object and end is to show us the reality. Remember the two-fold relation to us of the universe; to our bodies, as subserving our physical life, and to our minds; how much more essential the former seems to be; yet is this surely only a phenomenon, for what is our life, our body and mind, but simply *one vibration* produced on our spirit by the Divine act? When that ceases, still remains the spirit, still remains the Divine act. These are eternal and have no relation to time. Still is there passion in our spirit produced by the Divine act, still do we live. Our physical and mental life are but one form of the ever-changing phenomenal passion, nothing is lost or ceases when that ends; so the apparent primary importance of the physical life is deceptive or phenomenal. And our bodily and mental life is really as it were only one vibration out of the boundless series of vibrations which constitute the passion produced by God's action on the spirit. This life is one vibration of the music produced in the human spirit by God's action influencing it. Human spirits are like lyres which vibrate when breathed on by the wind, but the wind does not blow *for* them, or in order to produce that music. And our bodies and minds are one note of such music, which swells and dies away, but only to be succeeded by another and different one. I perceive that people are puzzled by confounding relations between phenomena with the view of the phenomenon as a whole: the *relations* of phenomena are not affected in any way by the subjective view. Just as the sun's path among the stars is merely phenomenal, yet as a relation among phenomena remains unaffected by the subjective view of the sun's motion. It is only *understood*, which surely is no detriment.

All phenomena and phenomenal relations are real in relation to our bodies and minds; as real as *they* are. Things, qualities, time, space, are actualities to our bodies and minds; really affect and influence them; these are relations between phenomena. We are apt to think of the external world as unreal in comparison with our own bodies and minds, but the relation of the external world to *them* is not altered in the least. In fact the phenomenon remains altogether just as it was, only we *understand* it. Thus no alteration is made at all in our common-sense treatment of phenomena, which are as ever in relation to each other, and our bodily and mental interests continue the same as ever.

As for the wonder of perception—sensation, thought, &c.—this is the fact of organic mind; and physiology must afford the explanation. Thus not only is the externality of the universe conceded in every possible sense, viz. its externality to our bodies, but the reality also in every sense in which there is the least evidence or possibility of it, viz. in relation to our minds and bodies.

It was a fatal error of Berkeley's to make the mind

a reality in relation to the external world as phenomenal; thus he denied the reality of the external world in an inadmissible sense. The mind being also a phenomenon, the full reality of the external world is maintained in every sense, except an artificial one, that might possibly be asserted by controversialists, but certainly rests on no possible evidence even of the least conclusive description. It is real in relation to men's minds and bodies; that is all they know or care to maintain, and that is true. The question is, What are it and our minds and bodies also? And this is the question of questions for all, though disregarded; it is the "*Know Thyself.*"

It is because the laws of nature exist in ourselves, have their origin and cause in us, that we know truth when we see it. We recognize its conformity with our own mental constitution; see ourselves in it, in fact. But then how is it that before knowing the truth we always err? Surely only because the universe is too large for us to grasp; we cannot for a very long time comprehend the simplicity of nature. Therefore we look wrongly upon things, but the error is in detail not in principle. The principles of natural doctrines are ever true, axioms do not deceive us, enlargement of view is all that is needed to help us to apply them rightly. And truth ever succeeds; it must indeed, for truth is but the *natural* action of the mind: and to "arrive at truth" is only this—that the laws and forms the mind imposes upon that part of God's action with which it has to do, should not be arbitrary but consistent. And the mode in which we err is most suggestive; for what is it but that we *invent* things and properties which have no existence. Error is the seeing what does not exist; seeing in fact many things where there is only one. The progress of truth consists in the rejection of multiplicity and the substitution of unity and simplicity of conception. But this shows what the prerogative and necessary action of the mind is. No one would say that we are made to err arbitrarily in our progress towards knowledge; these erroneous "creations" or forms imposed on nature by the mind are the legitimate steps of its advance. Its prerogative is not to receive but to give laws to nature: the work of science is how best to do this. Man is the ruler and lawgiver: *things* have to conform to him, not he to them. As he is more and more filled and penetrated by God's work, so does he rule nature better; so does he carry out to greater perfection his own mental action: and instead of many partial and discordant powers, properties, and laws, comes to see around him *one* act:—the normal operation of his own mind, and that alone, ever presented and repeated before him in that which God does. Knowledge is not a being filled to the brim; science is not a submission of the intellect to laws. Knowledge is power; science is dominion. Hence the twofold aspect of science: it sprang first complete into existence. Man gave laws and right laws to the world when first he was placed upon his throne: he enunciated right laws when by the first philosophers his statute books were written. But also he had need of larger knowledge of God, of a nearer approach to Him in His work, before he could use his power fully. Man by studying nature brings himself into communion with God, that from Him he may learn how to discharge his Godlike office of Lawgiver.

Man constructs Science as the bird builds its nest; the bird arranges things in a way accordant with its nature, and its sensations; it does what it must, it carries out its laws of thought, just as man does in Science: it puts them right, it groups them in what appear to it their natural and necessary relations, solely with reference to themselves—and then it is a nest! So Science becomes a moral nest, in which man's spirit reposes.

Woman being taken out of man affords an excellent allegory to illustrate the relation of man and nature. Nature is "taken out" of man; it is himself that he sees thus as something external and secondary, and subordinate to himself. Yet not himself merely—not a phantom or illusion—but God and he working together; not man without God nor God without man, but God using man, as it were. In nature God uses man's mental constitution to educe out of His spiritual action a material universe suitable to himself. Nature is thus, as woman was, the product of God's action and man's "substance." It is man's mental substance or constitution, which, brought into relation with God's (spiritual) action, is nature: i.e. man imposing a limit on God's action (itself infinite) perceives it as matter and motion. And the relation of nature to man should be that of woman to him—it should be his second self: it should be known to be so: it should be treated so. Man has degraded alike woman and nature to be his material minister: miserable error, miserable loss. Both are his spirit's peers and friends.

It was the old practical error of the a priori philosophers that theories to be true needed only to agree with the laws of our own conceptions; it is the recent practical error of the empirical philosophers that theories to be true needed only to agree with the facts. In each case the same error of defect.

Instances of the disregard of the laws of our own

conceptions in the formation of recent scientific theories are innumerable: in fact that vice pervades the whole scheme and structure of modern science. Either way, of course agrees equally with the facts; indeed the facts suggest rather the wrong than the right, and therefore by men who thought their only or chief business was to make their theories accord with facts, the wrong was naturally adopted. But the structure of our minds demands the reversal of these views: an entire turning round of science, a re-assertion of the laws of mind.

The a priori chimeras had at least this advantage, that in the very nature of them they were obliged to be expressible, and therefore conceivable; but the chimeras of experimental science will not even submit to this slight restraint. They float, many of them, in such an equivocal region, that when you want to speak of them, their enunciation is found to be no less than impossible.

That was a great error of Bacon's: he thought truth was in nature instead of in man, and that formulæ correctly expressive of natural facts must therefore be true. The very error of the a priori men, in another form, but still identical, for they believed that formulæ correctly expressive of laws of thought must be true. And has not this falsified science ever since, the idea that formulæ correctly expressing facts must be true? The error is palpable—those only are true formulæ which bring facts into accordance with the laws of thought. Is not this the error of the mathematicians; using hypotheses merely as means of calculation? . Bacon thought also that by changing externals he could alter internals; could eradicate a false intellectual habit by substituting a new method. Just what those men do who are for reforming mankind by altering institutions. It was the one-sidedness of men that wanted removing, and Bacon essayed to do this by turning men altogether to the opposite side. But I also am wrong in thinking that I could improve history. What is this alternate excess but a vibration, what the union of the two but development? We must excuse the vagaries of the period of liberty; variety and apparent caprice are its element. The future science shall embody both—the law and the liberty in one.

The law of science is, to make our *per*ceptions and *con*ceptions harmonize: thus it is altogether an internal thing. How recent science has failed even to aim at this, is palpable: of the two it is more important that our theories should rightly correspond with our conceptions than with our perceptions; [for after all these are what we mean by facts]. Laws may be true although not agreeing with facts, the facts being incorrectly observed or regarded; but laws that do violence to conceptions cannot be true. The universal error of putting phenomenon before cause, almost necessarily arises from the idea of receiving laws from nature instead of giving them to her.

How simple, comparatively, it makes the mystery of perception—that we are *the cause* of the facts which we perceive, i.e. the cause of their being as we perceive them. All that mystification about the "authority of the senses," &c., ceases.

Let us trust ourselves, trust our senses, our mental senses as well as our bodily ones. Now we place much reliance on our external senses and none on our internal, as, before, much on internal and little on external. We should learn to rely on both: for what is the good of talking about the external world, when it is absolutely ourselves that we study and trust. Are not the senses as much we, as the intuitions? Have the senses any authority which they did not derive from us? By the senses we acquire a subjective knowledge, viz. of an effect upon ourselves. By the internal senses or perceptions we learn, from this effect on ourselves thus known through the senses, the cause which is external to ourselves. The internal senses, the rational powers, are in immediate relation with that which is external to us, which the senses are not. By the senses we learn the effects on ourselves and their relations; that is their value. Our knowledge is entirely bound in effects on ourselves; this is the reason of the necessity for the use of the senses; without them no basis for any knowledge; we cannot know causes if we do not know effects. Our internal faculties, reasoning, intuition, &c., bring us into relation with that which is not subjective, with the causes of these effects on ourselves which we perceive by the senses; but these internal faculties can have valuable results only when they are employed upon materials gained by the senses. Without these they are, of course, misleading; trying to learn cause without knowing effects, is of course hopeless; for the effects are the causes in the "present," existing where alone we can know them.

In one sense the old philosophers were not too much subjective, but too little. They reasoned of things external to them, without knowing what was internal; tried to get at true external causes of effects on them, not having first learnt what those effects were. Our philosophy is becoming as extremely subjective as theirs was external. They busied themselves wholly about the causes affecting them without caring to know what were the effects on themselves; we busy ourselves wholly about the effects on ourselves and their relations to each other, without caring to know their cause external to us. This is the true relation of the two philosophies. Our material universe, as we consider it, is altogether an effect on ourselves (for our reference to God having once created it, or to His now and then doing or creating some things in it, is idle in the extreme). The old philosophy was full of guesses about what might be the cause or causes of the effects on ourselves; not knowing what those effects were, nor caring to know, save in the most superficial and inaccurate way. Put the two things together, and we have a depth, something satisfactory and worthy of manhood.

Here is the point for positivism: do we certainly know (as it affirms) that we do not and cannot know the fact and being of things? If so, how and why do we know this? If we know this much, surely we may know more; for we could not know this unless we knew why we cannot know it. It is "because of the subjective element in all phenomena;" but then can we not find out this subjective element? This "self," which must be perceived as external but is not, what is it?

The positivists do not see that they are cutting the bonds which have tied philosophy's feet, and then saying to her: do not walk. They do not see that their arguments about it, and the presumption from its failure hitherto, lose all their force in that very fact of the new starting point they give her. The question is altogether another one now, and susceptible of an entirely new treatment; now that we know that this assumption, that things exist such as we perceive them, is an illusion; and that the cause of our perception is not and cannot be this.

Positivism must aim to put us into one with the fact of the world around us. And this it does by saying: Sacrifice yourselves, live for others. Then this must be the fact of the world around us, not passive, not getting; but giving, *acting*. The positivist says: I speak of the *law* only, and that is self-sacrifice, love for others; but as for the *fact*, I will not even think what that may be. But none the less is it involved in this law that the fact is Love : is that which, in relation to us, is self-sacrifice.

The problem of science (of interpretation) always is, the phenomena being given by accurate observation, to find something which, being considered as the fact, the phenomena shall necessarily be as we see them; and where such a fact is found, as it does inevitably force itself upon the mind of some man, it is self-evidently true; comes with irresistible conviction; it is the fact, we cannot help seeing it to be; that which makes the phenomenon necessary is unquestionably the cause of it. This is a good way of seeing it; it identifies physical cause and connection in reason. Now the fact which makes the physical necessary (and has this self-evidence) is a subjective inertia of humanity. Cause is ever that which makes necessary; the motion of the earth makes it necessary for us to perceive, therefore it is the cause of our perceiving. Now surely all finding out of cause is interpretation in this sense; is it not ? And all other supposing of cause is hypothesis, making phenomena their own cause, as gravitation, e.g. : we have to interpret gravitation as gravitation is interpretation of planetary motions. And see the beauty of this; our perceiving is the primary fundamental fact, and necessarily so; we can have no other basis to start from or rest on. There is ultimately nothing else to explain or give cause for; all questions of cause resolve themselves into this, the cause of our perceiving, or of our sensations rather. This is as it should be; the final answer, too, must be that which gives some condition of ourselves as the fact.

The question respecting the universe is not, "How comes there to be a physical, or what *is* the physical world?" but "How come we to perceive a physical world?" He must be dull who cannot see that this is the "fact," the question, especially with astronomy to help him, in which the same history has been. Astronomers started with the assumption that the heavenly motions existed as such, and puzzled themselves. They did not ask the right question. In like manner we do not face the true problem; we have made assumptions instead of keeping to facts. The question is, how come we to perceive a material world? This we answer by guessing; we assume, we jump at once to a conclusion, do everything that is unphilosophical and sure to land us in error; we lay it down, without any reason at all, that it is because the physical exists externally to us. Let us keep to the fact and give our attention to the real question, How do we come to perceive a physical world? That is the question, and the only question; to be answered by investigating first *what* we perceive.

With regard to the question, "When did the physical begin?" I answer, "It began with the not-being of man, the Fall." It is like the question, when did the sun begin to move round the earth?—when man began to perceive. They are alike affairs of perception. All that *is* remains the same; nothing was altered when the physical began; but a mode of perception commenced in man.

When and wheresoever there is sin, suppression of moral Being, there is the physical, there is time and

Metaphysics. 17

space, there is nutrition; i.e. there is redemption or development. This is the great life. This constitutes the spiritual universe, this is our not-being from other spiritual Being, our nutrition-producing failure, our tendency and function. All other forms of life flow from, are included in, and re-present this.

What more is there in what I say than this: that God is all around us and we do not perceive him? It is this simply. But then our not perceiving God is our perceiving matter. Postulate Being instead of not-being; and that is the universe.

This also I see; the law of cause and effect, under which we see nature, is a form of thought. It is nothing real, truly belonging to the essential action which constitutes the universe; but a relation like that of time and space and motion, arising from our constitution; it arises as time does from the limit we impose on that which is unlimited. Hence its absolute authority, hence its absolute non-entity. It is one of those things which is and is not (like time and space). And now the value of this thought: this relation of cause and effect, succession of "second causes,"—what is it except the mode in which we view God's immediate action? Therefore when we say anything occurs under or by virtue of this law of cause and effect, what is it that we affirm? See if it can be anything else than that God does it? We see God's action as a chain of causes and effects; seeing them so by virtue of our finiteness of view, just as we see things in time. Cause and effect, because they are cause and effect, may be known to be God's direct action. And it follows that if cause and effect be God's direct action, God's direct action consists in cause and effect: and therefore to affirm *direct creation* is to affirm creation by second causes: the two things are one. To see the law of cause to be a form of thought removes that apparent difficulty also.

God's act is not the cause of things but the fact of them. When we ask for the cause, we ask for the cause in *time*; that which preceded it, which was and is not: which God's act cannot be, being eternal. The idea of cause, thus, I see to be wholly phenomenal.

If we consider God's act only as the cause of the *origin* of the universe we deny the existence of His act, for the cause exists only in the effect; and the effect has all the reality, the necessity, the fact, of the cause. The cause is not, and never was, more than the effect; the effect contains it in full. We have fallen into horrible confusions from this word "cause," using it with so little understanding. I see it now clearly; and that it is above all necessary to separate from it all idea of efficiency, that is, *acting*. We have confounded cause with actions.

In tracing a chain of "causes" we are not tracing a "thing" which really exists, but imposing upon nature accurately and wisely the law of our own minds. We are bound to *make* the "facts" agree with our "ideas," and do not see the facts until we have done so. Our idea of cause and effect is the true and only possible fact of cause and effect. There is no other "law" in nature but a law which we make. God is not the "Lawgiver" to Nature—He is the Doer of it; we are the Lawgivers.

This strong persuasion that there may really exist space, infinite space, without matter, is very striking; the actual is felt in it dimly and unconsciously. Space is "the unknown God;" it is our ignorance makes the

Metaphysics.

actual to be "space." We are in space because we are in God, and do not know it.

Being is a property of God; not-being of the phenomenon: they are parallel; the phenomenon is the Divine, but without its "Being." This is the puzzle of theology —a God *apart from Nature* is both asserted and denied. It means that the absolute of Nature is God; but this which *we* take to be, is not, as it cannot be, God. The old heathenism identified Nature and God; ours is a suppression of this, with a "hypothesis" of God. God *is* Nature—not the phenomenon but the Fact, the Being: this is the interpretation. So the classic life was more harmonious and whole than ours.

If we once get it into our minds that an effect on us, or passion produced in us, as sentient Beings, causes us to perceive material things, there is surely no more difficulty about the material world. Then all we have to do is to ascertain the cause of this passion in us, which causes us to perceive the material universe, and all is done. And this of course is a work of induction: how is it to be settled without any trouble, a priori? I want to know *what* this is, that I am caused to perceive. If I wish to ascertain a cause, all right reason teaches me to examine the effect. How is it likely we should be able to answer this question alone without taking any trouble? People say at once that the cause of this passion in us is that a material universe exists which we perceive. Now I do not insist upon the absurdity of this answer; I will suppose it to be possible, and even rational: but I say it is a mere guess; it is a priori: it is doing the very thing which the same men are never tired of abusing our forefathers for doing. We argue from our senses, which is the very thing that is under dispute; a most vicious circle.

Men who maintain cause to be a form of thought, an universal law of mind, do not see that if it be so it must exert an absolute authority over all "primary qualities"; that the mind as imperatively demands a cause of gravity as of the ascent of a balloon, and can no more rightly be put off by a reference to a direct act of God in the one case than in the other: both are equally God's act. That is why we perceive them as links in a chain of cause and effect. To call a thing God's act is to bid us find its cause that we may *see* it to be so—that is how we see God acting. The mind, in short—the man, I should say, humanity—rejects everything except *action*. One action it accepts as the universe; properties are mockeries, feeding a hungry and thirsting soul with dust. God! is its cry. Let me see God and I see all things. Blind me not, dare not to stifle me, with those dark veils of matter; clothe not the universe in sackcloth. Life pants for life. I wait for the Lord, my soul doth wait.

In affirming *action* the intellect is only doing for the whole what it does successively for each of the parts. It is the exclusion of a hypothesis, a "not;" or rather it is a transferring a "not" from without to within. It is but showing us why there must be this subjective passion in us, which makes us infer the external world (and such a one); viz., love acting on "not."—It is important to observe that the subjective must ever be first, and that what we call perception of the external must necessarily be second, a hypothesis. The not recognising this has put us wrong, has made us think of "our senses deceiving us." The truly instinctive must be that which recognises

Metaphysics.

sensations as *in us*. Surely this is before intellect properly so called. Surely intellect begins with the first inference, i.e. hypothesis. And is not that the first conception of the external? As for children, when they first perceive or infer the external, their apparent knowledge of "things," as external and acting in relation to them appropriately, by no means involves that they have any such conception as that of "external things," or that all is not purely subjective to them. An infant (even anencephalous) sucks immediately; but it knows nothing of any breasts. Children act well and truly in relation to "external things," not knowing that there are, or thinking whether there are, any external things at all, conscious only of sensations purely subjective, but prompted thereby to actions which are perfectly adapted to their relation to "things." It is the same with animals.

This suggests (among other thoughts) how we may be acting with a true reference to spiritual things, influenced by them and responding to them, and taking our place among them, while utterly unconscious and unthinking of them. While engaged with our own sensations alone (which material things are, when regarded as physical only), we yet are truly acting among, and in relation to, spiritual facts—though we are heedless of them utterly and do not perceive them at all. Yes, our unconsciousness of the spiritual, while yet that is the whole fact, is like a child, playing with "things" and educated by them, without any thought but of his own sensations. After a time, that which was to him a mere sensation becomes to him a "thing." The perception of physical "things" is an interpretation of the physical sensation. Humanity is such a child—taking no thought but of the physical, and educated thereby to see true existence.

It is quite right that man should perceive the material world; this is perceiving the "not," which is the great thing for him to know. Save as knowing this "not" in himself he cannot be saved; and he must first perceive or "suppose" this "not" as external, before he can know it as internal (this we know by the history of the human mind). This is why man is in a material world: to show him the "not" in himself, he must first see it as without (i.e. humanity must), and then he will come to know it as within. (In the meantime individual men, feeling it by conscience and revelation, are redeemed.) This is the infancy of humanity; and still, as we see in the animal world, the embryonic form remains. Humanity is just now waking up from perceiving only its own sensations to perceive the actual around; just as when a child first interprets its sensations into external things.

All mysteries are removed if we once grant our feeling not true. It does indeed seem strange at first, and unlikely, that we should be thus living a life of illusion—feeling as one thing what is another—but then this is just the mystery of our life: it *is* odd and unlikely we should have been as we are. Why not this oddness, as well as any other? There is this strangeness, in fact; whether we regard it as a mystery or as an unlikely fact: so far as expressing the case is concerned, we may take either view; we have certainly one or the other. In the untrue feeling is the basis and explanation of the practical wrongness of our life, and of the theoretical puzzles. But in fact there are mysteries and wonders any way; and this view too gives us the world as larger and more; it only means that we are too small.

And again: this fact (of an untrue feeling) is only strange at first, before it is reflected on and examined;

then it is seen evident and most natural; it is involved in our finite being only. And observe, this is putting one oddness, or strange and unlikely thing, in place of many. It has the law of parsimony on its side. If we do not grant that, we must affirm innumerable mysteries, and each of them beyond all proportion greater than it. And against it is absolutely nothing except a strong natural tendency the other way, which is involved in the fact itself that we do feel wrongly. Observe that Copernicus's was exactly the same argument; that we must admit one strange thing, that we are feeling wrongly, instead of many. And with regard to the moral objections which at first appear, they soon range themselves on the other side; it is a great relief to the moral sense.

Before astronomy was known, men necessarily believed there was a heaven such as they had impression of by sight. Till this time we have necessarily believed there is a material world, answering to the impression we have by touch. And clearly this arises from our relation to these bodies; but in the same way it was from our having sight—our relation to eyes—that men were obliged to believe in such a heaven. There *is* no such thing; but they, having eyes (and in relation with the true phenomenon) were necessitated to think so; we understand why, for our impressions are still the same. So is it not by our having muscles and nerves that we are compelled to believe "matter?" Being so sensed, and brought into relation with the true world, we must have believed so. It is surely to our senses we must look for the explanation of those necessary false beliefs.

Here is our folly, our damnation; not even for the sake of taking the deadness out of all the universe besides, will we consent to take it to ourselves! Let the universe be dead, but respect *our* life. Let sun and stars whirl round us like childish toys, but question not our stedfastness. So we seem to have control over Nature; it seems that the sun rises and sets for our convenience!

It is clearly wrong to regard the "not" as the fact, as we do with our material world; but there is also another erroneous way, that of Plato, the considering this world as an imperfect image of a world similar to it in all respects except that imperfection—the considering this as an imperfect *physical* world. To this I conceive is parallel the theological conception of the world as physically depraved, i.e. as having been originally in a superior and perfect physical state from which it is now fallen [and the same of man]. Plato's super-sensible world is the right idea; but it errs in this, that it is not truly spiritual or moral; and so also our conception errs. The Fall, the "not," relates to the moral; and the "not" of the moral is that which *makes* the world physical. But as physical, it is perfect, as much now as ever, as much as possible. Clearly it is so, by the axiom of least resistance. This is the point to recognise: that the "not" in the universe is a "not moral," and it is that which causes it to be physical; but that as physical, it is not, and cannot be, depraved. And seeing that this "not" is a moral, actual "not," there can be no longer any question as to the seat of it, viz. that it is the moral "not" *in us*. Our conception makes God intellectual, as conceiving ideas, instead of moral.

This parallel of the ordinary conception of the effects of the Fall to Plato's doctrine, shows how far it is from being an absurd imagination or chimera. And now one sees why the present doctrine of "real matter" was necessary; it was necessary that it should be seen that the "not" is the very essence of the physical. The other doctrine, that the physical was imperfect, would not do; because it implied that without the "not" it was still physical. Only by seeing that the very fact and essence of the physical is this "not," can it be seen that the true fact (apart from the "not") is moral or spiritual; that the Fall introduced the physical; i.e. only by the belief in a "real matter" and in the necessity of the physical processes and laws, could recognition of the spiritual be introduced.

Seeing that the "not" is the essence of the physical, and that it is only from and in ourselves, we see how the physical is from ourselves, is our mode of perceiving that which is spiritual or moral. Therefore men have invented a real matter, have introduced this hypothesis of "substance"; it was necessary before they could realise the moral Being that constitutes the universe. This is the function of that nutrition. The introduction of "matter" is the nutrition; its exclusion reveals a fact. And see—it was introduced by suppressing an instinct.

An act is an act or a passion, according to the view that is taken of it. It is an act in relation to the doer, a passion in relation to its effect on others. Act and passion are two words for one thing. The external universe is God's act, and at the same time passion in spirits; and regarded in this two-fold manner, it stands before us, as it were, completely revealed. When I used to think of the universe simply as God's act, the question would arise, on what does He act. We have been accustomed to think of Him as acting on matter; and we seem somehow to want a substratum or recipient for the action. This our own experience suggests to us.

And I conceive this idea is a just one in some sense; and that God's act is an act on something; viz., on the world of spirits. That God first created spirits, and that His act, which constitutes the universe, is His act upon them. Thus I approach towards the great question, "What is that act of God's which produces such passion on spirits, that we perceive it as nature?"

How difficulties and contradictions disappear by seeing the universe as an act, and not as a thing. And this simple view is again the first instinct; always, whatsoever we perceive, we first, and by our nature, suppose some one does it. This is the superstitious form of first science, to which last science returns.

The great difficulty in science seems to have been the want of seeing that all force, motion, or passion, must flow from, or rather perhaps, be the re-appearance of, some previously existing force or passion, precisely equal. See how this has vitiated physiology, as in the idea of "vital" force as a "property" of matter, or any "force" as a property at all; not perceiving that life was passion, and must be referred to equal pre-existing passion. So with regard to function, physiologists did not see that the force of the function involved an equal force as previous to it, which the function is, in another form: so that they talked about the contractility of a muscle, and its contraction *causing* waste. And throughout science, the false and impossible doctrines I think must all of them have rested on this one error, of supposing physical passion [or psychical] to *begin*, as it were, not recognizing the force or passion as ever the same passion with some previous form. Now the root of this error may be clearly seen and is beautiful. It is nothing less than that we are spirits, and can act; and our consciousness as agents has

Metaphysics. 27

led to our attributing in thought (though not designedly) active powers to "things." The whole philosophy of science, I think, lies in this; the source of all error, and therefore of all advance; i.e. of nutrition and of growth.

Our consciousness of acting has been a continual illusion to us in nature; we have thought that "actions" acted. Just as we have thought "actions" were real Beings, by virtue of our consciousness of Being. So simple and natural to us is this idea of "acting" or "free-will," that the whole advance of science consists in separating it from that to which it cannot belong. In brief this is science: to get rid altogether of "properties of matter," and to see all such properties as passions, the same in another form as some pre-existing form of passion, which becomes the property or passion in question.

It is no wonder there has been so much materialism, confounding as we have done, the spiritual with the mental. The mental is truly physical, one with the rest of the bodily life, and is only perceived as is the rest of it. It is our mode of perceiving that very same passion which constitutes our bodies, and of course it depends on our bodies; there is nothing about it other than physical, i.e. passional.

As to animals we are all of necessity poets. The poet says of a flower that it is "thirsty;" and he does not speak figuratively, but strictly. The flower is thirsty; if that which is in the flower were in us we should *perceive* the thirstiness, or as we say, "be thirsty." This is only the perception of a bodily condition; which condition does not depend on our perceiving it; nor can it rightly be called by any other name. The poet has true and fine perceptions; but the most ordinary man is a poet respecting animals, and says of them "they are hungry" or "thirsty." All recognise in them that which in themselves they perceive as hunger and thirst. Of course the animal is hungry, just as we are; but we are "a Being" to perceive or be conscious of the hunger; there is no Being to be conscious of or to perceive the hunger of the animal; it is altogether a *thing*. If the hunger were not there (independent of our perception), how could we perceive, feel, or be conscious of it? Does our consciousness create that of which we are conscious? How can we feel hunger, except because there is hunger to feel? We have been deceiving ourselves here—as if our consciousness or perception were something in itself, instead of a perception *of* something. It is just an inversion here of the fancy of a real matter external to us; we make in one case that which is internal external; in the other that which is external internal. Or again, how can I be conscious of (or perceive), under the form of hunger, a condition of the body in respect to proportion of fluids or of salts? It is hunger that I feel. These "conditions of the body" are hypotheses, theories. I do not perceive them, they are suppositions which I infer or invent to account for what I perceive.

This advantage for religion is gained by seeing that the phenomenon is effect and not cause of the subjective passion, viz., that though when the phenomenon is put first, some people may deny that it has a cause, no one, I think, will be found to deny that our subjective passion has a cause. This is the very basis on which the belief in an external world reposes; and has availed to maintain that belief all these years in defiance of the most conclusive metaphysical proof to the contrary. If it once was shown that it is the subjective passion which demands a cause and not the phenomenon, there is surely no class of men that will deny the necessity of a cause for that. Unfortunately by making it the *phenomenon* that demands a cause, unnecessary difficulties are placed in the way of a full recognition of the divine act as the cause. The effect does not agree in many ways, as is plain, and is shown by consequences, e.g., the referring of the act to a distant period; the dividing it into direct and indirect, or supposing it to consist altogether in the institution of laws, or to be amended and altered:—the whole series of inappropriate and unconceivable peculiarities which are supposed to attach, and one can hardly avoid attaching, to the Divine act as manifested in "creation." The one source of all the error is the attaching the idea of God's act to the phenomenon instead of the reality. There is but one cause appropriate to the universe, and that is a subjective passion of the human spirit. It is the cause of that passion which we must look for in the Divine act; and so seeking it we find it to be in accordance with its effect, what it must be in itself, an eternal spiritual act, having for its one emphatic characteristic, *holiness.*

Interpretation—perceiving true relation among phenomena, or perceiving phenomena to be subjective—is merely looking naturally at the facts, as it were closing our eyes and forgetting our former artificial ideas, and opening them again to look the facts fairly in the face. It is like a man who has perplexed himself in vain with an affair overnight, and after a night's rest sees the same matter under a totally different aspect and as simple as anything can be. Genius takes this morning view. The difficulty lies in the first false perception. At first we cannot see things in their true relation, we do not know the facts sufficiently: then as we discover the facts we assimilate them, arrange them according to our false view; and so at last require just to forget them entirely and look again naturally, to see how they really are.

To suppose that we can perceive "things" or matter or anything but force or passion, is an unsound dynamical view; it involves the origination of force or passion. For perception is a passion; and all passion is produced by passion, i.e. by force. It can of course be only force which produces the passion or perception. We only need to remember what we are talking about.

Is not a "thing" wholly an affair of relation to us [an image]? It begins and ceases; i.e. it was and becomes *not*; but that is because it ever is not; if it *were*, it could not cease to be. That it is not, is included in the doctrine that nothing (that is) can be annihilated. Now I see; time or succession does not relate to being at all; to any *thing* even; only to form, but that is surely only to "appearance": is not this also a matter of definition? How strange it is, we feel no surprise at *form* beginning and ceasing, in spite of our conviction that nothing begins or is annihilated. Clearly it is involved that nothing that *is* can be truly in time. Consider now how it is, and what we perceive as form.

Now I perceive: these forms (that pass away) are the *things*—the physical—they are the images of the spiritual: they constitute the physical. We know it; we say *things* cease to be; they become other things: the "thing" is the "form." Neither the unchanging matter nor the force is the thing. The universe is *real*, i.e. it consists of "forms," which become and cease; i.e. are not, are but images. It is the things or the forms that are images

Metaphysics. 31

of or correspond to the spiritual; it is the "thing," not the abstract matter or force, that is the symbol.

The question well arises: things are forms—forms of what? They say of matter or force; I say by no means; forms of spiritual action. In this sense I use the word "form" as an equivalent to that of "image." This is the thing to insist upon. What we "perceive" in this world is not mere matter and motion, but more, infinitely more. They are *things*, the forms or images of the spiritual; it is the materialists who deny it. They are things; "forms" replete with divine energy and meaning.

Thus it is that a real world is given to mankind; a world of *things*, which the present science denies, and substitutes an abstract world of matter and force. "Things" have meaning, they are forms; forms of fact or act, which matter and force are not. There are no "things" to science as yet, only to artists and poets; but when science has things it deals with meaning and significance. Think of this word significance. Things are " signs." Perhaps this word sign is better than image, for the relation of the real to the actual.

What a glory and brightness surrounds the world now to my gaze. That these things which science has taught me to look on with such cold curiosity, are in truth more real, more "significant," than ever enthusiast dreamed. Science outvies in meaning and depth of revelation the inspirations of the artist and the poet. "Things" are forms in which the spiritual appears. This is the basis of poetry and art, for the emotional is also in a true sense the spiritual. Let science give us back our *real* world again. It is the present phenomenal science that is unreal, is abstract, dealing with our own conceptions. The old "metaphysical" science had its faults doubtless, and of course was only a half; but at least it had a real world, i.e. a world of things, of forms or signs, each with its meaning or reality. It did not confine itself to abstractions as ours does.

I perceive that what I cannot tolerate are those primary or inherent properties — mystical values or powers: e.g. "contractility," "irritability," the "vital force," the "inherent tendency to specific form." I see that to go against these is what I have been doing from first to last: trying to see all as necessary; but that is, as *forms*. It is curious, for each of these aspects of life—function, nutrition, and form—there has been supposed an inherent primary property. This is how the case has stood: first, there is an inherent tendency to form; then there is a peculiar vital property; then there is an unaccountable irritability, a property of performing special functions. How clearly this is mere hypothesis; how miserably monotonous, if nothing worse. All the known, certain laws of physical action, adapted as they are to the results, are set aside as if they were not. The tension that must be from the manifest forces at work where life exists; the tendency to action from such tension; the necessary moulding into different forms—all these are ignored! And as for the recognition of these doing away with the wonder—the recognition of and reverence for God—let us be rational, and apply our wonder and reverence to *these*, and to God in them.

But the basis and foundation of all this is evident—it lies in the assumption of the existence of the phenomenon. The "primary qualities" must be supposed in some way or other on that hypothesis: there must be a *first*, an inherent virtue or nature. So that it is clear the rejecting these means the rejecting of a real matter. This is

Metaphysics. 33

in the nature of Science: its entire work is the doing away with these primary and inherent virtues; its work is precisely that of showing that the phenomenon does not exist, freeing us from this illusion, and thereby necessarily revealing to us the fact.

How a *process* may have effect like a substance, one sees in a jet of water supporting a ball; as it were by a solid mass. Is it not thus Nature is to us:—a process, an operation, felt as "substance" by us? And as for this view of the "actual" making us feel that our apprehension is so false and mistaken, is not that exactly right? Ought not science to press home upon us this very correction—that spiritual realities are our true concern, not such things as we feel? Surely that case of the jet of water supplies a good idea of "life"— the physical organic. The body is a process, appearing as a substance.

Surely it is right to call the separate forces, as electricity, "things." The forces are *forms*, i.e. things, and the one abstract force bears the same relation that the abstract matter does. The separate forces cease to be; therefore they never were. Surely the fact is just the same, whether we draw water from the earth by a bucket and pass it into a receiver, or whether we draw electricity by a machine, and pass it into one. The fact is as truly the same as the process appears identical; in neither case have we operated on any real matter, alike only on form.

I see in reading the writings of the mathematicians, so far as I can understand them, that my reasoning is a mathematics. I do not go into details and employ formulas, but as to the essential nature and self-evident and demonstrative character of their reasonings, it is alike. Mine is a mathematics of *things*, where arbitrariness has been. God writes in an unchanging present—"on the instant Eternity"—a Geometrical Diagram; and we deal with it in the strangest way. In the first place we are apt not to perceive at all that it is one, but to regard it as a series of isolated lines and figures, *arbitrary*, any part of which might have been otherwise without detriment to the whole; nay we even consider it rather irreligious to say the contrary. And these isolated lines and portions of the figure we endeavour to trace out in their relations to each other; i.e. to gather from them any consistent meaning that is most obvious: but to make them accord as parts of one whole, tending progressively to one result, does not enter our heads. We do not feel justified in insisting that each single group shall represent clear geometrical principles; we have no right, as we think, to do that, we only want to know what they are, we are "ministers and interpreters" only of Nature, and whether there be any strict mathematical relations between the parts we do not know. And then, stranger still, when we do find out such true relations, such logical connections of things—the meaning of each part—we straightway call them *causes*; and imagine that in these relations exists the power which produces the figures between which they hold. Only that which we cannot understand do we give God the credit of doing—i.e. directly: anything that is reasonable and intelligible we seem to think unworthy of Him, and as soon as we have traced its relations to other things we sever it from His hand. But this surely is simply a form of anthropomorphism; because we consider Him to be and to act like ourselves. *We*, acting on *things* only by taking part in God's action, i.e. only on something that is without—on a substratum in short — do really act primarily and secondarily; institute chains of causes; do some things directly and others indirectly; act "immediately *at first*" and "afterwards through the powers of nature" as Newton says. But this is the very sign of our imperfection; it is the result of our creative incapacity. It is because we are man and not God that we do this, and it is because the Creator is God and not man that He does not. This poor fancy rests clearly upon the idea that God acts and requires to act upon a substratum as we do.

Metaphysics in truth is but a species of mathematics; it is only more comprehensive. Mathematics we may say perhaps is the "metaphysics of quantity," but it rests wholly on the mental processes; and the fundamental conception of the transcendental mathematics is entirely metaphysical, i.e. it is simply a fact of our mental action, accurately observed. And metaphysics has the demonstrative character of mathematics, if it be rightly used— the words rigorously defined and kept to their meaning. It is then quite on a par with mathematics in that respect; both treat merely of the relations of our conceptions, and are absolutely alike; both having also direct and immediate application to things, mathematics not more than metaphysics. But the latter is larger, and therefore more difficult and less advanced. The processes of mathematics, I believe, will be found to be, in detail, precisely correspondent to those of a sound metaphysics; and hand in hand how prettily the two might walk together. In short, mathematics is simply a branch of metaphysics. But of late years it has been separated from metaphysics, and hence the misery of our Science, the load of absurd hypotheses.

Mathematics surely is so certain, and deductive or independent of observation, because it is seen to be a science of *forms* only [i.e. of relations]. Experimental science professes to be not of forms, but of that which truly exists; yet it is not really so: all science is properly of forms [which " things " are] and of forms alone, and when this is rightly seen surely all will be like mathematics in certainty and deductive character. What perplexes science, and puts us at fault, is the supposition that the objects with which it deals truly exist as such apart from us. The mathematician does not stand so in respect to his science; he admits an existence to which his forms relate (matter, &c., in space and number), but passing this by altogether, he concerns himself only with forms. Now all science must come to be thus; admitting a true existence, an actual to which all " things " relate, of which they are all forms, we must see that we, in science, have not to do with this existence at all, but only with forms. Then we may *know*. Should we not see " things " to bear some such relation to the " actual " as the mathematical conceptions do to " things "? Then as the pursuit of these conceptions a priori results in propositions which are true and necessarily true in respect to the " things," would the pursuit a priori of " things " result in propositions true of the " actual "? But here a new conception appears; is not our inductive science just such a pursuit of " forms " as the mathematician's; and do we not find what we have thus indirectly learnt of the forms, or things, to hold good of the actual or spiritual?

It is clear if the mathematician considered his " forms," or geometrical conceptions, as existing in nature, his science would be altered altogether; it would become then merely experimental, lose all its certainty and uniformity, all its value and use indeed. He never would find in nature, nor make, any one of them. His very definitions are impossible, they exclude that which is essential to reality. Just so " things " cannot be, in true actual existence; the very nature of them excludes that which is essential to true Being, viz. *action*. But it is interesting to note this parallel between the deductive treatment of mathematical abstraction and the experimental treatment of things; both are processes dealing with forms, which result in conclusions that apply to that which is relatively fact; abstractions give us results which apply to " things "; " things " results which apply to Being. So that, in truth, mathematical deduction and experimental induction are parallel rather than contrasted; they are the same process in relation to forms which have a different relation to us. Mental forms, or abstractions, are to be treated by mental induction, or a priori; sensational forms, or " things," by sensational induction, or by experiment. Is not the idea of sensational forms for things a right one ? The physical is a sensational form, even as the mathematical is a mental form. Experiment and observation being the same process in respect of the sensational that deduction is in respect to the abstract.

Let me think how observation and induction correspond with mathematical thought; both are a similar putting ourselves into relation with the respective subjects. They are using our senses, bodily and mental respectively. The mathematician does, in respect to conceptions, just what the experimenter does in respect to things. Both alike exert themselves, use their active faculties, bring themselves into relation with the subject of their thoughts, and vary their relation to them. Is there not a strict parallel here; the same *life* exhibiting itself in many forms?

I perceive now a more right way of dealing with the question of a real matter. By denying that there is matter we put ourselves in a wrong attitude; virtually conceding the very point in question. We speak of "matter" as if it were a thing that *could* be asserted or denied; while the case is that matter is not in a position to be either. "Matter" is a mere symbol or expression, without any meaning of its own, for some unknown fact. To deny it is no less absurd than to assert it: it is to be interpreted. Clearly if a mathematician were foolish enough to affirm as a great fact that some unknown quantity—say the diameter of the sun—were $= x$; we should be entirely beside the mark in affirming that it could be x; or denying that there could be x: the question would never be settled so; the whole dispute would be mere nonsense. So is that about a real matter. In truth the man who affirmed the x would have the advantage of him who denied it; for he could certainly show that we were obliged to suppose such a conception, to have some such symbol, to fill the gap which otherwise there would be.

Our ignorance exists only by virtue of our knowledge and capacity of knowing. We do not say a beast is ignorant; to be ignorant means that we ought to *know*. So, to be not-Being means that we ought to *be*. All terms of negation are necessarily relative. That of which we are ignorant we express by a symbol; but only because we know it must be, although we are ignorant of it. So our selfishness has relation only to a love which ought to be. We suppose a physical or inert in

Metaphysics. 39

nature, i.e. a symbol or unknown, because we perceive that a fact, a Being, is there which we do not know. We know it must be there, although we do not know it; and we call it (not intelligently, as the mathematicians do x, but with a poor conceit of knowing) "matter," "physical laws," "motion," "force," anything whereby we can cheat ourselves. Let us thank God and nature, who carry us on in spite of ourselves, and will not let us rest in our symbols, as we fain would do.

Now, how come we to perceive that there is this unknown fact and these circumstances and conditions of it whereby we determine our symbols? Can I see how the mathematician, starting from the smallest point of known value, lays hold of more and more unknown; converting more and more into the known, by means of relations established between them? So we, starting with some true knowledge, some spiritual, some consciousness, some conscience rather; some love or sense of holiness (yes, all consciousness flows from the conscience, the moral Being; the physical is a symbol standing for an unknown *moral*); starting from this Being or known love, and brought into relation with other Being or love which is not known, is not in us (we being selfish)—this unknown love is "passion" in us. And we, perceiving that it *is*, but not knowing what, use a symbol for it, and call it "physical" or "matter." This we do by virtue of our ignorance, even as the mathematician does. Only the mathematician does not mistake his symbol for the true existence he is in search of; and we do. Because in reference to our moral Being there is a "not" in us, which there is not in reference to our intellectual.

Scientific speculations are very well in their place, but

do not let them intrude into other regions. It is very well for physicists to speak of "matter"; but for men generally to call this "a material world" is an absurdity. Should we call it an x-world it would mean as much, viz., that we do not know what it is. Matter is a symbol for an unknown fact; the world is not a material world, it is a world of *things*. To call it an x-world would be a gain, for then we might suppose there were some reality and meaning in it at the bottom, if we could find out what it was; whereas this word "matter" passes with us as a sort of voucher that there is truly nothing, no significance, in the world at all. Let us abstain from calling it matter until our wise men have given us a known quantity for the symbol.

Again, see how the unknown quantity is that for the sake of which mathematics exists altogether. So it is in Science: it is by hypothesis that it exists, and for the sake of the unknown. And only by means of the symbol for the unknown (the hypothesis), and by using it as a reality, can the progress, the interpretation, be. Even so, in all thought, we must *use* our hypotheses as if they were real facts; we can interpret, or do away with the hypotheses themselves, only by so using them: to refuse so to use them because they are *only* hypotheses, would be like turning out the unknown quantities in a mathematical problem. Berkeley's idea is just this. It is easy enough to prove "matter" to be merely a non-entity; but that is the very reason why we should work with it. We must use this symbol in order that we may know what it stands for. By bringing it into all sorts of relations, more and more complete and extensive, with the known, we are able at last to say, "it means *that*." How we might advance in thought with this conception we 1 held in view! Surely all thought then may have, must have, mathematical precision. It is a mistake to suppose that mathematics is so certain because of the peculiar nature of the subjects it deals with: it is not at all so; quantity has no peculiar certainty about it; the certainty lies in the method. Mathematics, dealing with so limited a subject, has been able soonest to arrive at a practical (not indeed a theoretical or intelligent) realization of the right method—that is all. All thought can be as certain as mathematics; and even mathematics itself may be much beholden to other thought for an explication and extension of the method which it has unintelligently instituted.

I say with reference to the life of thought, that nutrition must precede function; that we must think wrongly before we can think rightly. It is only saying that before we can know an unknown we must have a symbol. Think what we lose by clinging to hypotheses as real; to a real matter as if it were the thing we were to rest in. We lose nothing less than *all*; we stop short of the very point; we take up with "nothing," when that very "nothing" is given us only as a means of getting at *something*. We deprive ourselves of all that is of any true value in our Science, just as if a mathematician rested in his unknown symbols.

Is it not one chief advantage of mathematics that it goes straight on with each inference, without this reference to other considerations; that it deals with each sequence of ideas solely in and for itself? It does not profess to deal with the real absolute truth, but only with what is under the given conditions, only what follows from definitions and axioms. And therefore going straight on and never swerving, it does arrive at the real truth, and does interpret nature; because it has assumed its right position. All reasoning must become similar, and then will avail equally. We must learn to remember that in reasoning we have to do, not with that which really exists, but with our own definitions, postulates, and data; and to see what follows from them, and that only, quite irrespective of whether or not anything "external" agrees with them, or with our deductions from them. Acting thus we shall have an available art that will not fail us. In a word, we have to give up the idea that thinking is a means of arriving at truth, and to remember that it has its own purpose and use for which it must live freely its own life. The contradictions of mathematics to nature are most interesting here; they are such as would never be tolerated in any other form of thinking; and the superiority of mathematics as a mode of thinking, which is so inseparable from these "absurdities," is a good demonstration of the nature and right relations of the thinking process. The question is not are the things true, but are they good natural mental life; if so, no fear but they will effect their function. Suppose the mathematician were to falter, and qualify his deductions respecting the triangle because no perfect triangle exists in nature? Mathematical truths are not true to nature. We let the inadmissibility of a conclusion vitiate the process of deduction, instead of reacting upon the premisses; we let the bond go, the bar yield. It is as if a mathematician, landed in a result which gave him a part greater than the whole, should refuse to apply his axiom, instead of arguing back as he does. The reason of the greater advance of mathematics is partly the simplicity; but partly also that mathematical reasoning does not bring the intellect and the heart into opposition, as philosophical reasoning seems to do, and so has never been vitiated by that stress. It is no matter that a mathematical deduction should be inconsistent with the facts of nature; no moral difficulty arises; there is no forcing of the mathematical argument to make it agree. There is no remedy for philosophy but to draw the distinction between the truth (or belief) and the life of the intellect. If our thought be natural it will in the end be sure to agree with nature. Would it not be well to have the axioms employed in philosophical and moral reasoning explicitly stated, as those of geometry, and referred to, and unflinchingly adhered to; and the definitions and postulates also? The simplicity of mathematical ideas is not directly the cause of the great advance of mathematics; but this and their very limited scope have allowed thought to proceed unchecked in those respects, and hence its advance, as a lower form of life. There has been *resistance* to the higher. I seek to make all thought truly mathematical, to extend the mathematical process to all. They develope in the same form.

Do I not see this in respect to the point, that it is the only infinite? This is what mathematics does when it deals with the infinite; it simply gets rid of substance, becomes spiritual. The point alone has no bounds, no limits, because it has no dimensions. So soon as ever we arrive at, or think of, the infinite, we have laid aside the physical; no limits mean no "matter." It is wonderful that in order to treat of the real, or things, mathematics must go to that which is immaterial; only from thence can we gather the power: as the physical flows from the eternal, so must the interpretation. The point is infinite; it has no bounds. It is *all* in one; not only the circle and ellipse in one—the two dimensions—but all three, all absolutely in one, are the point; and this is the idea of the point, and so absolute unity involves infinity, and infinity absolute unity; i.e. no dimensions, no physicalness. Thus the absolute unity of God involves His infinitude, and His spirituality. The point is actual [the atom with no substance]; and it is one, and infinite.

The " point " is the symbol of God. We look wrongly at this; the point is the denial of substance, but if there be no substance there is the spiritual—no-*thing*, but therefore spiritual Being.

The infinite is to space as the eternal is to time; it is no space at all, it is neither much nor little; or, if either, still less much than little; to assert infinity is to deny space. The conception of the infinite as very large, is parallel to our conception of the eternal as very long. Surely there must be something bearing a similar relation to time that the point does to space; that we consider *nothing*, yet is symbol of eternity; something which has neither past, present nor future. Would not such a conception be aidful to Science, even as that of the point is; be to metaphysics, perhaps, as that of the point to mathematics? Are not our metaphysics perplexed for the want of it? If mathematics wants to be freed from substance, surely much more metaphysics from duration?

This mode of conceiving infinitude and eternity as very much of time and space instead of as having nothing to do with them, is "natural," it is true, to *us*, who are by deadness in a physical world, and in absence of the physical see absolute not-being. Our way of regarding the point as absolute negation, our physical conception of the infinite and eternal, is proof and exemplification of man's actual deadness.

Metaphysics. 45

Again, with respect to the point: consider how all physical conceptions relate essentially to molecules; e.g. gravitation of masses is only gravitation of molecules, and of masses through them. But the only true idea of a molecule is an ultimate molecule, that which cannot be divided; but this is having no parts, which is no dimensions, no substance; it is a point. Here is the true conception of the atom; it is that which has no substance; it is only the physical conception of the point: it is the "infinitesimal" physics, that is all. It is at the basis, like the point in geometry. Have not much of our confusion and difficulty arisen from not seeing this, but introducing the idea of substance into it? Is not this what makes mathematics so superior to all other Sciences —its spirituality; its having discarded the idea of substance? With *a-chrons* for metaphysics, and true *atoms*, or points, for physics, will not an equal exactitude be given? Clearly I see this about the atom; physics is essentially "non-substantial." And surely here is the reason metaphysics is behind; as the greatest, of course, it is the least developed; it has not yet emancipated itself from the conception of time, as Science has from that of space. The perplexity that still is in physics is probably much from the atom, or molecule, not being yet recognised as a true *point* (or infinitesimal); the conception of true substance still adheres to it, though not entirely. Here is the philosophy of Boscovich's conception, surely, as *points*, surrounded by infinite spheres of force; but was he not wrong in introducing space again? Is not the true infinite the point itself? Substance comes, in physics as in metaphysics, from action of the point, the atom or molecule; it is secondary, and not primary.

I must think of the full bearing of this; that physics

too is wholly based on action without substance; how it clears up that great mystery of the molecular constitution of bodies, that infinite division which yet is not infinite! Mathematics and physics alike derive things from points, and interpret them by it. And do I not see, it is chemistry that especially relates to the atomic or molecular, i.e. to the point or infinitesimal? It is in this especially distinguished from physics; and here is the key to it: it is the Science of infinitesimals. How strange that we should think of it emphatically as the Science of *substances!* The doctrine of atoms is the doctrine of *points*. It corresponds with the infinitestimal mathematics; the other portion of mathematics with physics proper. The doctrine of the molecular constitution of bodies lies at the basis of all, as the idea of the point does in mathematics; but the infinitesimal mathematics is "atomic," i.e. chemistry.

A physical thing or body no more truly "consists of" molecules or atoms than a mathematical "thing" or figure consists of points, for an *atom* cannot occupy any space, any more than a point. Space cannot be *atomic*. Therefore atoms cannot constitute, or make up a body, any more than points. A million points occupy no more space than one; and just so a million atoms. We must introduce the mathematical conception here. Its "things" do not *consist* of points, but are generated by *action* of points. So physical things do not consist of atoms, but are generated by action of atoms, i.e. action without substance; by pure action, i.e. spiritual action. Is it not plain that nature is spiritual? Physical science refuses to have it any other way.

The true use of metaphysics and science is *together*: metaphysics, alone, is a failure; science alone unsatisfactory and "superficial." They have one object, and should be employed in union. It is as if touch and sight were used separately; how, in that case, touch alone would fail of any clear or intelligible result; and sight would give us knowledge merely of appearances.

How palpably the faculties science employs answer thus to sight! But the existence of that unsatisfactory metaphysics demonstrates other faculties, which might be the very ones to make the knowledge of phenomena the interpreter of fact; as knowledge of appearances is of "substance." The phenomenal relation of science, and the failure of metaphysics, give no ground for any conclusion; like touch and sight, they may be the very things which mutually give the needful completeness to each other. The failure of each alone surely is what ought to be.

We have previously argued that the physical (scientific) and the spiritual (metaphysics) are one; let us treat them on this plan, and see if metaphysics will not be fruitful (certain and practical), and science penetrate below appearances: e.g., in physics all action is *vibratile*; all the "laws" = no external change; therefore subjective, &c. [Metaphysics, in fact, thus is Science.]

This presents us with another parallel, viz. that of science to sight, and metaphysics to touch. Like touch, metaphysics assures us of something more real than the objects of science, but gives us no satisfactory intelligence of them. Science, like sight, must be the interpreter for it, recognising the relation of the phenomena it deals with.

The true revealer has a sort of wonderful power of making things quite new and different from what we thought them. But there are two kinds; the one showing us unthought-of wonders and problems in things of which we previously were ignorant, and knew we were ignorant, and had only vague impressions, but no *contrary* ones; another presents to us, in entirely new lights and ways, shows us unsuspected wonders in things which we felt and were convinced we perfectly understood. So the latter meets with an opposition and refusal the other does not encounter.

People think that philosophy can never be in itself influential on, or regarded with interest by, the people generally. I am not so sure of this, when philosophy is renewed. It was so of old, when it referred to matters of universal interest, to the instincts of truth, justice, piety, in a word, to rightness. Why may it not become so again? I grant the modern is not, and cannot be, but the reason is plain; our modern philosophy is nutritive—force-absorbing—has no power in the nature of things. But a philosophy that brings home nature to man's heart, and sees in the universe the very passions that are agitating his own bosom, is another thing. Whether men can find time and attention and love for that, remains to be seen. Why should we prejudge so? We always think nothing can be but what we are used to. Absolutely all that our modern philosophy has for the heart is proof that God is very wise and very powerful, and, on the whole, rather good than otherwise; and strangely enough these proofs are made to consist in what we can understand. Moreover, our philosophy and science have been not only divorced from but almost ever opposed to religion—never one with it,—and it has been therefore watched like a thief, and men ever sought to bind it in new chains as it burst the old ones.

Abstract philosophy—" interpretation,"—the answer to the question " why " in its ultimate form, the *moral* why, was ever man's passion, is now, and ever will be. This is

Metaphysics.

re-introduced with all the added scope and power of five centuries' nutrition.. Our modern nutritive science has been doing all it can to put it down and keep it from operating, and in the main, though with hard struggles, it has succeeded, as indeed was right and necessary; but the passion, the tendency, is there still as ever; becoming indeed more powerful the more it is opposed (as chemical affinity does in nutrition): it will have its way again at last, indeed the nutrition exists only that it may, and that in doing so it may effect objects higher than itself— the *function*, that is, of Science.

Surely platonism arose from a kind of positivism: indeed it is necessary that the reality of the physical should be denied, before a doctrine which puts another reality in place of it can be conceived.

So here one may clearly see the tendency of positivism. One may point to experience, and say to the positivist: "Yours must come to a more spiritual doctrine. Look at platonism; it could only have come into existence by aid of a doctrine akin to yours; and as your denial is deeper and more complete, so shall the resulting spiritual doctrine be also. The platonist fails because of still keeping hold of some kind or degree of true reality in the physical: this defect you must remove." The doctrine of a present and only real spiritual waits for and solicits some one to remove the reality of the physical.

Positivism must come to an *actual* doctrine of the universe: it carries a new platonism in its bosom. It is like the chrysalis to the butterfly, or the bud to the flower: the restraint and coercion are for development. Positivism is negative now, by accident as it were; i.e. by the law of the case, this must precede the positive.

But a positive form must come: there must arise some view of the existing.

Platonism, as well as actualism, is a system based on a correction of our impressions and tendencies to think: i.e., considering the subjective elements, it is essentially the same. Positivism, or science, taking away the reality to which the platonist holds, demands the platonic process to be repeated in new relations.

But the former platonism is proof that this will and can be done; it failed because not complete enough.

One chief thing I want to do is to show the *life* of metaphysics; how it has been working in a necessary way to a most important end; how all has been good; how even the nonsense and contradictions are hypotheses by which the fact is revealed, and the "not" more and more excluded. How, e.g., less and less value is being attached to arguments for the existence of God from the visible world; and yet the rejecting all such arguments, as some have done, saying we can know nothing thereby, is just an anticipation, suppressing hypothesis, but not putting the fact in its place. (It is as "spiritual," not as physical, that the world reveals God.) Is it any better argument, that to create "mind" the creator must be intelligent, than that to create "matter" he must be material? Matter and mind alike are from "not."

Let me come nearer to Thee, oh God; know more truly what it is Thou doest. How sad a disappointment it is to me to find that these principles of Thy acting, as I have thought, are but shadows projected from myself! I would know, not more of myself, but more of Thee. I beseech Thee, show me Thy glory. Hide not Thyself from my desiring eyes. What is nature to me, of what value are beauty, delight and use, of what satisfaction the simplest and the grandest laws, if Thou be not in them? May I *never* know what Thou doest? Wilt Thou be recognized alone by faith and love? Dost Thou say to me, in these earnest but futile strivings, "Who by searching can find out God? But with that man will I dwell who is of an humble and a contrite spirit, and who trembleth at my word."

II.

NATURE KNOWN BY THE MORAL EMOTIONS.

Man's response to right—The actual is known by the conjoint use of sense, intellect and moral being—Man fell by the conscience—Men really judge by their feelings—The evil of thinking that God acts for results—Mysticism is allied to Science—The Mystics are interpreters—The intellect attains freedom by subjection to the moral sense—The physical is the moral—Nature is Holiness—Nature is man's bride—Nature is "the hands of the living God"—We must recognise negation of Being—Love of God is the love of all things—The world as a work of genius—The organic is not the highest in Nature—The future Science—Nature's secrets are won by sympathy—Evil of the doctrine of special creations—"Design" is a necessary consequence of the assumption of matter—Science is done for love—To be natural is to love—Nature is perfectly beautiful, therefore ideal beauty is less perfect—Nature is God's ideal—All mental life is the representation of Nature—To account for error is to show it beautiful—Evil is nutrition—Painting recalls to us the spiritual fact of Nature—The function of Art is to reveal the holiness of Nature—Art will advance as Science has—The future of the world.

THE strongest feeling in human nature is our response to right; deepest in man's breast, and ineradicable, lies that fundamental passion; it is king and ruler, and though driven from the actual throne by meaner feelings, never abdicates its authority. "People will fight for truth and justice, or that which they think to be such," says the *Times*. If we can therefore but make nature embody to us the idea of *right*, how much more it will be to us; how much profounder and more over-ruling our love.

It only needs to use our whole being in the induction, and then we know the actual. By sense alone we only know the apparent (not the *real*); by intellect alone we only know the abstract. Now taking both, and so bringing to bear a larger part of our being, we attain a better and truer knowledge, i.e. of the real. But sense and intellect still are but part of us: by them we can of course only know the real—still the illusion, though not so merely an illusion as sense or intellect separately. But where is the moral nature? That which the sense alone learns cannot be true for the intellect also; that which the intellect alone learns cannot be true for the sense also: so that which sense and intellect alone learn is not true for the moral being also.

The definition of the actual now is: that which is true for, which answers to, the whole being of humanity; that which will bear investigation by sense, intellect, and moral being, the latter correcting the former two, even as they correct one another. It is that which is learnt by the joint action of sense, intellect, and moral nature.

And here one may think further respecting that "it is not good for man to be alone." Take this idea of the woman as represented by the moral "faculty." Is it not remarkable to see how well then the old Greek philosophy will answer to man's state? For that philosophy wanted precisely these higher elements. It was "very good," but it was not well for it to be alone; and a help meet was given it in the newly-awakened, almost newly-originated, *conscience*: and see, it *fell* thereby. As is well seen in the early ages of the Christian Church, in the unscientific, unphilosophical, superstitions of the Fathers, dictated, evidently, by the moral element.

Thus we see how natural, how necessary it is, that men

should turn with such admiration and delight to that old classic literature. It is like the longing look back to Paradise, to the true, right, attitude of man; nor can this cease till the same attitude is restored and perfected: and this is what we should seek, or at least be ready to welcome and expect. And may not this be the true reason for man's clinging to classical studies?

What a strange thing it is that people imagine they decide on doubtful points by their intellects, and not by their feelings; and they are even angry if the contrary is suggested. What a putting of the inferior above the higher nature: but how beautifully herein does God attain His higher ends even by human error! What is really done when a person with sincere and earnest heart undertakes to weigh the evidence on a doubtful religious point—such as future punishment, personal reign, &c.— is that under the idea of letting his reason judge, he listens calmly and intently to the voice of his inner nature. Painfully and with prayerful resolve he lays aside prejudice and passion, he puts off indolence and *judges as he feels*. Herein is a deep beauty. To what good all this toilsome process? Certainly not the attainment of truth; because equally earnest and capable people arrive by such means at opposite results; and evidently not, because such a process has in itself no adaptation to lead to truth; and the less, the more purely intellectual it be made. To arrive at truth involves many conditions in the person which in the vast majority are sure to be wanting. What then? Does the process fail of its result? Are the prayers, the tears, the hours of meditation, the agonizing renunciation of old ties, all of no avail? Not so. They fail not of God's purpose, which is the discipline and development of the moral nature;

the education of the soul. In this strife the child grows into the man: the end is gained. What he thinks about future punishment or millenarianism is of no consequence: that he should bring his soul before God, and struggle earnestly to do the right, that is the point.

The doctrine of virtue or moral rightness being that which most promotes happiness (Paley's doctrine), goes with that view of natural theology, which sees in creation only God's wisdom in the sense of design and skill. Nature truly viewed teaches a better lesson; she is law; she does not exist for results. God in nature acts according to an absolute rule independently of results. What an infinite (yes, and eternal, for it is moral) meaning there is in this *law* of science. God acts by an invariable rule, and not for results: blessed be the men who have sought to establish this as a fact of science. Therefore He does not act in time; He acts morally.

We think we exalt God by attributing to Him an optional creation, a supreme and absolute self-determination apart from any law. We forget that love includes law, and can only be by it. It is true *we* act, or seem to act, optionally, or without any determining power: but this is our misery, our degradation, our death; it is because we are passional, inert, not loving. There is no mere optional with Him, all is holy. Our own true human characteristics and dignity are entirely in abeyance in respect to those things in which we act optionally.

It is amusing how, with all our Science and triumph of common sense, Mysticism is not put down; here it appears again in its extremest form. The cure for it has not been found yet. Nay, it is clear that Science cannot put a stop to it; Science only feeds it. For see how these Mystics have been the very men who have had the largest grasp of Science, have done most in it. Not to speak of Moses, passing by Plato also, let us come to modern times—look at Swedenborg and Newton. It is clear that we must look elsewhere than to the prosecution of Science for the cure of this disorder of the intellect, if it is such. As Science grows so does that tendency, that conviction gain increasing power. Nay, it allies itself to Science, rests upon it, turns to its own use the means brought for its destruction. It urges on to perfect fulfilment all those discoveries and tendencies which are announced as its destruction.

In this unity of the sensible and spiritual, one sees the basis of ceremonies in religion; why, too, they are so misconceived and misused from our separation of the two, from our thinking that the sensible has any other being than that which is one with the spiritual, and that therefore, as sensible, they are of spiritual power or value. "This is my body;" "As *often* as ye eat it;" that is, in all eating.

It is interesting to trace the different states of feeling on the subject of necessity in Nature. The ordinary supposition—of design, i.e. arbitrary will, not necessity— implies that we do understand, that we know all about the thing, that our faculties are tests and capable. Seeing it as necessary, we feel that we do not understand it, that it is something infinitely wonderful *to be* understood. So we gain, not only a grander conception, but also a hope of a future understanding above any that now we think possible. Those who rebuke the belief that we can understand, do not see the humility that is its source.

They are too modest to think that men ever will understand—more than they themselves do.

Think how the Mystics are the *dynamical* men: men who ask *why*. (See Newton especially.) This is their character. The mere laying out of phenomena in order does not satisfy them; they insist on the knowledge of causes. Hence they discover the physical causes; and hence too they see the physical as efflux and effect from the actual, which is their Mysticism, especially so called. It is one tendency, one faculty, that makes them discoverers in Science and Mystics. They show causes; they cannot rest in appearances, but must go to fact; that is all. Find the fact of the physical, and we have the actual, the absolute: this is what they do. They apply practically Comte's principle, that the intellect has to do only with relations; so in regarding the fact they go constantly to that which is not in the intellect, to the actual. This is the fact to them, and necessarily they see the physical as an "appearance" flowing from that; as indeed Positivism shows it cannot be anything else. For the fact that the intellect cannot deal with the absolute, by no means shows that we are cut off from it—it only shows that we cannot intellectually know it; but we have other faculties, other Being and nature besides the intellect, which Comte seems to forget in this connection, though he fully recognizes them in others; as where he shows, e.g., the inferiority and subordination of the intellectual to the moral. Comte is, in truth, a Mystic himself; only stunted; if he had carried out this last idea of his he would have had a lofty place among them.

The Mystics are precisely interpreters: they show the phenomena necessary and also they show the fact. The non-mystics, the men of talent or theory, do not, in truth, seek causes at all in any genuine sense. They virtually say of the phenomenon, it is " because it is." This is the sum of it, though of course they put it under a pretence of cause; all these ultimate inherent properties of matter or things are nothing but this. As for saying, God made them so because He chose, this is truly an irreverent thought. It no more applies to them than to any other physical fact or process to which superstition might assign it; yet the feeling that there must be an ultimate of which this is true, is a wise one : why does it not lead men to see the eternal fact which alone truly is ?

Sense alone gives the phenomenal; intellect alone the abstract; conscience alone the moral; sense and intellect alone the scientific; sense, intellect, and conscience together, the true real, actual or spiritual, which alone truly *is*. But I do not say this is true Being; it *is* as much as we are; but it has our own negation in it. The true Being is not man, or such as he, but God. So I may admit that true knowing is impossible to man; but I say that man can know according to his whole Being, though his knowledge must be subjective; that he can therefore know altogether more than he does now, in an entirely different way; that this knowledge of ours does not answer to man as he really is. This is the basis of actualism: that we are as much mistaken as the men who believed appearances uncorrected by reason.

Comte's position practically is just as if, in old days, any one should have said: Do not trouble yourself about the intelligible world; this sensible is all that concerns us, meaning us to put up with the uncorrected appearances. Now this would not do. It was because this did not answer to the whole man that the "intelligible" was invented. Yet would such a man have had a certain right on his side; for the separate intelligible word was a chimera. So has Comte; but his real does not answer to the whole man, and will not do; and because it did not do, the separate spiritual was invented for the conscience to have its full development and scope in, just as the intelligible was for the intellect. But the intellect was given to man to interpret the sensible by; and so is the conscience. The real world will fulfil, and more than fulfil, all our moral demands, if we will employ our moral faculties on it; even as the sensible world contents our intellectual faculties when they are employed on it.

See how, by union of sense and intellect together, an entirely new "reality" is given to the world. It is a different thing: the "intelligible world" has ceased to be a chimera. So from the union of real and spiritual a new universe is given, and the spiritual ceases to be a chimera. The eternal is no longer an "everlasting time," no longer future. Of course we cannot understand the eternal, with our *separate* real and spiritual; our spiritual is in fact only an abstract sensible; just as the old intelligible was the sensible, not truly different, only chimerical, with the same sort of "eternity" as ours.

Bacon said: "You must take the sensible into your intelligible, and not go dreaming." So I say of the spiritual: we must take the sensible into our spiritual, and not go dreaming. Only so, by conforming our imagined spiritual to the sensible, shall we know the true spiritual. What we talk about now is our imagination merely. What an apparent reversion in my thoughts! Yet the spring of it all has been intolerance of the chimerical spiritual, the Design argument, and the "sensational" heaven. I have come to this through the medium of metaphysics, from the love, not of the sensible, but of the spiritual. Now I can understand Bacon better It was not that he regarded the sensible especially; but he could not endure the old chimerical "intellectual." He saw that to be worth anything it must be conformed to the real or sensible; in short that the sensible was not that mere phenomenal that it was supposed to be, but was more. "Conform the intelligible to it, and see," he said. I say exactly the same; the sensible is not the mere phenomenal that it is supposed to be, it is more; conform your spiritual to it, and see. So it was by metaphysics too that Bacon did his work. He was not an experimenter; his world was in the intellectual.

The essential point in inductive science is the authority of the intellect over the senses. This is what distinguishes it. (E.g., our knowing the stars for worlds.) It is the only means of discovering truth, the only true science; because the only one subordinating sense absolutely, and compelling it to conform. The "actual" philosophy deals by the intellect as the "inductive" by the senses, denies its authority, and subordinates it, and makes it conform to a power or faculty, together with which it uses it in investigation. Thus, of course, the "actual" makes more use of the intellect, even as the inductive does of the senses. This denial of the authority of the intellect, taken with the assertion and employment of the moral sense, constitutes a new inductive science, in which the intellect bears the same part as, in our present inductive science, the senses do, is at once the foundation, and yet subordinate.

It was only by subjecting the senses to the intellect that they could be properly and freely used. So long as

Nature known by the Moral Emotions. 61

they were held to deal with the real, they were neglected, held so fallible, and a limit placed upon their use; because they gave results against the intellect—against a part of man *felt* to be superior. So Bacon necessarily liberated them; stimulated, and indeed gave unbounded play to their use, and relieved them also from the stigma of being unable to discover. Bacon said: "Do not take ideas superficially abstracted from the senses." Now just such is the case with the intellect. See how it is unused, neglected, repressed by some; and by all, friend and foe alike, held incapable, except under narrow limits. By subordinating the intellect to the conscience, I think it is set free; its use is stimulated, rendered certain and unlimited; and the idea of its incapacity overthrown. This does for the intellect what Bacon did for the senses. Refusing to accept from it as truth anything that does not conform to the demands of the conscience, it is compelled to go on, and Nature is subdued again. All the reasons which now repress it are removed. First, the religious reasons: it is no longer opposed to the part of man felt to be superior to it. Second; the reasons that make men say we cannot know by it; just as Bacon removed what made men say they could not know by the senses, the attributing authority to them. Now we see that the intellect can explore absolutely, that it has a boundless field, that nothing it can come into relation with can be beyond its exploration. Of old the intellect had to be trained and developed before the senses could be rightly used; i.e. made servants, not masters; so the conscience had to be trained and developed before the intellect could be rightly used.

Is not the future attitude of thought to be this:—that what the woman's emotions demand is to be thought;

that *that* is to rule, as intellect or conscience does now; but that its demands are to be rightly interpreted, by sense, intellect, and conscience, *working*. For here it is, as it was with intellect of old: its true demands could be found only by uniting it with the senses, and actively working by them. The ruling faculty, without this, takes too little; invents something not enough, based on the acceptance of the uncorrected impressions of the inferior faculties. What union, harmony, beauty and delight will there be, when men and women are united thus; each understanding their position, and each using it! This were, indeed, a making of twain one new man. And into what harmony that discord of the faculties will then be resolved; the discord comes from what the earth abhors—the servant-faculties taking upon themselves to rule.

Man has various "faculties" to exercise on one world —the world that is; but his plan has been to make as many worlds as he has faculties. Of old there was that absurd "sensible" world, through which the intellect could not work, and an "intelligible"; even as we have an "intelligible" world, morally absurd (through which the conscience will not work) and a "spiritual." We must invent a world for a faculty that comes into active exercise, if it will not work in the already recognised one; and surely the tendency to do this is felt as each faculty comes into activity. So now our spiritual world rests on conscience, as the old intelligible one on the intellect: the invented world rests, for its evidence, on the faculty which demands it; and this is the relation which ever wants inverting. Very instructive and interesting is the reference to conscience to prove the spiritual world: what it proves is that the other (known) world needs to be differently seen.

Note how the intellectual life of man simply *re-presents* the moral history, springs from it, exists only by relation to it. Not the moral is *like* the intellectual; but the mental is only a partial and typical, or veiled, presentation of the moral; and the physical, as corresponding with the intellectual, repeats it again. Now may not this life, which to us is bodily and intellectual, be in truth moral, a true spiritual life, only seen by us with an inertia in it, and so *to us* physical? This, that we see as physical, necessarily corresponds to the moral; because it *is* moral; it represents it to us in a lower form because we do not perceive the moral element in it. We suppose cause and effect, &c., not seeing that it is true action or love. The physical is the moral with the love left out; and therefore the form without the fact. All the physical palpably is just that—the form of the moral without the fact. So the law is as we see it; yet truly it is the very fact of love; the not-love, which constitutes it "Law," is only in us. And so of all: so of the physical world; it is the very fact of love; the not-love which constitutes it physical, is only in us.

The way to understand nature is by patience and gentleness, being willing to be ignorant, not using force. How violent and arbitrary, and therefore unmeaning, is that idea that we perceive things as we do because they are so. It is an invention forcibly introduced. Let us be content with that which nature gives us; not being in such a hurry and so violent. There is no possible connection between things being as we perceive them and our perceiving them so. Let us think in least resistance; not insist on making a thing clear, but leaving it obscure if necessary, above all things distinguishing thoroughly between things that differ, not forcing things into unnatural union.

The moral sense cannot say of the intellectual phenomenon that it cannot be thus; or it must be thus—it cannot deny the phenomenon. That would be like the intellect asserting or denying what is or must be to the senses. Scientific inferences or theories should never be affirmed or opposed on moral or religious grounds. The point is, not to assert or deny respecting the phenomenon as such; but to show the phenomenon to be only phenomenon, and to learn the fact from it.

I see two things in Nature; giving as it were a double solution to the problem. One of them has reference to the reality, the other to the human perception of it. The latter is *vibratile motion in direction of least resistance;* the former *God's holy act.* The language of sensation translated into the language of reality, or the reality deduced from, and seen in, the appearance; rising from the phenomenon to the cause :—this is the course of true Science. And this last deduction is the truest Science; Science cannot stop short of it, it is her mission to deduce causes from phenomena. Nor is anything in Nature truly known until it is thus known; till it is seen that moral action is the very being of all things, Science is but on the threshold of her domain. She is busied with subjective impressions, with sensations and ideas which she professes, and rightly, to despise, and has not entered on her true work, which is to explore the objective reality. It must rise to spiritual facts and moral deeds or it does but sport with illusions, and remains an idle classifier of sensations. What you would say of him who thought to study optics by comparing, arranging and grouping colours unenquiring whence they arise, holds true of all who trace the laws of matter and ask not what spiritual fact is there. And here is a new branch of knowledge

Nature Known by the Moral Emotions.

opened; the correspondence viz. of the spiritual and moral world with Nature; the parallel, I should say, not only of Thought and Nature but of character and Nature. If Nature be holy action, then shall holy action be in some sense Nature. And we must seek to trace all things not only in the intellect but in the moral sense; not only truly to understand Nature by seeing her repeated in intellect, but to appreciate her by tracing her again in the virtues. Then Nature shall be known.

What a glory it casts over the working of the laws of Nature to regard them as expressions of holiness! How it changes them from darkness into light, and renews the face of the earth! God will not do anything for any one, nor save anyone from any evil (as we see He will not), except according to those laws; not because there is anything in the law, but because it would be wrong. No necessity is in the laws, only rectitude in the deed; no iron bonds of matter, but only free choice of right. This we do not tremble at, nor submit to, but love. Fearful and appalling are those laws which work generally for good, but do harm sometimes; and with a lurid ludicrousness superadded, because they are represented as binding the very hand and heart of God. Because it would be *wrong* otherwise, it is that God drowns him who saves others from a watery death; that God cuts off by quick disease or wasting penury the best and noblest men, capable of the highest deeds; that He gives no success save by means adapted to secure success. It would be wrong: and therefore we who suffer thus are glad, and will rejoice. Co-operation with God in the laws of Nature is choice of right, the spirit's life.

What madness can be like that of living in the midst

of eternal verities and busying ourselves exclusively with a few subjective phenomena, as if we and our thoughts were all? Matter, and the sciences founded upon matter, are subjective, and touch not the real basis of things; our knowledge is but a well-ordered dream, until, opening our eyes to the real light of heaven, we see that each thing has its place as a moral deed forms part of a holy act; *is* that. What we perceive it as, relates not to its essential nature, nor is the question true science takes cognizance of, except to enquire why we so perceive it. We are not mind and matter; we are spirit, and our true concern is with moral beings, and moral action. To that all things tend; all material, all mental knowledge is but a stepping-stone. The bringing all things into relation to the spirit, seeing them as moral, is the end and meaning of all knowledge and all experience. Until things are spiritual they affect not us; they are outside us; far, far away, as material things, nay, even as intellectual things; dreamy mysteries, unintelligible, strange, fantastic; in which we see a glimpse of meaning here and there, but the whole is a riddle; filling us with joy, indeed, but with a joy mixed with awe, almost with terror, and full of strange misgivings. If we can see Nature to be a spiritual deed, a holy act, then we understand her, then she is ours. A right act? There is no mystery in that; that is native to us; what we were born to and would do. It draws us absolutely; not one thing too much, not one too little, if it be right; our inmost spirits claim it all for ours; the mean and the noble, the painful and the pleasant. If it be right it is man's, it is human; it is our very own. God has done it for us; we, had it been our place, would ourselves have done it. Yes, this world we would have made, with its darkness and pains and sorrows, its mysteries and doubts, its aspirations that end in disappointment, its temptations that rule with a sway so bitter.

The love of Nature is man's instinctive and unalienable joy in right action; it is the attractiveness of virtue, but working as yet blindly, and without a just appreciation of its objects. And, in truth, herein lies the real meaning of that relation of Nature to man, which so many have expressed under the image of a marriage. Nature *is* the bride of the soul: not wedded yet, indeed, but to be wedded. And is it not with man's love for Nature as ever with love? Beauty excites it first; it is an irresistible drawing towards the lovely, but that is not its end. Its end is for the inmost soul. This play of charms leads us on through a path of flowers to most serious duty. When man truly weds Nature he will find that he has taken to his heart, not a beautiful body, but a deep and earnest spirit; not his sensuous or intellectual faculties, but his spirit, his conscience, will be mated there.

"It is a fearful thing to fall into the hands of the living God." The "hands of the living God" are what we call the "laws" of Nature. When God is spoken of as the "living," it is ever with special reference to Nature. It is Nature, the creation, that is the *life* of God. It is thus, in respect to ourselves; our life is that which we produce by our self-sacrifice; we are living in respect to that which we have so created by self-control. Thus the passage means what we daily see. It *is* a fearful thing for a man living in this universe to be wicked; Nature infallibly and fearfully avenges every wrong. Not that I mean to bring down the awful meaning of these words to a mere passive operation of physical and moral laws; that is just what I wish not to do. This universe, these "laws," these facts, are God, and there is none other. I mean that this avenging of sin by Nature is the falling into the hands of the living God; that this one fact is stated truly, as it actually is, in the Bible; and falsely, unperceivingly, by men of science and moralists. We have to lift up our conceptions from the dust and raise them even to heaven, and to see that it is the hands of the living God that lay hold upon us in these natural circumstances. Think of this which we have so overlooked: the power of Nature to *make* us sin, i.e. act wickedly, if we are selfish. Is it not a fearful thing to be unloving, dead, inert, in a world of action, which operating so on us makes us the willing instruments of crime?

Because I assert all Being to be Divine, or God, I do not therefore assert that *we* are Divine, or that matter is. Even as in asserting all motion, or light, to be vibration, I do not therefore assert darkness to be vibration. I assert (relative) not-being also; i.e. not-being affecting us, or appearing to us, as Being. Here is the great error: men, having assumed the negation which affected them to be Being, were compelled to suppose some Being not Divine. Hence all the mystification, past and present, from which no system has escaped; not even Pantheism, though it has altered the form of it, and asserts the negation to be Divine. For clearly here is the error of Pantheism: it asserts that to be God which is not-God; i.e. it asserts that to be Being which is not-Being. This is the true relation of Actualism to Pantheism: there is no harm in asserting all Being to be God, if we only recognize negation or not-Being. The main error of philosophy is this of not recognizing negation.

Is not this, in part, why love to God is so much a true

passion, an all-absorbing joy? It is not only a love of some unseen person hard to conceive, from which love to creatures flows merely as corollary; it is a love of the universal, the absolute, the infinite Being, that is, the love of all. It is being united to the source of all delight, the very height and consummation of all beauty. It is to be one with Nature, to love, to know God; what man longs for, has longed for, in all ages. We need not wait to be dead for that; we may be it now. This is the bridal union of Nature and the soul. To see God is to love Him, to see in all Nature that one fact of God Himself, and to be joined with it in love. Nothing is now unloved, nothing unloving. Now we know her; know why she has stood before us so long with deep sad meaning in those gentle eyes. She has wished us to know and to love her, but our blindness would not let us; we have felt indeed what she must be, but we could not truly know her. When we sought to clasp her to our hearts—oh horror—it was a corpse cold and dead, a painted image with no heart within. But now we know her, and know it was our own death alone that made her dead. This is the love of God, the being one with Nature, the being holy: no more enslaved, no more doing as we like. It is the glorious liberty of the sons of God. *Words* cannot tell it; words, which have been poured forth in vain to paint the joy of human love, how shall they tell of the Divine? Yet words must be used; for when was joy silent?

It is thought alone that is "material"; man has made matter, made it by his sin, his selfishness. We see matter, because only love can see love; and where there is not-love is matter. Christ Himself would have been but matter to a crocodile. Alas, to how many of us is God only "matter" for the same reason. Our taking all this world to be mere matter, and using it only for the supply of our animal wants, and generally for our physical and mental purposes, is like a wild beast devouring men as if there were nothing in them save so much food for its stomach. The reason is plain; we have not eyes, we are not alive, we are not-man. Poor miserable lost creatures —miserable herein, that we might be better off. The Africans stole the glasses of Anderson's telescope to ornament their bodies with; it was merely "matter" to them. So we use the world, laughing in our ignorance at those who remonstrate with us.

Logic is a lever by which we elevate ourselves. But for that purpose we must use it firmly. It is like a pole by which pressing on the solid earth we push ourselves up an ascent. But we, feeling the resistance, are so apt to cease to push; we come to a "paradox," and say, "Ah, this is beyond the reach of reason, we must not adhere to logic here, it is above that." Fools! let us push and push and hold hard to our pole; and though in truth we shall not move the solid earth, we shall move ourselves, which to us is of much more consequence. Logic may prove nothing; certainly it alters nothing; but it may rectify our premises.

We know of God's gifts only by finding that we have them. The earnest work given to Science, the faithful, self-denying loving labour, live to end in better than mere material knowledge. Love, aspiration, hope, and toil of the soul, yea, spiritual life and love, have been given up, freely expended; is the result to be merely material knowledge, sensuous advantages? Oh no; for spirit spirit shall be given. Love for love. Life for life. The weary brow, the throbbing pulse, the aspiring heart,

Nature known by the Moral Emotions. 71

the longing sighs addressed to God for knowledge of Himself, are not squandered *thus*. Men have sought to know God, that is the good of Science, and lo! God shows Himself to them.

Physical things prepare the way, fit us for the revelation; but they are not the fact itself. The fire and the whirlwind are the knowledge of the phenomenal; spiritual science is to the phenomenal which it follows as the "still small voice." The true deep impulse to Science is love for God, desire after Him; and if God gives not to man love in return, He is still the debtor. For love can only be paid with love; not with material gifts, not even with such as are God's gifts to man. Science is man's prayer: "I beseech Thee show me Thy glory." How can God answer it but by showing us His love? In Science man has given himself to God; he cannot be repaid with universes. Shall love be repaid with "things?" To repay Science God must give Himself. The eyes of shepherds turned long ago to heaven, thinking that in those stars they saw the very heart of God. They were not deceived; we, their late descendants, do see in those stars the very heart of God. They poured out their love, not that we might exult in knowledge and traverse unerringly the seas; this were a poor reward. Their love, their life comes back to us as love, as life. The true desire of Science has been to know God, not His works; and it must end in knowledge of Him. It was our spirits, *we*, that desired to know, to know that which is like ourselves.

I cannot express truly the sight that flashes on me; yet it is the very fact. The material and psychical world *is* (as I have seen it must be) passion in spirits; i.e. conscious passions, emotions; it can be nothing else. Therefore it "becomes" in us conscious passions, i.e. passion in our spirits; we are surrounded by an universe of feelings, sensations, hopes, fears, sorrows, joys; an universe, in a word, of "passion." Here is the foundation of poetry; here the truth of imagination; here their marriage with logic and with Science. This I have been saying so long, and did not know it: that the universe was passion in spirits, not seeing that this is sensation, thought, emotion. Thus it is that we have no words for spiritual things, but those derived from physical; the physical *are* spiritual.

If I have any power of investigating Nature, it is because the world is a work of genius and I love it. God's heart is in it, and I know it as a friend. The solemn throbs and pulses of its vast vibrations are not merely mechanical events to my eye, I feel them as the beatings of a heart pressed close to mine. I throw myself on Nature and press myself upon her bosom in the passionate embrace of a friend; our *thoughts* are one because we *love*.

The imaginative view of God—that which attributes to Him the human, as "passion," "the world a work of Genius," and so on—goes to the heart of theology. It is not itself the truth, but the road to it. The introduction of fictions, the theory which leads to interpretation, is the living theology; the imaginative view of things, which gives to them human attributes is the truest. But, alike in respect to things and to the Deity, it should be remembered, that this imaginative view is not final, but only a means to an end; that it is the introduction of fictions, necessary indeed, to enable us to grasp the phenomena, but whose design is not to remain for ever, but

Nature known by the Moral Emotions. 73

to reveal the fact. [This idea was seen afterwards to be one with that of the *calculus*.]

It is truly therefore mind, design, thought, emotion, that are at work, and embodied in Nature; even as in our thoughts, feelings, and so-called "actions." And surely our mental passion may appear "a world" to other beings. It is design and feeling that are in Nature; but not God's. It is His act, His Holiness, which becomes feeling, emotion, and all those human passions, when it becomes passion; i.e. as it affects created spirits. The design, the goodness, the wisdom, are in the passion, the result; not in the act; they are phenomenal.

As in a musical composition each sound exists because the musician chooses it, but each is as it is because it is right; and to show each note to be the right note is to show the cause or reason of its existence; so Nature is music, and each vibration in it is such because it is the right vibration; the only reason for its being is that God chooses so to act; but acting, God acts *so* because that is the right act. Herein appears again the likeness of Nature to a work of Genius. Both are right: but the rightness of a spiritual act is Holiness. That other rightness of material adaptation flows from this, and expresses it. It is a secondary thing, having relation only to those Beings who perceive God's act as matter.

The laws of Nature, as we call them, are the relations or connections of our sensations. They are beautiful, nay glorious; they are well worth knowing; they must be known; they constitute the very basis of all our knowledge. They are what bring us into relation with God's action, which is the thing to be known. But they are not themselves the objects of knowledge, but only a means to it; as we use colours and sounds for learning optics and acoustics. That, in our sensation, motion must take direction of least resistance, and all motion be vibration, and develop by interference and subdivision, and follow in the definite order of cause and effect, and so on, is beautiful, interesting, and absolutely necessary to be known. But all this is not what we want to know. This is not the fact; this is the effect upon ourselves: it is the cause of all this that is the true object of knowledge; *what* is it that thus affects us?

Nature being thus a representative and expression of moral rightness, how she justifies and repays an unbounded love! *Right* is the only thing we cannot love too much. Will it not be a good thing when the separation of the love of Nature from the love of holiness is no longer possible? Shall we not be willing to submit, and to take part with her? Do we not acquiesce, nay do we not rejoice? Can we not lay even our torn and bleeding hearts upon that altar?

Nature obeys the man who acts right, for he takes part with God. In right action Nature has her origin and her existence; to right action she owes an absolute allegiance. Hence it is, sin works its own punishment: there is no deception, no defect, no error in Nature's justice; each wrong, however it may seem for a time to succeed, is fully avenged. No criminal can overrule her process by his power, no secrecy elude her vigilance. It is indeed a fearful thought: weak as an insect as man is in Nature's grasp, absolutely and passively within her power, how shall he dare to put himself in opposition to her! Inevitably those fatal wheels will crush him; yet this he does when he does wrong, for Nature is holiness. The earth's motion, fearful as it is to contemplate, hurts us not, because we move with it.

We are so constituted that the fall of one loved one outweighs, in our feeling, the happiness and good of any number; and so Christ speaks in his parallel of the hundred sheep. Why have we that feeling? In what lies the charm, to a loving heart, in the wandering and sinning of a loved one? Is not our heart so because God's is? Does not the fact demonstrate some unknown value and meaning and depth of fact in such wandering itself, which we have yet to learn? And as to the illustration, on the other side, of the multitude of seeds of which only a few develop, is there not an inversion in our view, arising from our perception of the *organic* as the highest in Nature? Do not those seeds which are restored to the inorganic reach the highest place?

That is a beautiful thought of Shelley's, that the dead are one with Nature. Cannot he who sneers at it see that Nature is infinitely more to the poet than to him— so much more, that it fills the poet's mind with an emotion and enthusiasm unknown to him; making him even willing and happy to die?

I rejoice to think of the future Science. How our children instead of being overwhelmed with the vastness and multiplicity of Nature, will delight in her simplicity, will play with her as with a child, and take sweet counsel with her as with a friend whose whole heart is open to them. And what a friend! One who is pure and fresh ever from the hand of God, holding before us constantly a pattern of the right, answering to our unceasing enquiry, What would God have us to do? "God does this."

Nature is gentle and "easy to be entreated"; all her

secrets may be gained by sympathy, by self-devotion. The way to comprehend her is not to put her to the torture, and attempt to wring out her laws by crucial experiments. She gives deceitful answers in her agony, or indignantly refuses to respond. Confide in her, love her, talk with her as a friend, woo her by secret, silent, reverential dwelling of the mind and heart upon her beauties; be a lover to her, and she replies with love, and makes the heart that thus with self-abnegation devotes itself to her, the participator of her most cherished secrets. There is no limit to such a man's insight into Nature but his own power of comprehending what she tells him. All this artists and poets have long known. They have wooed Nature, and not in vain. In their verses, on their canvas, her inmost heart stands revealed. But men of Science have done otherwise. With brutal violence they have sought to wrest from her those pledges of affection which are due to love alone, and they have rightly failed. Science and poetry and art are truly one, and must be cultivated in one spirit. When men of Science are reverential lovers and worshippers of Nature, as artists and poets are, then shall they also, as artists and poets do, comprehend her. The study of Nature is a study of physiognomy, needing for its successful presentation not the scalpel of the anatomist, but sympathy.

It is so far from being the fact that our knowledge of the laws of Nature is founded on microscopic and telescopic observations or indeed on minute examinations of any sort, that in truth our knowledge of the laws of these remote facts is based upon their analogy with those facts which are obvious. It is only in so far as we can reduce the former to a sameness with the latter that we know anything about their laws. Hence e.g. it is right to call the two forms of polarity male and female. Herein also lies an idea full of joy: as the external and obvious in Nature is full of artistic and poetic beauty, so also must that be which is remote and concealed. The excessively minute, the overwhelmingly large, are one with those exquisite forms of which our eyes can realise the beauty and our art idealize. As the external superficial world has a moral meaning, a sympathizing heart; as it speaks to us of our own joys and sorrows, and raises within us tender emotions and lofty aspirations, so is that world which is hidden from us bound to us also by ties as close. The stars that roll through space, the minutest particles of which millions constitute an atom, are our brethren also, even as trees and flowers are, share our emotions, reciprocate our love. This noble work the men of Science have, to extend the artistic and poetic appreciation of Nature beyond the scope of the senses, to show that she is the same in the vast and in the minute as she is in the forms which we speak of as forms of beauty. I feel within myself the spirit of those old Greeks who symbolized Nature and man's relation to it under so many legends and in so many statues. Science is the "loves of man and Nature:" Cupid and Psyche speak to me of it; but it is love fraught with no disaster. Tearful, painful, full of doubt it has been indeed, unconscious of its divine and joyful nature, a blind yearning, torturing and harassing the soul of man all these long ages, while he knew not what it was; his soul passionately smitten with the beauty of Nature, yet knowing it not, nor how to express his vague yearnings, knowing only that he was miserable. Such is ever the dawn of love. Inconceivably removed and unapproachable appears to us the object of our passion. Enough for us it seems to kiss the hem of her garment, to adore her at a distance; we shrink into utter insignificance before her. Thus appears to each man's heart his destined bride, thus to the universal heart of man has Nature yet appeared. Oh miserable days and nights of tears, prophetic of unutterable joy! Loved even as he loves, although he knows it not, one soft reply to stammering, half-uttered words, raises him to bliss he had not dared to dream; gives him the empire the dearest to his soul, his rightful empire too, for there enthroned he has his home. Does man love Nature, and Nature not love man? It is not so; she is his bride, his wife; bone of his bone, flesh of his flesh, soul of his soul. Oh union made in heaven and yet to be accomplished on earth, has not thy day come even now?

To affirm special creation, is a step towards atheism. The certain effect of introducing God specially into the past is to exclude Him just so much from the present. A reality is exchanged for an hypothesis; a seen and felt reality for an inconceivable hypothesis. The universe in truth is *full* of God; so full that nothing can be added thereto. No possible mode of regarding Him as working can bring Him closer than He is. Only those whose God is afar off can even conceive of Him as brought nearer. It is our privilege, and a privilege full of exquisite joy it is, to see that God does all things so directly, that it is impossible He can do anything more directly. No cause, nor chain of causes, has intervened; God did it: God does it: just as directly, just in the same sense, as He is supposed to "create a species." If any one says this makes no difference, I repeat that he cannot know till he has tried how much he loses by referring God's *immediate* agency to the past. If that idea has any excellence or virtue, if it be glorious or delightful, if it be true, let us have it now. It sanctifies the world and makes it holy; a sacred, awful, joyous thing is that which God is doing. And worst of all, the best of people with the best of motives, are committing Christianity to a scientific hypothesis. It must not be. Christianity is too precious to be, not indeed imperilled, but impeded so. It matters not whether the hypothesis be false, as we think it, or true as so many hold; the point is, that the oak shall not cling to the ivy. The remedy for apparently irreligious scientific dogmas is not to affirm a contrary scientific dogma, but to show that Nature is so full of God that no scientific doctrine, rightly stated, can be irreligious. True science teaches the same thing as the heart dictates; puts only into definite expression the indefinable emotion.

If creation had been, as is supposed, by design and contrivance of each particular thing, it would have been as Ruskin describes the "*un*-imaginative" painting; and just as far from its present perfection. Indeed it surely is our perception of what we think failures and defects and evils in Nature that makes us take this view of it as arbitrary, or as a work of talent. Once let us see or realize its absolute perfection, and we shall immediately conceive it rather as a work of genius.

Here come a group of vibrations sweeping through the air, mere matter and motion; and lo! they fall upon a human eye, a human ear, and straightway are become thought and emotion, an overwhelming passion of love, or joy, or grief; virtue or penitence, or heroism. If those vibrations were truly matter and motion here is a miracle. But what if those vibrations, as we thought them, were, in very truth, God's spiritual act; His thought, emotion, passion, surging against another spirit's bosom? What then more natural and just? The miracle resolves itself into sympathy. How can we so stultify ourselves as to think that what originates and ends in love and gladness, becomes matter on the way? Poet nor madman ever feigned such a metamorphosis! I adhere to common sense. That which is once spiritual is spiritual for ever.

We have to introduce design because of our assumption of "matter." To deny that, and leave the "matter," is manifestly bad: but the inadequacy, the impossibility of design, its making God *in time*, and indeed altogether denying Him in fact—all this is proof of the wrongness of our conception. The "design" is a hypothesis necessary from the wrong assumption. It involves the personality of God too; and the very impossibility of it is evidence of the wrongness of the view, and the means (in part) of rectifying it. So I find this idea of design to be as it were the "evil" by which a negation is removed: and the atheistic argument—holding matter but denying design—is an anticipation: it does not show us *why* we perceive design. We must perceive design in Nature because we perceive it as real or in time (putting our own "condition" into it); only by seeing it as eternal can design be excluded: for as truly as there is cause and effect, there is design. Now if we know *why* we must perceive design, we can exclude it; just as, knowing why we must perceive (or infer) the epicycles, we can exclude them.

This I must apply more widely. The feeling of intolerance which some experience towards the "design" idea is like that of Copernicus towards the epicycles. He felt that it could not be so, even though he might not be able to show it otherwise. Probably he denied them long before he showed the motion of the earth. But the assertion of actualism is involved in this feeling against design; even as the motion of the earth is latent in the disgust at epicycles. Design cannot be got rid of without making the world eternal, spiritual; otherwise there is a blank, a denial of plainest facts. We cannot deny that we perceive design: and seeing the actual as "real" involves seeing it as design; like seeing God as "personal."

That God is the direct doer of every thing in Nature, that this present world is full of Him, is not so much seen with the intellect as felt with the heart. I feel it throb through all the pulses of my life. I cast myself on the great ocean of Nature, on my mother's bosom, and feel God's arms around me, and His loving heart pressed to mine. It is no longer Nature, it is divine love and holiness that hold me in their embrace.

In my own experience there is a good illustration of the identity of two opposite opinions. For example: formerly I could not be brought to admit special creations, because it appeared to me that all was law, and accomplished by second causes. Now I see that there is no special creation, because all is God's direct and special act. Formerly I saw the law, now the liberty; but not two things: these are one, the chain of causes is God's absolutely free and direct action. These two are one, just as in Nature necessity and freedom are united in motion in direction of least resistance. The advance is to see the liberty, but not to see it as exceptional, and opposed to the law. Because law and liberty are one it is that God's direct act appears to us as cause and effect. One sees that God does as He choses in Nature, and holds a special providence; another sees that Nature is the expression of an absolute law, and holds it to be a chain of second causes, with which God does not interfere. But we should open both eyes, grasp Nature with both hands; embrace the Deity with head *and* heart. When we have most enlarged ourselves still is God too great for us, but how great He is we cannot see while we shut ourselves up in less than our native littleness. How God sets our distinctions at defiance, and bids us learn from each other. He does as He choses in acting by law. The chain of causes is His free agency, His direct and immediate act. The incompatability of law with freedom, of direct action with unvarying causation, lies in our imagination alone, is the fruit of our weak and corrupted will. Let us not bring God down to ourselves, but rise rather up to Him. Law is His freedom: be law our freedom too. It is the only freedom. The absolute Right alone is liberty. Nature thus, in her primary conception, in her very foundation and essence is moral: she is spiritual in truth, as man must have her to be. Nature is law and liberty because she is right action—the holy deed of a spirit, and regarded every way teaches that great lesson of the conformity of the will to right. Trace matter back to its essence and it is found to be Holiness. This is involved indeed in saying that the universe is a spiritual act. The great principle which Nature embodies, its essence, what it means as a great chain of causes and effects, is *Rectitude*.

The question may be brought to this: we are to believe God—now why? Is it because the facts warrant belief? Or are we to believe for the sake of some advantage to ourselves, because something will *happen* if we believe? To ask the question is to answer it. And this is, in truth, the design question over again, whether it is holiness or contrivance in nature; whether the thing was done because it was right; or in order for some advantage. Our systems form a whole; our believing for design, and creation by design, are all one thing. Well may theologians tremble so to have Science touched. They are right in feeling that their sacredest doctrines are involved: Science and theology are one. The chain, though hidden, vibrates to the slightest touch; it is vain to talk of holding them separate.

Science is done for love. Now what man, that is a man, would repay a woman's affection with jewels? And shall not God too give love for love? Man has been struggling, blindly, madly often, to pull down this barrier that rises up between him and God. Science is the record of this effort, the achievement of this end. At last—behold infinite eternal love: *this* is our God; we have waited for him. Wherefore hidest Thou *Thyself?* What to us is this infinite array of suns and worlds, this thronging life and innumerable shapes of beauty and delight, if Thou be not in them? We cannot, will not have them; through and through we search them and pronounce them all a vanity; not in them is that true fact for which we long, which we must attain or die. They are inert; our flesh and our soul crieth for *God.* With earnest, passionate, self-immolating toil man has sought for God, for the true Being in nature. Is he now to be told that he must be content with physical advantages? That he must be content with getting? That there is no Being to whom he may give himself? Oh weary, longing, steadfast heart, believe it not. Shake thyself from the dust . . . arise, shine, for thy light is come.

"To be natural" therefore is to love, and willingly to do the right. Nature is voluntary or spiritual rightness; moral goodness: spiritual because absolute freedom; right because absolute law. We are surrounded therefore by, exist in, goodness; hence the discord with Nature of moral evil, a discord how powerfully felt, how fearfully seen, in human life! Every voice of Nature to man has this meaning. "Choose the right. Make your liberty conformable to law; in conformity to law achieve and maintain your liberty." Not driven and compelled, but how sweetly solicited to good, is man. Each softest or sublimest object whispers in its beauty, "I am right," or in its grandeur thunders, "I am right." This seeing, God pronounced it good. All good but one thing; and that the one that Thou madest, oh God, in Thy image, the crown and glory of Thy creation, choosing right like Thee! How long shall he be thus dishonoured and abased, walking the earth with step erect, but with heart crushed down with evil and face bowed in shame? Teach us, I beseech Thee, to see Thee so in Nature, that Thy moral beauty there revealed may win us to be like Thee; Thy holiness fill us with shame, Thy tenderness melt us to penitence. Lead us through Thy works unto Thy Gospel; by the condemnation teach us to seek the pardon; by proof of ruin and corruption subdue our hearts to renewing and sanctifying love!

And that this law of Nature—the law and liberty seen in motion in direction of least resistance—is given to it by ourselves, is the expression indeed of our mental constitution, how it shows us to be made for good! This is in us intellectual rightness; the sign and proof of that

Nature known by the Moral Emotions. 85

spiritual rightness which is our native but now lost inheritance. This world could have been made only by a good, or holy, Being; its very structure involves it. Right is stamped everywhere. Holy, holy, holy Lord God!

Have I not solved that question I proposed to myself so long ago: What is that action of God's that we see as matter and motion? It is His Holiness; His choosing the right. Nature is right, and right by His choice, therefore not infused or filled with the moral element; it *is* morality. Each true thing I have ever heard seems now to come back to me with a new kind of truth: this for instance, that the glory of God is His moral character; even His creative glory. The universe proclaims not only His power and godhead, but truly understood His moral excellence also. God answers prayer. In my earnest wish to know something of what *His* work in Nature was, I prayed, "I beseech Thee show me Thy glory." And He has shown me, sufficiently for mortal comprehension, what His glory in creation is. The rightness of each object in Nature is an instance and evidence of the spiritual rectitude of its Maker. Beauty, being, as I have seen, conformity to the universal law, bears this testimony: He that made me conformed His will to law. The word is infinitely beautiful, because God is infinitely holy.

A miracle cannot be an interference with the general course of nature, because there is no general course of nature to interfere with. How can a being interfere with his own action? How many cases there are in nature of mischievous result as well as of good: e.g. bees are destroyed sometimes by the adhesion of pollen which they are conveying to the stigma. Thus natural theologians have never been able to look nature fairly in the face. In truth the idea of nature is not that of use and design; it has a deeper basis. Nature is right, and results shift for themselves: there being the innate compensation in it, because it is right, that every evil, every failure or loss, becomes tributary to a greater good. The true idea of nature is that of a work of art; what it expresses is not contrivance but passion; its end is not use but self-expression; its spring not benevolence but the necessity of producing; its law not adaptation, but rightness. This is the truth that God's object in creation was not the good of His creatures, but His own glory, "For Thy glory they are and were created." Creation sprang from God as pictures grow out of an artist, or melody flows from a musician; because it was in Him and must come forth. Thus the universe is music. It is an impassioned act; full of a meaning deeper than thought. Man cannot know nature, starting with the idea of design; alter the conception to that of passion, and it is clear.

The idea that the universe is music was with me the result of a purely scientific induction; the studying of material laws alone developed the conception, and simply in reference to material phenomena; yet it contains the moral secret of the universe as well.

I do not agree with that view of "ideal" beauty which represents it as more perfect than the true beauty. Nature is really perfectly beautiful; infinitely above any ideal of beauty we can form; it is blasphemy to say or think the contrary. Is it not God's act; and can He not conceive better than we? The imperfections and ugliness of Nature are relative to us only. The real beauty of Nature as it is, is absolute, infinite, God's act being so;

but we see it under limit of our own nature, partially and in time; therefore to us it is defect, and want of beauty. I object to this in Plato, that he finds the real world not even beautiful enough for him! It was a false direction (i.e. though right then) that he gave to thought in sending it to the region of the ideal for its highest conceptions. But this, observe, it was emphatically right to do; it was the separation for perfecting.

Man's thought cannot surpass, nay for ever shall fall infinitely short of God's act. Higher thoughts, more glorious conceptions, a more perfect beauty, a diviner truth, a purer and profounder holiness *exist* here in the facts of actual Nature than our most elevated imaginations could ever approach. Nature is perfect and infinite in beauty and in every form of rightness. That we find her not so is because we see her wrongly; in parts and not in whole, in time and not in eternity. Yet is this right also; our proper mental discipline consists in not seeing all things beautiful; it is needful for us, this perception of the beautiful mingled with the ugly. But to accomplish this good for us it was not needful that God should deform His work and really mingle bad with good; it was enough to place us with our littleness in a world of perfect good too large for us. That is all: what makes our evil—apart from sin—is only too large a good; our ugly is a beauty on too grand a scale for us. The senses delude us here as everywhere; we perceive an ugly and we think therefore that the thing is really so. Here as everywhere the first step towards true knowledge is to learn to emancipate ourselves from sense.

Now I know what the "ideal" is. It is to us what Nature is to God; that is, a fact perfectly beautiful. We cannot see the true and perfect beauty of Nature, because it is too large. Because it is only a part, it has innumerable connexions with other things which we do not perceive, and so it appears to us defective. Therefore we conceive for ourselves something smaller, something that shall be a whole and yet not too large for us; a single fact that shall represent to us the universe, isolated, and without any connection with any other fact; and that we conceive of as perfect and complete in beauty, in itself. This is creative art, the work of genius; but this to us is just what creation is to God. The universe is God's Ideal perfectly acted out. Our effort to attain the ideal is an attempt to do what God did in creation.

This is the meaning also of creation being a work of Genius, of Nature expressing God's *passion*. It is God carrying out His ideal. Little sympathy have they with God who deem that He did anything worse than He could have done it; even an artist worthy of the name will not do that. No man who can legitimately claim the title of *Poet* will do less than his best: shall the Great Poet be the only one to link shame with the word? "The heavens and the earth, and all that is between them, think ye that I have created them in jest"? Does not the Koran rebuke the Christian? Did not the Great Heart glow, the Almighty Hand thrill with joy, when the Ideal of the Universe was realized in act? Nature is God's ideal wrought out with no shortcoming. We have the gift of conceiving an ideal in order that we may know what Nature really is, if we could see her rightly: and that we may share with God the joy of creation; share in the joy, though not in the achievement. God will not keep even that joy to Himself; all He has He gives to His dear loved child; the joy of holiness, the joy of love, the joy of making others happy, and even that joy we might have thought truly incommunicable, the joy of creating. But it is a poor return for this great gift, yea rather a most melancholy abuse of the gift itself, to claim for this petty ideal of ours a superiority over God's own ideal; to call His creation poor and mean, defective, marred, and incomplete, and our conceptions perfect and surpassing :—they are but toys.

The absolute and perfect beauty of creation is involved in its *holiness*; if Nature be really partly ugly, it is partly unholy; this is no strained analogy, it is mere certainty. In Nature we perceive a mixture with the beautiful of that which is ugly, and we conceive a perfect beauty; but this is only to teach us that in Nature as God sees it there is nothing ugly. For *sin* is not in Nature, not in God's act; it is man's act, and corrupt as it may be it cannot pollute Nature's purity.

As our sympathy with God increases, we shall understand more what His ideal is; i.e. as we grow holier; for sympathy with God is holiness. Therefore it is as I have said: the source of a true knowledge of Nature lies in rectitude of heart, in love of right. When we have a perfect sympathy with God, so that our ideal corresponds with His (save only as respects our poor capacity), then we know Nature to her inmost heart, she is our ideal also. There have been men who have attained near to this in all ages, I believe; for it does not depend on great knowledge. The true poets have come near it; martyrs have seen it who have beheld in dark and loathsome dungeons the path that leads beside the still waters, strewn with sweet flowers, and overshone by the sun and a thousand stars; who have seen in burning piles the altar of a glad and grateful sacrifice, in chains and cruel stripes the gems which glitter in the crown of life. Yes, even we, unworthy to be martyrs, may see it too, if we can learn to see in care and want and toil, in self-control and sacrifice for right, a bright and joyous life.

Is not this God's ideal of Nature, that is, of Life—Love duly regulated? If we ask, What is Nature? the reply should be, What is your ideal? That may not be, nay certainly is not, the very truth—but it is the nearest you can come to it.

Now our ideal is to Nature as if some one unable to comprehend or appreciate a musical strain as a whole, should take the single chords, and seek to make each one complete and perfectly beautiful. He would add more notes, or alter their arrangement, or leave out the discordant ones, or cause the chord to be played by more instruments. He would make each chord an "ideal." But this could not really be done without spoiling the music, and we should say to him: The whole strain just as it is, with what you call these imperfections, is to us just so perfect, just such an "ideal" as you seek to realize in the separate parts. The ordinary view of the ideal, regarding it as above Nature, has inflicted on us woeful injury. It has misrepresented to us alike God and Nature. It has made Nature teach us false lessons; it has closed our eyes to the holiness that is in Nature, so that we have not in truth really seen Her. And, pitiful loss indeed, it has taught us to look for our best, not to God's conception, but to our own. How could we ever rise, when our own ideal was our standard? What can our own ideal express or contain, but ourselves? That was not what we were endowed with the ideal faculty for, but that we might by its means be emancipated from the tyranny of our senses, and see Nature with our hearts as she really is. So knowing in our inmost soul, taught by our hearts that Nature is really perfect, we shall be led to explore and study her, we shall seek how we may see mortality swallowed up in life; pain, evil, and defect absorbed and lost in perfect rectitude. And thus studying Nature our heart and thought will be itself expanded.

"Man sees nothing that he does not say." I perceive science, philosophy, art, that wonderful impulse to "represent" nature, which is so specially evident in the artist, but is equally the fact of all our mental life, is the child's instinct to say what it sees. I have noticed this in my own children; whatever they see or think of they say; before they do anything they *say* it. That is the primary idea and use of language, as a means and form of our own mental life; to communicate with others is a secondary application. It is clear we must "represent" (or say) that which we are, which we understand, or are the substance of.

Now, incidentally, as our mental life thus *is*, and consists in, re-presentation of nature; so, certainly, does our bodily. Our physical nature is a "saying" or "representation" of nature; all life indeed is so; i.e. of physical nature. And the human body, as the ultimate development of the physical life, is a complete representation of nature. When our mental life attains to be a perfect representation of nature, then will it not have attained to the stage of manhood; a perfect "saying" or representation of nature?

There seems to be one way in which the unbeautiful phenomenon already reveals the beautiful reality, and that is man's most distorted works revealing the beautiful working and development of the human mind. So that when we look at the ugly we no longer *perceive* the ugly although we see it, but perceive by its means the absolutely beautiful. I have long ago seen in so many cases that human errors and follies were among the most beautiful of all facts; that to account for or give the reason of anything was always to show the good and the beauty of it. I have seen this long before I saw that it was so because it is all life; that evil is nutrition, and nutrition necessarily of absolute and equal goodness; all except sin.

Life always appears to us beautiful and good. It is a very synonym for good, indeed. But wherever we see a whole there we see life; therefore if we saw the whole, we should see it to be life; i.e. absolute beauty and good. Ugliness and evil are *not-life;* types of sin, which is death. Ugly, evil, false, mean simply that we do not see the life; they are phenomena of which we are unable to see that they are vital parts of a living whole.

Art is the interpretation of Nature by the intuition of Beauty.

Nature has no secrets which she hides from him who knows that she is holiness; no love that she withholds from him who loves the holy.

As I look on a painting I see that its calling is to make us see that nature is not really matter, but a spiritual fact which thus appears to us. By painting we are recalled to the reality of nature. Painting and Science both deal with the one question: What causes us to perceive the phenomenon?—Science for the head, painting for the heart. It is the higher spiritual function they are destined to achieve that binds man to the arts, although he knows it not. Nothing *he* seeks in Art or Science is the real reason of his impulse towards them, or can redeem that impulse from being unworthy, but a higher end which he cannot foresee or intend, because it is to raise him above himself, to elevate his spiritual standard, which nothing he can himself conceive can do.

As the *function* of Science is to reveal that Nature is a holy act of God, so the function of Art must be to reveal that holiness in the actual facts of Nature; to show the holiness of Nature. All Nature is beautiful, and beautiful because holy; for beauty truly is spiritual, and the work of Art is to display this, but it must be done in Nature's living way, and by no short cut. The phenomenal is God's road to the spiritual therefore, it is man's.

What course Art will take in showing the universal or absolute holiness of Nature, one cannot say, but it must be so. When Science, or the mere tracing of cause and effect, becomes thus spiritual, in the true sense of moral, how can Art fall short? It must have even a higher function, to point out the holiness, not to our intellect, but to our heart. Art is truly above Science; Science makes us see the holiness of Nature, Art shall make us feel it. And Science as the lower first attains its development; Art follows and depends upon it.

An ideal beauty above Nature must be laid aside, and Art must sit down to Nature accepting her as absolute beauty, and making her ideal correspond thereto. It is not hard to see that there must result a complete revolution of our conception, or rather of our feeling, of Nature altogether. It will show Nature to be only phenomenal and the reality quite different. But that is what we want. In order to rise above Nature we must first put Nature above us. We are truly above, no doubt, and shall safely rise again; but this inversion must be or we are left in ignorance.

Of Poetry also as well as Art this must be true. So long as Poetry deals with an ideal beauty above Nature, it is in its infantine stage; like the science of the dark ages:—not wrong absolutely; this has been a stage all the mental life of man has passed through and it is only right, but it must pass.

We err altogether in thinking the dark ages time lost for Science: it was, as I have said, the preparing of the instruments; it was infancy laying the only possible basis for manhood. So now of Art and Poetry.

In the same way, we must study the evil phenomenon as *good*, and it will reveal its good reality. We should say, evil is a subjective phenomenon, produced by a good reality. Holding it to be good, and studying it so, in all its details, mastering it *phenomenally*, it will reveal to us what that good reality is which causes us to perceive the subjective evil.

I cannot but believe that human life may become glorious, beautiful, and happy to a degree almost beyond our thought by the fulfilment of the promise of such a Science, when through the false phenomenon we see the true reality; through the ugly phenomenon the beautiful reality; through the evil phenomenon the good reality. Shall we not, must we not, be happier then; more conformable to Nature; yes, better, without which we cannot be more natural.

It is striking—first we use the phenomenally true to interpret the phenomenally false, then the phenomenally false when interpreted to interpret the phenomenally true.

First we interpret the life above by the life beneath; then the life beneath by the life above. For as we interpret, more and more comes to require interpretation. Thus, at first, we divide nature into two portions, the inorganic and organic, or unliving and living, and first get a certain knowledge of the unliving, which we use to interpret the living. Then when we have interpreted this, we use it again to interpret the unliving, and see that the whole is life.

Surely Art will advance as Science has done: by nutrition and function, first by making the ugly appear beautiful; and then by letting it reveal the beautiful which constitutes it. And this will continue as in Science, making more and more phenomena which now appear beautiful to us appear not so, until the entire phenomenon being seen to be unbeautiful will reveal the real or spiritual beauty. This is the " function " of Art from the first, unforeseen by us but not less to be worked out by us. And it is (as in Science) only a renewal of its childhood.

How beautiful appears that childish instinct to believe and to admire everything; it is not a childish folly, it is the instinct of humanity to trust in God, and God honors it, makes it the great, the only instrument of revealing to man the really true, the really beautiful. Only those who trust Him so implicitly as to believe *all* His work absolutely true and beautiful, will God conduct to a true knowledge of Himself. Knowledge can only come through trust and love; and cannot be when there is not perfect sympathy.

We imagine to ourselves a God, and then love Him; but do we love the true actual God who does all these things in the world? Is our will one with His? We must enlarge our conception of good by all the evil that there is; that is God's ideal. How poor a thing we should have made of His love and mercy; it would have been self-indulgence, not self-sacrifice. Here is the failure of our ideal, the false ideal. Thus Christianity is spoilt by such "ideal."

Science and Art have done, like other children in their childish period, only that which they like. It is the mark of manhood to know that the important things to do are not those which he likes, but rather the opposite. He has to do his work against his inclination. Science has set herein a noble example, and by mere instinct of advancing years; seeing indeed some reward, but not knowing at all the best. Nor can it be known; how can the youth who quits his play and sits down reluctantly to business know the best results that will ensue; the place among men, the home, the power that he is creating for himself. He acts for immediate ends, he gains respect, he gets a little money to spend, and so on. But what he *does* is incomparably more than these, though he little thinks of it. So Science set herself to her weary phenomenal task like a good boy leaving school; she saw a new scope for her activity; she saw immediate useful ends to serve, and she has had her share of these; but she does not foresee God's design for her. *The* thing she was accomplishing, to which all these were as nothing, she did not know; nay she can hardly believe it when it appears. See too how habit becomes second nature. This experimental course which Science was so loth to enter upon has become so pleasant, or at least so usual, by long custom, that it is hard for her to do anything else; or even to believe anything else is to be done.

How the men of the old pseudo-spiritual science must have scorned the idea of a science wholly material or phenomenal, founded entirely upon nature and observation. They had been diving into essential being, talking of deep "spiritual" reality. The mere phenomenal must have been distasteful in the extreme. We cannot wonder that the struggle was so long. Perhaps the greatest apparent degradation of the human mind, in the whole history of humanity, is that abandonment of a real or spiritual science to take up with a purely phenomenal and natural one. Yet instead of a descent it was a rise no less than infinite, as we see now.

We say, with the poor Israelites of old, to man: "Speak *thou* to us, but let not God speak to us lest we die." Alas! the sad mistake—God's "words are life;" for they are spirit. But life is a painful, tearful, striving, failing, desolate, discontented thing; we do not like it, we fear it, we think it death and say again: "Speak *man* to us; lest we die." We cling to the "ideal," to the human; and dread to plunge into that great ocean of the phenomenal wherein God's voice alone is heard. For He speaks in thunders, and lightnings flash from His eye; He utters His voice when sorrow chills the heart and forms of horror affright the soul. In illusions that bewilder, in anguish that overwhelms, in loathsome shapes that terrify, God speaks; and we in our folly say: "Let not God speak to us lest we die." But we grow wiser at last, and weary of man's empty words; athirst, and finding only broken cisterns, we brace ourselves to our solemn task, and say: "Let God speak to us, that we may live." Then we apply our lips with resolute and trustful heart to the bitter fountain; we grasp with shuddering yet undaunted hand the abhorrent fact, and say: "The cup the Father giveth me to drink shall I not drink it?" And we prove that the words He speaks to us are spirit and are life. The fearful or the sad phenomenon reveals the joyful fact, the false and ugly evil melts into the holy.

Will it not be glorious, this future of the world, when Science, Art, Philosophy and Poetry shall join in showing to man that Nature is a divine and holy deed; its truth, its beauty, its good, all spiritual, and revealed by perception of false, of ugly, and of evil; when ugliness and evil shall be to us only as wrong perceptions are to our sense of truth:—the means only of revealing to us, bringing at once and of course before our minds, the higher, larger beauty and goodness, which, except by them, we could not know.

To affirm the absolute beauty of Nature is at once to affirm that it is not material, because the material universe is not absolutely beautiful and cannot be. Has not this, partly, kept Art back and prevented us from identifying the ideal with the actual; she has waited for Science. But when Science also affirms matter not to be a reality the way is open for her; and for Poetry also, in the affirmation that Nature is absolutely good, although phenomenally evil.

And what a new world thus opens before us—what untold, unthought of treasures of beauty and good lie hidden in the ugly and the evil! It will re-create our world for us to "interpret" them. I thank God there is so much ugliness and evil—so many illusions—because each one of them is the voucher for a beautiful and good reality, as each illusion of the sense in Science is evidence and voucher for some true scientific fact. I clasp evil and wrongness to my heart, and love them by anticipation: they are life; they are God's tenderest love; and He says to me in them: "Look, my child, and tell

Me what I am doing; 'tis painful to you at first, but you will love it when you see it." By faith I see it even now, my Father; and love it though unseen because Thou doest it. Blind and ignorant children that we have been, that we would not look to see *what* our Father does, but turned away our eyes, calling it ugliness and evil because it affects us painfully. Yet is this ideal Art right, as a step; nor is this vain attempt to rise by our own ideal up to God, really in vain. Sad indeed would be a phenomenal Art, or Science, or Poetry, if it had not first been hallowed by the upward flight towards the throne of God. Once having learnt to see that the ideal is in truth *divine*, Science, Art, Poetry can descend safely to identify it with phenomena wherein the stamp of divinity seems almost lost; once having soared the soul will soar again. Therefore the false ideal precedes the true. God's is too large for us at first; uninstructed by the teaching of the fancy we should never comprehend the glory of reality; as a child is taught by toys to deal with the reality of life.

It is God's voice and not man's that I want to hear in Music; and in Science too, and in Society; and in all human works indeed; for in all this best knowledge is to be attained. *All* man's works may and shall express this higher meaning—even human life. We try to put society right, to carry out our own ideas; so long as we do this we shall certainly put it wrong, but, thank God, it will be *vitally* wrong; and in the end it shall express a meaning beyond any thought or design of man, or possible to man; an idea written there by God; accomplished not by our efforts, but in spite of them, although by them only rendered possible.

III.

MENTAL PHYSIOLOGY.

Moral and emotional facts stand on the same basis as physical facts—False perceptions are the condition of mental life—Nature is always first misunderstood—There is no method for discovery—The relation of logic to imagination—The place of those who want logic—The significance of paradox—Sleep in mental life—Breathing in mental life—Genius and talent—Talent is nutrition, genius function—Man's mind is female, woman's male—How genius and talent are affected by paradox—Genius is common sense—Mental life arises from failure—Men are parts of a whole—May genius be found common?—In humanity, as in genius, there is no design—Nutrition and function are the life in thinking—Submission to the thought of others is disease—Saying is seeing—The mental life of humanity.

We perceive not only physical facts, but moral, emotional, intellectual facts. These moral facts are as much external to ourselves as the physical; and they nourish, constitute, are food of, our emotional and intellectual life, just as the physical facts are of our scientific life. This is important to observe; because though our entire mental life depends upon observation of physical facts, yet these physical facts are not only physical, they are intellectual, emotional and moral, as much as physical. For instance, when I perceive a person fall in the street, I perceive a physical fact illustrating gravity; but I also perceive an emotional fact, a fellow creature injured; a moral fact, a call for my assistance; an intellectual fact, or process of thought and motion. And these emotional, moral, intellectual elements are as truly in the fact I see as the physical ones. I no more create them than the other, indeed perhaps even less; doubtless the physical elements, those which involve space, time, and matter, are much more dependent upon my perception than the others. Thus each psychical fact is three-fold, physical, intellectual, moral; nourishing our three-fold mental life.

Our emotional life is only one form of the emotional life of the universe. And observe that our minds must be nourished with emotional elements in wrong or organic relations. The entire process of nutrition and function exists here also, and will reveal itself to patient thought. Thus an emotional organization is produced, so that perception of " physical facts " sets up long trains of feeling. It is psychical facts that we perceive in nature. But the question returns whence and how come those physical forms of thought, space and time and matter? I know what is wrong; I have a nutritive view of the question; I put the phenomenon before the fact, effect before cause; this it is that perplexes me.

It may be objected to the statement of our perceiving emotional and intellective facts in nature, that we only perceive these by virtue of our own consciousness, because by our own experience we have learnt that they must be there. When we see a person fall we do not *perceive* a sentient being in suffering, but know from our own experience that it must be so. Now this helps me to the very fact I have been wanting. I grant that our perception of emotional facts in nature is based upon our own experience; but this statement is equally true of all our perceptions, of physical as of emotional. We can perceive nothing but that which is homogeneous with what we have experienced. The foundation of all that we perceive lies in what we feel; here is the foundation of our perception of space, time, matter. Let a man once perceive a new idea, excite him in a new emotion, and from that time he sees everything new. What he sees depends on what he is himself. A child perceives no "things" in the facts of nature until by his own consciousness he has obtained the idea of himself, of his body as a thing, or occupying space, as being solid; nor of time, until he has experienced in himself the lapse of time. So he perceives in the facts of nature no ideas, no emotions, until he has conceived ideas and felt emotions himself. Thus the facts of nature constitute our minds and yet are independent of what we perceive in them. The "things" bear the same relations to the reality as the ideas and emotions do; they are all, as perceived by us, self-derived, and yet true.

Our solemn conviction of a real universe around us would really be almost laughable if it were not so glorious; this wrong relation of our ideas is our nutrition, the very fact and basis of our mental life. It is, in fact, because of this wrong perception that we have a mental life at all. I am truly overwhelmed with the grandeur and solemnity of this thought; our perception of a world external to ourselves is the source of our mental life, the stimulus of all our mental activity; in one word, it is our mental nutrition from first to last. All our mental life comes from obervation of Nature. Consider how useless it would have been for all purposes of mental life for us to have perceived Nature as being merely a passion in ourselves; or, if instead of seeing the sun moving we had directly perceived that we were being carried round it.

In this necessity of our perceiving passion in ourselves

Mental Physiology.

as external, I conceive I approach to a solution of the question as to the sense in which our mental life is maintained by organic or wrongly-arranged materials; to seeing how the elements are in themselves organically arranged. Until the illusion of a real external world had had its full nutritive operation upon us, it could not be done away with. Berkeley and other spiritualists attacked it in vain; its work was not done. And now, if so be it is overthrown, Nature has another sort of work to do for us, not less but more. The illusory motion of the sun was the life of astronomy up to a certain point, but when that was seen aright, there were other nutritive errors in astronomy, and it advanced faster than ever. So when we see matter aright as a passion in ourselves, there will be other nutrition from Nature, and Science will advance faster than ever; for each function is a nutrition. And see how the nutritive elements of each former period are cast off, excreted, when they have performed their function and become decomposed or disintegrated; with what contempt we look back upon the idea of the sun really moving round the earth (though not upon the men who believed it); so shall we before long upon the idea of real matter.

I see, too, that books presenting new truths, must be first misunderstood; men must be so as well as Nature; this is nutrition; there can be no function without it. All new facts of observation must be first organically arranged; it is the very law of life. Perhaps we may say he never really understands a fact or truth who has not first misunderstood it. A new truth is presented by a book just as by Nature, and will certainly, by all who really perceive it, be organically perceived, although the rectification or function may immediately ensue: the new, true food, must be first assimilated, i.e. its elements arranged in vitally wrong relations, in conformity with the previous life of the individual; it could not else effect its function. And why should men complain? It is not a thing to feel hurt about; they only participate in a common lot with Nature; surely this is enough. Nature is ever misunderstood at first, and most by those who most earnestly study her. Did not she show us, as plainly as it was possible to put the thing, the earth going round the sun; and did not we, for ages, think that she meant that the sun went round the earth? It was too bad, and really very hard for her, for we are her pet children; our education is her dearest delight. But we could not help it, and she has had most pathetic patience with us, never one harsh or angry word; she has only said: "Look again, see this fact, how can it be as you think?" And when we put *that* wrong also, she has still only smiled, and caressed us gently, and said again: "Look here." Fact after fact she has tenderly laid before us, until at last we could not but see it as she meant it. But still how far we are from her real meaning. Nature deals with us as with children; when we see one thing wrong she does not scold us nor explain it to us, but shows us other and other things, yet truly one, till we cannot help seeing them aright. Hers is the true scheme of education. And the true scheme for a writer is not to explain, but to show fact after fact. Ever by men as by children, a new fact (and especially a new theory, which is the fact of facts) must at first be wrongly seen, and assimilated to that which is in the mind before.

That is a radical error, the idea of a *method* for discovery. There can be none, any more than a method of growing and developing. Mind developes as the body does, by passion in direction of least resistance. Men have supposed they made the mind. Have we not hitherto taken more pains to do God's work than our own; there is but one work that He commits to us, and that is moral control of passion; to do right is the only thing we have to do, and can truly *do* at all. All the rest is His doing. There is no method for thinking, or prosecuting Science; thought developes by alternate nutrition and function, like other life. If we must have such a one method it is this alone :—sympathy with Nature; love, which is life. Life is the " method " of the mind, as of the body, as of the universe. The mind grows like the body; the conditions are, in each, plenty of wholesome food and air, and plenty of exercise. " Which of us by taking thought," is as true for mind as for body.

This has struck me respecting logic. The logical faculty helps thus: Every one has certain basic or fundamental ideas, in accordance with which, more or less, he arranges all his conceptions and views. Now if a man have not logic he can arrange his views inconsistently without feeling them to be so, and therefore can rest satisfied, looking at subjects as he likes, seeing them all under the glow of his favourite moral perfections, as e.g. of God's goodness and wisdom; not perceiving that his opinions are more or less inconsistent with such general idea. Hence he is eloquent, active, can talk and interest, and in a word be "charming," Indeed, " imaginative " men are very much characterised by this deficient logic, and poetry as yet involves it. See Mr.—— e.g. "The world is holy;" not perceiving the illogicalness of calling a *thing* " holy." Hence I think, in a great measure, the weakness of poetry, and that class of thought. The poets do not perceive the illogicalness, but practically the world feels it, and even to the best of us, such thoughts seem to be a thing apart from the real and actual world; we call it "imagination," meaning fiction. [As indeed, in a high, noble (i.e. a vital) sense it is. And, by-the-bye, surely imagination altogether, as Ruskin defines it, is the vital introduction of fiction, preparing only for the function.] Now, the logical man is very different; to him it is necessary that his conceptions should be really consistent; hence he is ill at ease, does not know what to believe, does not find that he can ordinate all facts and phenomena under any such beautiful basic idea, is therefore at a great disadvantage; cannot speak, has no beautiful things to say, finds poetry mystify him, has no brilliancy, is in short a mere dull, useless simpleton. But his turn comes, the illogical man rests content; the logical man advances. With patient toil he arranges his ideas consistently; but then he finds that they require another basic idea; by his logic he overthrows the fundamental conceptions, and introduces one consistently with which all the phenomena may be arranged; making thus an absolute advance or development in knowledge. The logic works to and fro, as it were,—vibrates. It is a lever by which he overthrows his own basic conceptions. I have the image of stone-work in my eye; he first lays a rest for his logic, then by means of that, as with a lever, upheaves his own firm standing ground. He gets "revelation" in fact, that is, he interprets. I seem to arrive at this (though it appears strange to me): that logic is emphatically the interpretative faculty. Logic puts right the ideas arranged theoretically, or in vital wrongness; and by that means reveals or inducts the new basic idea or general conception, i.e. the function; or in Science the development, the new and higher life. This seeing that the elements of any theory must *go so;* this instinctive putting right, and so interpreting, is in truth the logical faculty. The interpretation is emphatically logical. I think this must be so. This "logical faculty" is simply that instinctive perception of right relation. And here is the relation of logic and imagination; imagination is nutrition, theory, fiction; logic the function, interpretation, exclusion of the fiction or vital force. Thus imagination is the nutritive, the theoretical, the converse of the logical. Here should be the love between them. Imagination and logic are man and wife—one; the blessed parents of truth and mental life. [This agrees strictly with Ruskin.] The logic cannot be without first imagination; but imagination exists for logic. "Without poetry can be no facts."

What a strange divorce and unnatural hatred it is that has existed between imagination and logic; or rather, not unnatural, but only that natural aversion between boys and girls, which I have noted so widely, and which is the precursor of the marriage union. But how wonderful it seems that I should find the logical faculty to be emphatically genius. How oppositely we usually think; but it is so. The gift of genius is to exclude fictions, to permit the elements to assume right relations. (Boys, at a certain age, have just that same contempt for girls that logical men have for imaginative.) Mozart wrote music logically; and so of all interpreters. It was very clear in Copernicus that he treated astronomy logically. Imagination is theory, after all. All this is merely the old common sense and instinct of the world—that imagination and strict reasoning should be united. Logic works first forwards on the phenomena, then backwards upon the stand point. My own logic has worked thus. I never could see that the facts of the world agree with God's skill, wisdom, and goodness, as the "idea of the world." Accordingly I worked logically upon the phenomena, and then my logic worked back again, revealing to me a different, higher, and truer "idea" of the world, viz., that of holiness; revealing it by the interpretation of the phenomena, or rather, of the imaginative theory of them. And this holiness, which has been revealed to me as the "fact" of the universe, is not a fiction, but genuine, real, and logical holiness, viz., the holiness of a deed. It has been said before, imaginatively, i.e. fictitiously, the world has been called a "holy *thing*."

And here one sees the nature and the use of that class of men in whom logic is wanting: they can deny results without denying causes (or systems); can deny conclusions, leaving the premisses uncorrected. Now, so far, this is a defect, doubtless; but does it not enable a thing to be done which otherwise might not be? Is it not by such people that the evil and wrong of certain facts, or results, are felt and insisted on? To these men it is owing, surely, that others (in whom the logical connection of things will not be ignored) are made to feel the wrongness and impossibility of the results; and *so* the system gets altered.

Thus, in fact, three sets of men work out the *reductio ad absurdum*. One set deduces the impossible results, and gravely sets them forth as facts; another denies and denounces the results, and insists they are not legitimate consequences, &c.; then a third sees what each of the others points out, and so makes visible the demand to correct the premisses. Is it not a beautiful *organic* co-operation?

It is interesting to note the dependence of the class

Mental Physiology. 109

who correct the premisses upon the other two; how they need not be able—doubtless are not able—to do the other's work, not logical enough to make the deduction, nor sensitive enough to feel decisively, for themselves, the wrongness; but capable of seeing both when shown them, and putting them together; endowed, that is, with the faculty of seeing what the new premiss must be. And doubtless they do that work not by more or stronger perception, but by a *less resistance;* i.e. others may see, as clearly as they, both the proofs of the results and the objections to them; but, not perceiving any way of escape, they remain passive. The man who finds the new premiss may do so simply because those forces, as it were, are able to move in that direction; there is an opening, a channel, in him, there. His perception of a new fundamental conception is a direction of not-resistance. So it does away with the stress, or tension.

No man can tell you anything *new;* for in knowing one thing you truly know all, and until you know one thing no man can tell you another. The one thing that is, and only can be, known is *life;* and all that can be known is only life. More and more life you may be made to know; more can be told you, but not different, not new.

How gloriously Coleridge said in answer to "What is life?" "What is not life that truly *is?*" His instincts led him to affirm truths of which he did not see the mode, or strictly the evidence.

The existence of a particularly difficult and manifest paradox is one of the best of signs; it is the indication that the time has come for an advance in thought, for its development or advance to a higher grade. The two opposite opinions must be put together, not by a compromise, nor by holding two contradictory opinions, or making one yield, but by maintaining both in their fullest and most absolute sense, and seeing how they agree and are one; i.e. by adding another element to our knowledge and raising the level of our thought. Strong and startling paradoxes are ground for hope and not for despair; they are the things which turn the course of thought when in that direction it has reached its limit; turn it and elevate it, if dealt with aright, in a spirit of manful boldness and earnestness, and not of cowardice and compromise and distrust of power. In fact paradox is in mind the analogue of that condition which caused development of species; two extremes, two polars. And what did Nature do—sit down and talk about the limitation of her powers? She took the two, each in its completeness, and putting them together, educed a new and higher race; setting us there, as ever, an example. A paradox in point of fact is male and female. Paradox is the puberty, the adolescence, the nubile state of thought. In each new development of thought the sexual or polar distinction is there from the first, but latent. Boys and girls grow up together and we do not perceive the opposition or mutual adaptation at first, but by-and-by the two groups declare themselves; at first in very trifling differences, then more deeply, at last absolutely; then thought has grown to the paradoxical state. Male and female each assert their nature and will not yield one atom to the other. We have, not many views or ideas of like kinds, but two opposite kinds which each maintain an absolute and indefeasible footing, and will not be put down. At first they repel each other and are shy, even quarrel and dislike; but Nature at last asserts her purposes, mysterious sympathies grow up; each one admires and respects the opposite and is drawn unconsciously towards its incomprehensible difference from itself. The magical charm overcomes pride; love is established, but at first the talk is not of marriage but of friendship; they will retain their individuality and opposition but live in amity and mutual kindness and goodwill; in short they will make a compromise. Short-sighted ideas; short-sighted even as mortal men. You shall not have your friendship; your touch is fatal; it is the vortex of a Charybdis upon which you enter, which will draw you certainly within its gulf. You are not two but one; and one you shall become by a power higher than your will. This is the nature of paradox; it is polarity, and its issue is a bridal day.

In animal life, when development ensues, the creature gets into a paradox: i.e. there are two opposite tendencies or forces with which nothing can be done but by a union into one. In animal life this is done by instinct, as in thought it is done by genius. The work of genius in raising the grade of thought is the very same as that of instinct in raising the grade of life, and is done too with as little foresight and design. The instinct and the genius have no reason for what they do except that the thing "must be so of course." It is their nature to put it right. Genius therefore is love, or sympathy, as I have said; and marries male and female thought; unites the law and liberty in one. For this also is marriage; it is the law of liberty. And this is a further insight: not only is the law of right the law of liberty, but the law of love also. Law and liberty in one are holiness and love; absolute freedom and absolute law. And Nature, being the law of liberty, is not only holiness but love. The holiness the law, the love the liberty: one in God. This union is a true marriage, to be attained as man's spiritual development. Male and female are holiness and love; at war now in man's moral being, as are paradoxical opinions in his intellectual nature; but they must be one. Thus the progress of thought is a perpetual wedding feast; the intellectual repeats the social state of man; this is why love and marriage are ever the sources of deepest and intensest sympathy. So is a true marriage of Nature and man. They are truly wedded, and all the arts of life spring from the embrace. All is one: the great fact of human life is the great fact of Nature's life.

In our mental life we must be content to live and conform to the laws of life; to eat, and drink, and sleep, and be nourished, as well as perform functions. At the same time fully believing that, by such conformity, all we aspire after and much more is finally to be achieved; not despairing, for the general mind (Science) is the universal life, to the attainments of which no limits can be placed. It is no argument that as the powers of the human body are limited, and pretty well known, so are those of the mind; the analogy does not hold. The human mind, in the sense in which it advances from age to age, is one living organism, which has a course to run quite unknown, unknowable until it is revealed in fact. It can no more anticipate its future than can the child its manhood, still less can it conceive a greater. Nothing can conceive a greater than itself; anything that is growing and developing must of necessity outstrip its conceptions. Youth indeed casts a splendour on the future; but it is never anything more than a pleasant present; which is just what our Science anticipates, an everlasting "feast," forgetting that such a feast would become intolerable torment. Better than that, there is before it a noble succession of feasting and working, producing development which may not be anticipated.

What is *sleeping* in the mental life? It is the period during which assimilation most vigorously takes place, with no eating and very little function. It strikes me it must be a period of *a priori* reasoning; just such a period as preceded Bacon's epoch, not so badly called the dark ages. This is no legitimate term of reproach. What greater blessing than the darkness of night? What period of greater or more beneficial activity than natural sleep? Do not the alternation of light and darkness from the one motion of the earth, represent the vibration, day and night; being as function and nutrition?

I think I shall best discover what mental respiration is in myself. Thus thinking is like breathing to me. It is my breath of life, and I cannot leave it off or am compelled soon to begin again. And the respiration of the mind of the whole, is it not some constant passion which cannot but be done; and the effect of which is to cast off error and arrive at larger truth? Is not this work of mine one respiratory act of the great mind of man?

The human mind is the external world to genius, the productions of which he seeks to interpret. To say that a man has genius is to say that all he effects is truly and entirely the result of others' labors and done by their power; that he is merely a stimulus, and owes his influence solely to his relation to an organization built up, and a functional power accumulated, wholly by others. It is manifestly so; the disproportion were else too vast.

See how many men must labor and die to produce the edifice which genius with one touch reconstructs. It is of course because the power is not in him but in the elements he uses that his power seems so great. To attribute the deed to him would be like attributing an explosion to a spark, forgetful of the gunpowder.

The men of genius are sure to exist, yet they can occur only at intervals. Genius must be waited for; talent can be cultivated. Men can always do something; they can always observe; and this they must go on doing patiently, assured that if they thus effect the nutrition the function will not fail. They know that in due time they shall reap. But our experimental science sows and sows away and never expects to reap.

We must hold fast to the dynamic view in mental physiology—nothing is done without an equivalent expenditure of force. Genius does things without force *because it does not do them*, as the fall of an uplifted body needs no force.

About transitive and continuous vibrations: a falling stone and heat resulting must be taken together. If we take the fall alone, we leave off where no end is, if the heat alone, we begin where is no beginning. So also of spirals; they are transitive and continuous also, and in one form or other, universal; continuous in the earth's motion; but every possible motion is a transitive spiral, for every motion is three motions at right angles; and all motion also is vibration. Therefore all motion is three vibrations at right angles, i.e. a true spiral. For there is in nature no motion that does not involve length, breadth and depth. This is as true of motions as of things. Consider the complexity and the simplicity; how every motion is accompanied by an opposite while it takes place, and is succeeded by an opposite when it ceases, doubly vibratile, and each of these opposites is similarly accompanied and succeeded.

Talent absorbs force; genius reproduces force and passes it on. It is continuous and transitive again. He whose work is the result or expression of his passion has no exterior force. He whose passion is the *result* of his work has operative force. Take a painter; he has a passion, a conception, he expresses it in a picture, when he contemplates it he sees the re-presentation of his passion, he admires it, delights in it, accordingly; but the picture can be only admired by others; it has produced no passion in him, much less in the beholders. But another painter paints by instinct, by his nature; he has no conception or passion to express, but he must paint so, and as he paints, behold, his picture reveals to him something he had never conceived nor could conceive, and produces in him an overwhelming emotion or passion. This picture has power in it; it is a functional picture, a force-producer, and it excites passion and emotion in beholders. It does for others what it has first done for the author. The thought that moves the thinker will move the hearer too, and only that; not the thought that expresses or is produced by a passion, but the thought that produced a passion. So Goethe is a nutritive poet. His thought produced no passion in him, and it produces none in others. I do not say that the nutritive men are not deep feelers. I do not speak of them, but of their works. I say that they absorb the force of passion as nutrition does; and that the force can only be reproduced by just inverting that process. But the force of genius is only the force of talent thus reproduced; first the nutrition, then the function, and only then. [By-the-bye, the logical people who will have the function without the nutrition correspond with Berkeley, little as they think it, and just such was the old pre-Baconian science.] The men who produce this nutritive, imaginative, forceless work, must indeed be men of deep feeling. The work expresses or is the result of feeling or passion; passion is the only force; the powerlessness of it arises from its being the result and not the producer of passion. We only need to understand this, to see the vital relations of different men, and we shall put them to their right uses, and not find fault with them for not being other than they are. We do not look for work from the growing child, but we reverence the child not less than the hard-working man; the latter produces and the former does but absorb force; true, but the force-absorber is but the force-producer of the future; he grows that he may work; nay he may be of greatly higher order than the present force producer, and be destined to a work greatly more noble. We must be content. Both force producers and orce-absorbers we want, and of different grades.

All things, all men, all thoughts, all motions, the universe indeed, is divisible into the two classes of force-producing and force-absorbing; this is the great distinction. In other words all is *vibration;* for these are precisely the two halves of a vibration; i.e. all is life, or nutrition and function. The universe is vibration or life: may we not say, *a* vibration, *a* life. Then, if a life, whereof?

Talent has instinct as well as genius. Vegetables have instincts (as for food, light), as well as animals. But in talent and vegetable they are much less marked and extensive; they do not give the character as they do to genius and animal. In the vegetable the object and result of all is the nutrition, the growth; in the animal, the instincts are for its functions. Observe, in both the instincts for food, &c., for nutrition; in genius superadded those for function. Also note that instinct ever in both is the result of organisation, and depends upon a functional process. The idea of talent is nutrition, as of vegetable. The idea of genius is function, as of animal; in each both processes go on necessarily together, but they are differently subordinate. The vegetable world is to the animal as placenta to embryo; so talent to genius.

How familiar and common-place to us are the facts which threw into infinite delight those who first saw them! How Copernicus's heart must have throbbed when the fact of the earth's motion, so indifferent to us, revealed itself; and future generations will coldly take as matters of course what the men of this glow over with delight. So when we see the men and women in the streets, we little think how for each one a mother has groaned and rejoiced. A man of genius is the mother of new life; his the female part in the history of mind; his the throes and toil, the exultation and delight. He gives birth truly to new life. The man of talent does the work of the man; exerts his own powers and effects his own objects. The man of genius quietly nourishes unknowing in his own bosom, and feeds with his own life, patiently, in sorrow and depression, too often amid cruel taunts, his living burden; moving him sometimes to strange fancies, unappeasable longings and restlessness, until his time is come. And then his proud eyes weep happy tears, as he folds tremblingly to his heart the image and inheritor of his soul's life.

The cause of the difficulty in receiving the work of Genius is the wrong position of the eye, as it were; people think they are seeing one thing when in reality they are seeing another. They have not yet learnt to recognise the universal human mind, which performs functions, and of which the individual minds are but parts, elements, or organs—or rather, perhaps I should say, the universal humanity as a living existence, of which individual men and women are merely the " organic molecules,"—so that the functions of this higher "life" take them by surprise; they cannot believe the function because they have not recognised the organisation and nutrition. They have not seen that all the labours of men of talent constitute a nutrition, and produce one living organisation with power to perform functions. They have not seen in fact what they have been doing; in other words that they have been acting instinctively; accomplishing a higher object than any they had in view. In fact men have not seen that the human mind is a *life*; just as they have not seen that the whole universe is a life. They look upon what individual men do as isolated things. It is as if some being with microscopic eye should watch and register the individual processes which constitute the nutrition of a human body, without perceiving the bearing and meaning of them; should see the various particles mutually reacting and arranging themselves without understanding that all this made up an organization and accumulated force. Of course he would be astonished enough when the function was performed. It would appear to undo so much of that the doing of which he had been watching with so much interest and satisfaction, and which he imagined was done for its own sake, being, as he might remark, beautiful.

Man's mind is female; it does the nutrition and re-production; it absorbs into itself. Woman's mind is as man's body; it gives itself, is instinctive. As the female body is united with the male, and only so reproduces, is not man's *female* mind "quickened" by woman's and only so rendered truly re-productive? And development, in mind, is only from an union of the woman's mind with man's. In the ordinary progress of mind do we not see, in fact, that only as man is "quickened" by woman does the mental life multiply and extend? For the acquisition of knowledge is truly a growth, it is a taking in, not a giving out. This knowledge of the external world is in the strictest sense subjective knowledge. It is *in us*, all this phenomenon. The woman's mind that cleaves to the moral, acts by instincts, gives itself away in love, is the externally acting mind. Man's mind grows and re-produces itself; woman's mind performs external functions. And as woman's body is quickened by man's through mutual love, so is man's mind by woman's through mutual love. And in the true development, or Genius in its most perfect sense, the man and woman's mind are united into one. The new grade of mind is the male and female in one.

This in fact is just the difference between Genius and talent: Genius holds its own in spite of paradox, because it knows it, sees it, and does not care; the thing is so. Talent gives up at the sight of the paradox; it has not seen the thing, it has only supposed it, to see if it will do; and of course when it finds it will not, it gives up and takes that which will do best—a compromise; it is its business. It is necessarily so; and this produces all sorts of differences; Genius is bold; talent timid; talent builds up, Genius throws open; talent seeks to attain an object, Genius does the right, and the object is attained. But the great thing is this: Genius is one with the infinite, i.e. with Nature; talent is finite, limited, expresses the man. For Genius comes never to an end; recognises the infiniteness, the unbeginning; talent makes a closed circle; so it is talent that invents the chimeras, which are always beginnings; the specific or inherent qualities, primary properties, or God's especial act. Talent will ever have a primary beginning; its chimeras are ways of attaining that; it is, and invents, the arbitrary. Genius ever recognises rightness; ever carries knowledge higher up, sets aside the chimeras and shows cause; shows necessity for arbitrariness, infinitude for finiteness: its end and true object ever being the spiritual. It is, in truth, an infinite, an eternal, we have to do with; talent shuts it up in chimerical beginnings and ends; Genius throws down these barriers, progresses step by step, ever larger and higher, towards the eternal; her goal is the spiritual; ever as herself is rightness, so her home is the Right.

Common sense is genius, and genius is common sense. Common sense is the not going by appearances, not *making up*; it is interpretation; it is letting things come naturally, not using art and contrivance; therefore it cannot be first. Genius is common sense in its origin; it is the first application of common sense to a subject; it is common sense in respect to that which has not yet been known. That which is genius in one man or age, is common sense to succeeding ones. The Copernican astronomy is common sense; it rests upon common sense.

Common sense in Copernicus discovered it; but then it was the *first* exercise of common sense on that subject, and that is genius. So common sense belongs to women (the male mind); it is the woman's reason—" of course it is"—"it must be"—"it is because it is." Common sense and genius do not prove; they show. Proving is only hypothetical truth. It is curious that genius should be thought the opposite to common sense, deal with what subject it may. But genius brings new views, opposite to what has been thought; does away so with former common-sense conclusions (or interpretations of smaller nutritions) and so *appears* opposed through its greatness which swallows up the smaller. For common sense is the interpretation of genius, appropriated by men not of genius. It is a part of the work of genius to distinguish between the instincts and fashions; and say, that is an instinct, this is a fashion (the instincts being ever the true). Those who " want common sense" have not appropriated the results of former genius. And it is curious, and curiously right, that these are so apt to have a genius of their own. Also it is well called *common* sense; the self-element, the individual element, is put aside, which is emphatically the work of genius.

That which makes us go wrong is that we are constantly making up a system, making a scheme for ourselves perfect and complete; this is sure to be false. The interpreter is just the man who does not do this; who suspends his judgment, and whenever he does not see an absolute *must be*, says, "I do not know." It is nothing to him that this or the other "supposition" would make a very nice, beautiful, and every way desirable system; *must be*, or right, is his law; his act is the act of love, of necessity, alone. He has no *talent* to construct; he does but overthrow; overthrow chimeras, set aside inventions; reveal, unveil, that which was concealed by hypothesis. He is the simplifier, the putter of one for many, which is the great *must* of the human mind. And on the other hand, as when he does not see an absolute "*must be*," no consequences can tempt him to say: "I see"; so also when he does see this "must be," no consequences can deter him from saying it. It is so, and he says it, come what may; it is no matter to him that a system thereby is shattered and none seems ready to take its place; still less does he attempt to supply one. He has faith, and is in no hurry, knowing that every termination will be found the beginning of an illimitable expanse.

It is beautiful to see in the mental world how life arises from *failure*, from dissatisfaction. When I try to express an idea I do not satisfy myself. I try again; do it over and over again, and better and better: that is life. So life in its very idea involves development; it is not a stationary condition of activity, but always and necessarily a development. The question whether life has truly developed itself is absurd; if it does not develop itself it is not life. And so the indication of a capacity for a higher life is ever a dissatisfaction with the present. Those who advance the intellectual life are first discontented with that which exists. It must be a precisely parallel process in the physical world that leads to the development of animal life. And the parallelism may be traced into the very details as it were; the passion resisted by other passion. For what is the reason that a theory or view that satisfies one man does not satisfy another (capable of judging) but that in this other's mind there is more thought which *resists* the other thought? A conclusion cannot be reached; the passion fails of its accomplishment; that which seems right to the other to him is absolutely wrong, because there is more than that view will embrace. It is ever more passion, as it were, in the same limits, which causes development; as I have seen in life, it is more vital passion in the same space; this is the doctrine of development by pressure.

Why does the silkworm produce silk? Because it acts out its nature. Thus all truly great and valuable deeds are done. It is God that acts when nature acts, whether it be the nature of a worm or of a man. In relation to God, these acts of nature are moral acts; they are His spiritual and therefore holy deeds. If we would act like Him, we too must act morally: in spiritual activity lies our capacity of acting as God does. Here is the true difference between men; the difference between a great poet, an artist or philosopher, and the most untutored labourer who does his work but rightly, is none; it lies only in appearance; their acts are the same thing from a different point of view. But between a man who acts rightly and one who does wrong, the difference is wide as the poles. Do we thank the silkworm or the bee? Not so: we take all they do as a matter of course, and thank God. Just so should we deal with the men of genius. No thanks are due to them; they have simply done what it was their nature to do. Take all that as of course, and thank God.

The difference between talent and genius is precisely that between doing right for an object, as to obtain heaven or escape hell, and doing right simply from love, or because we must do it [that "must" always means love: it is the fact of attraction].

What lives, is not that which is *like* what is being done

at the time, but that which is unlike. That truly carries out the tendency of the age which is the very opposite to that which it has been doing and which is in fashion and approved. That which is in the spirit of the age, and meets at once with universal approbation, plays but a subordinate part; that which seems to go utterly against it is the true function. It is true that afterwards this function is seen to be a genuine expression of the age, and to have had many foreshadowings; but it did not appear so at the time, and these foreshadowings probably had not been noticed ot all.

Each man's (or woman's, or child's) special incapacity, or dislike, is his specific resistance; that which directs his force, gives him his specific form or being, and is the great source and secret of his value. There is no more inestimable gift than a well-marked and powerful "resistance."

In respect to *defect* as the source of our strength—or at any rate of what we contribute to the general wealth of mankind—I am aware how it is by not feeling the necessity for practical action and results, by being able to be content without them, that thought can be maintained unbiassed and absolute, and the true relations demonstrated and affirmed. And here one sees the mutual excluding of negations by opposites; *together* these results embrace the work of those who cannot be content without abstract truth, and those who cannot be content without practical right and good; and so the perfectness is given. Must not each be content to say: "*I* must insist upon this, *you* see to that; and putting these together, let us work altruistically"? Is not this the true attitude for thought?

This struck me in reading Lynch on Poetry:—Are not those who are able to dwell so beautifully and invigoratingly on the goodness and beauty of the world and of human nature, and who feel this so deeply and satisfyingly gifted *by defect?* Are they not capable of being thus satisfied, and therefore have the sensitiveness and appreciation by the absence in them of the necessity for higher? And from this "defect" comes a positive good, help and use for others; for the world wants that sensitive appreciation of, and bright light upon, wordly beauty and good; it is one of the elements it ought to contain, and in that full prominence and relief which only such men can give it. So there must be others, small enough to be content with the abstract, to give *that* also to the world, which wants and must contain that too. And since the world wants also the practical phenomenal life in its perfectness, must there not be those small enough to be content with that?

Is there, then, here a key to the *partialness* of men, that men must be small enough to be content with the part, in order to give it perfection? Is it not an evident fact that men are parts? Might we not as well say an eye was an individual by itself, as a man? Look not only at its dependence, but its function; the thing it can do implies a body, a whole, for the sake of which it is done, and alone is worth doing.

One sees how these not-perceiving men must even be fools, relatively and for a time. They do not perceive by their senses as other men do; it is for this reason indeed that they perceive the fact. Meanwhile, before this perception of the fact (which constitutes their discovery), necessarily they do not perceive at all, neither by senses nor intellect, and are really at a disadvantage, and the world is right when it calls them fools. May it not often be that men who pass for fools all their lives, and never do anything to redeem themselves, may truly be men of genius? Perhaps the possibility of the intellectual perception was never given them; perhaps not the requisite data; perhaps they never came to sufficient self-consciousness, never turned attention to what they could do, and so wasted their whole lives in attempting to do what they could not. I see it is a happy accident that produces an acknowledged man of genius; there may be thousands who merely fail.

This opens a good prospect; most likely men of genius may be indefinitely multiplied, and the world found full of them, when we know how to act towards them. Is it not certain that all "not-perceiving" men will be found to have that faculty of genius, and if rightly guided will prove capable of using it too? The defect, if there be true rationality, in them, necessarily involves the compensating power. It should be encouraged; such men are snubbed, and really think themselves fools; they should be taught sensible phenomena, and encouraged to look at them in their own way, or say boldly: "*This* must be the fact of *that*." As it is now, genius needs to be extraordinarily self-confident or it is altogether repressed. The man of genius, if he be not strong also, is afraid to speak his thoughts; he meets only ridicule, which cowes him; so he denies his own nature, endeavours to imitate the sense-perceivers, and, necessarily failing, he remains a poor, useless, foolish-seeming person all his life. So it is there seem to be so few men of genius in the world.

By the fact of the man of Genius doing better than he can conceive, is shown the possibility of the accomplishment by *man* of more than man can conceive. So the work of Genius is truly in one sense superhuman (taking *our* sense of human, in which the self is put for the man); in Genius *man* is seen; the self cast out and gone. Here is an image of the true being of man in the destruction of the self. It is so in the intellectual sphere.

So men of talent think Genius "cannot be understood;" they think that there must have been a *conception* before the work. Just so we think of nature; that there must have been a "conception" of it beforehand; so we cannot understand it. It is "a work of Genius," and we take the "talent" view of it. We think it like a work of talent, full of "contrivances." Our studies of nature are like the man of talent trying to understand the work of Genius; he can see a great deal; admirable design, results secured, &c., but cannot fathom it altogether; there is evidently something more, some organic unity, some "necessity." Is not this partly the meaning of that unity of plan which is seen, and which cannot be comprehended in "Design?"

I see the *life* in thinking, how each interpretation makes a new nutrition by suppressing some existing instinctive or "arbitrary" opinion or thought. After more thought I bring back the fact which I had suppressed, as one with the opposite which resulted from its suppression; and this giving me the truth of that, repeats again the process of nutrition in respect to some other subject, causes me to suppress some other view, and so it goes on, ever; there is no end to this process, as there is none to the life of Nature. When this can be clearly seen as the life of thought, how simple and satisfactory thought may be; we shall never be afraid to suppress, to oppose; always giving freely, yet in absolute obedience to law. We shall introduce our hypotheses knowing them to be unknown symbols; suppress our instinctive views knowing that Being is only in self-sacrifice, and that that which dies does so for a higher life.

The most effectual and most decided opposition to wrongness of all sorts is involved in the knowing and showing it to be nutrition, that it exists for the sake of the good, and in order that it may be put right or corrected. This view, so far from rendering us less earnest in correcting error, or rectifying wrong, renders us necessarily more so. We see not only the evil to correct but the good, else unattainable, to be gained by correcting it. Yet also it makes us tolerant, calm, loving, reasonable, patient, hopeful; full of confidence, indeed, and smiling through our bitterest tears. It gives us double power, greater fortitude and earnestness in doing, greater calmness, patience, love in the mode of doing. Not tolerant of error or wrongness, but rejoicing in it as a means to truth and good. In truth, embracing instead of opposing. It teaches us to say to the doers of things wrongly: "You too are good workers; you express the phenomenon; but this is the fact: this we owe to you, it is the fruit of your labours; receive and enjoy the reward of your toil." Is not this better than saying to them: "You are doing quite wrong; leave off and be-gone, or imitate me." Which is likely to have most effect as a remedy for wrongness? Nay, which man is likely to work most consistently, trustfully and earnestly, and therefore perseveringly, for the remedying of wrong-ness? In fact it is the same thing as in physics; wrongness is the result of force, and can only be averted by turning the force to good; physical evil and good are theory and interpretation. We see the beauty of our instinct of putting wrong right, of opposing all evil and falsehood. It is instinct in its truest sense, the tendency to function; we overthrow the wrong to reproduce the force, and obtain its function through the organisation.

We should revere our own thought, if it is genuinely our thought. It is God's very deed. To yield to fashion, to take another man's thought instead of our own, is ugly, evil, everything that is bad. If we could get our eye right we should see that it is disease, a passion not conformable to our life. That operation of an extraneous force is disease, the very essence of it. Disease is not so terrible, because it is in itself a bad thing; it is equally good with the best, simply a part of the universal life; but because it is a passion in us not conformable with our life, a passion imposed on us by extraneous force. This is just like having a thought imposed on us; it is mental disease; a little more of it were death. To make another man's thought our own, to see and understand it, become one substance with it, is another thing; that is to grow and develop. The passive submission to, and the living appropriation of, another man's thought, are two opposite things; development and disease.

What is the use of saying, or trying to say, that which we do not see? For example, that we perceive things in time and space, &c., because they really exist so; or that animals have a certain form because they have an inherent tendency thereto; or that matter has an inherent gravitation. What comes of it? What, in the name of common sense, is really said after all? *Saying* is *seeing*; and if the two be separated they are useless both—especially the saying. There is no perception contained in or involved by such expressions, and thus in fact as nothing is perceived, so nothing is said; the words are no more than the rattling of a stick. God uses them, however, and by their means reveals something to us which we can perceive, and in saying which we say something. We cannot say anything we do not understand; just as (consciously) we understand nothing we cannot, do not, say. These expressions, which are intended to convey incomprehensible ideas, are really meaningless. We know nothing but that which we comprehend, see fully and completely all about, not only that it is but that it must be; it must be involved in our fact of thinking, or we do not know it; and what is the use of saying that which we do not know—the idea is an absurdity. And yet surely these theories must be said; like the cycles and epicycles they are things unreal and impossible, yet having a reality to us until they have revealed the real. It is just so with matter, which is a theory, phenomenon, or chimera, a thing not only unreal but impossible; which cannot be said, because it cannot be known; yet it is real to us until it has revealed the reality. Thus matter is a theory, an invention, like the epicycles; necessary to the conception of the phenomena until they have revealed the fact.

This is the way those theories came to pass, those attemps to say what we do not see. We perceive or feel that if they were so the facts or phenomena would be as we perceive them; then we come in the strangest way, I suppose by familiarity, to regard that which we have invented as the easiest way for us of accounting for or conceiving the phenomena, to regard that as a fact, as certain; and we cling to it with the most wonderful tenacity, forgetting that we do not see it. We think that is the very thing we do see. People think that matter is the very thing that they see. It is all the result of our intuitive conviction of cause; it is our life; if we do not perceive a cause we invent it (and quite right too). This is the assimilation. Thus we come to be trying to say what we do not see, to express what we do not know—a ridiculous position certainly in one sense, yet not to be laughed at, and one at which God does not laugh; far, far from Him is it to mock His children's life. And all this ceases by falling by its own weight; the theory yields to the interpretation. Instead of our supplying unknown causes, the facts show us their cause, which thus seeing we know, and then can *say*.

Our individual minds live and die, constituting the whole, the great universal mind, the mental life of humanity; just as the individual elements of our bodies live and die, constituting thus the body itself, the physical life of the man. This relation of the individual mind to the universal mind is the grand presentation of the problem of continued identity, the transitory elements and the permanent whole, individual minds and the universal mind; as cells are formed, grow, and decay in the body, and by their decomposition produce functional effects, of development or other.

This is the mental life in Science. The theory yields to the interpretation, but the interpretation yields a new phenomenon, i.e. a new theory and basis for a new nutrition. Thus in astronomy the motions of the sun and stars, interpreted, reveal the motion of the earth, which is now the phenomenon, and forms the basis of a new nutrition, i.e. a new theory. So in Science as a whole. The phenomenon is interpreted as a subjective passion, viz. as motion in least resistance; but this reveals the holy act of God which is now the phenomenon, and forms the basis of a new nutrition, i.e. a new theory.

The motion of the earth has been theoretically regarded as an original motion deflected by gravity. So now that Science presents the holy act of God as the phenomenon, we shall have to treat that theoretically, to invent many things respecting it which of course we cannot foresee; and to reveal new truth by interpretation, which can still less be foreseen.

To understand how all is life, the great thing is to have an unbounded faith. This is life, that all evil is nutrition; by faith essentially it is to be seen. By faith indeed even the interpreter acts; he sees that which is invisible. Faith is the source of life; of mental, of spiritual life. Physically even, the analogue of faith must be the source of life. To believe and know that everything shall have a higher end and issue than we can see, this is to see life, to feel it in and around us.

The Art of Thinking. 133

IV.

THE ART OF THINKING.

How to think rightly—Truth is suppressed and comes back in higher form—All thought is necessary—Opinions are like institutions—Necessity of surrendering good opinions—Opinion is form only, and must change to preserve its value—We only know form; to know the fact is to love—That which must be thought must be distinguished from that which is true—Use of analogy—Thought is Nature, and therefore cannot be false—All opinions are true under their conditions—The danger of fear in thought—The value of logic—What are axioms?—Newton's work great by its incompleteness—Truth is the union of opposites—The minus in thinking—Necessity of sacrifice in thought—The nature of hypothesis—All advance in thought comes by right use of words—No ends in thinking—Thinking is an especial work—Parallel of thinking to art—Imagination the chief element in true thought—The Art element in true thought parallel to the Gentile element in Christianity.

No other art is so easy as that of thinking; and the reason it has been thought so hard, and is so backward, is because people have not seen its easiness, and have been trying to do something difficult; to *do*, instead of suffering to be done. For thinking is a passive thing, a life that is lived within us.

A rule for thinking is, that when two things seem opposed, and both appear true, not to deny one for the sake of the other, but ask: "If it be thus, how can the other be? So going on to see both right; not by means of hypotheses, but as necessary, as each involving the other. And this necessarily comes through seeing what the nature of the phenomenon is, its relativeness, and dependence on us. We must embrace, not exclude.

Were it not well if the advance of thought up to this point had been peaceful and mutually helpful, instead of so much fighting and disputing? Or, if that were necessary (as doubtless it was), were it not well if for the future it ceased to be so? This may and must be by the recognition of two laws:—(1) the necessary falseness of hypotheses or opinions formed in ignorance; and this even if they agree with the phenomena (as gravity, e.g.); that only shows the hypothesis to be good, not to be true. If it did not do that it would not be tolerable, even as hypothesis; it is the business of a hypothesis to agree with the phenomena; only so can it answer its purpose at all. And (2) that the true must be suppressed for restoration. To recognise these two laws heals all intellectual strife.

Are not all controversies between men just this:—one saying to the other, "You have not fulfilled the conditions"? And if that were done *consciously*, what a mental millenium it were! There need not be doubt or quarrel; not fulfilling conditions *means* not making all agree.

There comes to be another rule in thinking, viz., that we need never waste our labour on resuscitating any opinion or view which the world has rejected (Idealism, e.g.) unless at the same time we interpret, or perfect it; doing away the defect which caused it to be rejected. This is, truly, to unite with the opposite; incorporating

The Art of Thinking.

the added phenomenon or details. But also, is not all interpretation, all putting right, a restoration (although perfected) of a previous opinion?

We suppress a truth in order to have it back again more truly. With regard to this law of thinking, however, the suppression must always be necessary, not arbitrary. We cannot say: "Now I will suppress this and get it better." Not so, but seeing that which is opposed to it, let us think boldly, truly on. We are so embarrassed in our thinking now because we are afraid to suppress that which we hold to be true, i.e. to hold opposed views. When we come, in thinking, to that which seems opposed to anything which we must hold to be true, we stop, to avoid contradicting this truth. But let us suppress anything whatever; we can only suppress it because it is arbitrary to our view, being assured that it will infallibly repeat itself with fuller, deeper meaning, and in absolute oneness with that which seems now opposed to it. For this is what occurs now: un-religious men think on and suppress religious truths; then at certain intervals it is shown that the religious truths are quite compatible with these opposite doctrines, and indeed require them, are best seen by means of them. Now this will ever be the case; but then, why need this process be gone through *hostilely?* Why should not religious men do this work of advancing their own doctrines? The *life* once seen, the thing is done. The suppression of a true view is not a rejection of it, but merely a vital process; like burying a seed and letting it die that it may bear fruit. We do not despise and reject the grain that we put into the earth; we put it there that we may live by it. We do not repudiate the passion we control or suppress; on the contrary, we suppress it that we may exercise it hereafter in nobler form and to better purpose.

This is the confusion: we have supposed that holding an opinion opposite to any given view involved a denial of the truth of such view. This is an entire mistake; we need only admit that we cannot see all truth at once. Practically we have been counting ourselves omniscient. What we do is to lay aside for a time, to suppress in its relation to ourselves, a certain truth while we look at the same truth in another form; and the more intense and entire our belief in any truth, the more easily and confidingly we shall be able to do this, and we do it for the purpose of seeing that truth itself better and more fully, as one with its opposite; or rather, we do it in order to think, to know, to live; because it is right, and in faith.

A true thing is never new, because that which is true is always first erroneously said.

The way to think, is to think *anything*, to hold nothing certain or fixed. There is nothing to start from, except a certain state of consciousness, something which makes me conscious of self and perceptive; there are these phenomena. This is the only fact. What causes the phenomenon to be such? Nothing is to be held, and refused to be given up; anything is to be thought, no matter what it denies. Indeed it is certain that all which we naturally think is illusion. All opinions and prejudices of men are for calm investigation; not to be set aside as mere evil and folly, but to be seen as parts of the redemption, and their necessity; why and how this must be; the ignorance that is their source. They are *necessary*. We must trace it by a physical passive necessity, a necessity having relation to the mental, or states of consciousness; but the true necessity is their being necessary for man's redemption, of which the scientific passive necessity is but evidence and sign. Especially apply this to men's ideas about life, and why they will not allow it to be reduced to mere physical necessity, why this feeling must be, whence the confusion that makes them feel a physical affair to be so inseparable from the spiritual.

The distinction between logic or laws of thought, and intuition, is this: the laws of thought are "thought in least resistance." But for this there must first be the thought itself. Surely our putting logic up as all, is just like, in physics, resting upon the laws of nature, as if the laws were all. An opinion answers to an institution; it is an embodiment and expression of some fact or condition of us, some necessity in the life of man. An opinion is only good while it is this, i.e. while it is according to the other conditions of knowledge, which makes it a true expression of the "fact" or life. Like institutions, opinions must change in order to maintain their value. Both alike are forms, which must change, in order that the fact may be. In our hold of opinions, as of institutions, we put form for fact, and continually sacrifice the fact to the form. So we should be ready to change opinions which have done so much good, proved so valuable, so necessary, under which, and dependent on which, so blessed a life has been diffused. The power is in the fact, not in the form. That opinion is life-giving which expresses life, love, self-sacrifice. Keep, not the opinion, but the self-sacrifice. The evangelical doctrine is powerful while appealing as a doctrine of self-sacrifice, but soon loses this attitude and becomes one of self-seeking. Here is the key to its history; the reason that it can do so much and yet so fails.

That a thing is wrong, does not mean that it ought never to have been done or thought; but that it ought to be left off. Its good and rightness and necessity are in its being cured. So in respect to opinion: here is the struggle. When a thing is proved wrong, people think that it ought not to have been; but this is a mistake; it ought to cease, that is all. It is "in time." All this matter of opinion, all the physical, is form merely; its being wrong is merely appearing wrong. There is no true wrongness; such phenomenal wrongness is in the fact of right and Being. It is necessary to think wrongly before we can think right—we starting ignorant. Nothing should be more welcome, more natural and expected, than to see our opinions wrong. We should know it must be.

We cannot give up our opinions, because we derive good through them, and are conscious of honesty and zeal for God in holding them. So Paul says of the Jews, they were "zealous for God." But we cannot believe that the men who in former ages had to give up their opinions derived good from them and were honest in holding them. This has been the difficulty—that the form is held for the sake of the fact which it has embodied. All that is, is from Good; these forms were every one of them the result of good, and therefore held. And therefore too so harmful; because when, by the negation or defect in the good that formed them, there was more good demanding a new form, the old form struggled against it. Good produces the forms and opinions; but it is a good necessarily defective. More is ever being added; therefore the forms and opinions must change. We must learn to see that those before us were just as honest and as good as we; and that life consists in the honest and zealous giving up of opinions.

That we have made opinions the condition for salvation is just an instance of how we put the " not " for the fact : being inert, of course we supposed that truth was intellectual. Opinion is form only, and cannot affect the fact; nay, under different conditions the fact demands a different form. See how the change of form in Nature is simply because the fact will not change, and in order that it may not. So to retain the actual truth, it may and indeed must be needful to change opinions. The entire intellectual regard without any exception shall alter, shall be of every form; and in truth, the intellectual history of the world is the form changing that the fact may not change. A part of Nature is in this also: opinions necessarily change *because* the fact will not. Here is a guide to intellectual culture, to thinking. Let opinions, the mental forms, change indefinitely; they must, in order that the fact may be the same : with every changing relation these intellectual forms must change; clinging to them is doing violence. It cannot alter the fact indeed, but it produces tension. When an opinion is held longer than it entirely corresponds to the fact, or is the opinion which would naturally by laws of thought be in such a man's mind if not for old association, there is tension.

What constitutes the difficulty of receiving new opinions is men's unwillingness to give up those opinions which are best and wisest. It is so now as ever; in every advance men have had to abandon opinions sanctified by devoutest feelings, confirmed by vigorous inquiry, founded on the best evidence; than which no other opinions were possible. We may be taught to see this, and so be prepared in the future. We may be taught that our opinions may be right for us, and yet not absolute rightness. There may be opinions which it may be quite right and necessary for us to hold to-day, but which we ought not to hold to-morrow. The demand ever is to us to give up, not that which we may have thought doubtful or bad, but that which has been best and dearest (always excepting that which we *morally* know). Because a new view runs counter to the best-established and most valuable views, it is not therefore to be rejected: but this may be demanded—that it be *inclusive* not exclusive. It must not merely suppress, but show as necessary. All advances have been thus inclusive; yet how they too have been at first rejected. So Christ supersedes Judaism because He includes it; it could not otherwise have been set aside. Think how great a shock to a Jew the demands of Christianity must have been. It could only be complied with by seeing that it is an *addition;* that it embraces all the fact, and shows the form necessary.

To embrace an interpretation is not to reject, but to fulfil, a form. Only so could the Jew have been at liberty to receive Christianity. So is actual in relation to our sensational religion. Men cling to the old conception; feel it is Divine. Only by seeing that the actual fulfils it, not denies, contains all the fact and shows the form necessary—only so can they embrace it. Will it not be to the orthodox as Christianity to the Jews? Only a few of *them* will receive it; but the unbelievers may, even as the Gentiles accepted Christianity.

Is not *faith* essential to true knowledge, for the very reason that knowledge (intellectual knowledge that is) can only come through giving up conclusions, and utter unfixing of convictions—a course which only faith can enable us to go through. Without faith we cannot intellectually know, because we cannot and will not fulfil the conditions of knowing; will not give up and alter, and utterly distrust ourselves. Is not this dependence of knowing upon *trust*, beautiful? Is not the fact dimly expressed by some old sayings? An absolute trust in God—i.e. in that which *is*—independently of all things, and especially of our being right, is essential to knowing, because essential to learning: without it we infallibly cleave to our ignorant impressions, and dare not let them go.

All opinion is meant to change. The sole valuable thing is our being made to love, which can be in most varied opinions. That very opinion which produces love at one period, may crush it at another. The opinion is that which it is necessary for us to think, and is determined by two elements: one constant, viz. the fact itself; the other variable, viz. man's condition or relation to it, i.e. his ignorance—a positive and a negative. The negative must be in opinion as such. It cannot correspond truly with the fact because only the actual can do so. Love is the fact; we know or comprehend it when we *are*, or love. This is the only true knowing; then only does the subjective truly answer to, i.e. become identified with, the objective or fact, because the fact is only this. Here is the meaning of "knowing" being the "oneness of subject and object." To know is to be that which is known. So opinions about Christ too must alter; why should they not? The love, the life, will remain; the fact be more truly, more widely comprehended, the phenomenon seen as necessary. How can we think we know enough to know aright the history and nature of Christ's relation to us? Is it not necessary that with the removal of ignorance that fact must appear to us (as all other facts) in ever new ways? Does not the fact demand ever changing forms, by virtue of our being intellectual? My opinions are in ever fluctuating "form," varying with ever-varying conditions, according to the resistances; they affect no fact; *fact* remains ever the same, it is not in relation with my intellect. I distinguish broadly between *that which I am obliged to think* (by least resistance), and *that which is true*. An opinion, as such, is necessarily false. It should be ever ready to change on the least good, or even probable, reason shown; never held fast; it is a perpetual flux, a life, a part of Nature; and only so is good. Holding fast to *opinion* is like introducing stagnation into Nature.

Thus we should think: in the first place, our opinions must be according to our best means of judging; but they will certainly be not the truth, if only because partial. Second, the truth is certainly better than our opinions. Therefore we must be ready at any time to conform them to whatever evidence may appear to demand it, for to know more truly must be to know better; remembering that the office of the intellect is not to determine the *belief*. People hold as opinions what is against the best evidence, because of feelings. This is a total confusion. To see the relation of opinions is the only way to be free from this bondage. To do this is to cut oneself off from the chance of rising to know that better truth, is against the axiom that the truth must be *better* than our thought. We should be willing to give up a most pleasing opinion for one most repugnant, if evidence demands; knowing that this is the road to the

The Art of Thinking.

best. Say, if you like, this cannot be true; but it is according to the evidence; therefore it is my opinion, held as means of discovery and advance, but not my belief. The doctrine of "anticipation" is a great help here: it enables us to admit and embrace all. Where there is not sufficient evidence, think as you like—only remember that you do so. Do not fancy you have evidence where you have not. In science as well as theology what power and what freedom this gives us.

As a man's knowledge increases, either his opinions must change or *he* must change. So a man who retains his opinions, either refuses to learn more or does alter himself in order not to alter his opinions. This last continually happens, especially in successive generations; the men who retain the opinions of preceding generations, who uphold them, must be different men in order to do so. It is quite clear that if they had been such men they would not at that different time and different state of knowledge have had those opinions. The men alter themselves, they do violence to some feelings, they coerce themselves; that which was genuine expression of the entire man, and therefore left the man free and whole, is no longer so, and therefore distorts the man. There is nothing for it but to see that opinions are *forms* only, and do not touch the fact. Here is the essential and radical failure of orthodoxy; it makes faith include a certain intellectual view. Is not what is wanted a plan of thinking which should retain every old opinion as a phenomenon in its own place; never abandoning it absolutely, but seeing that in a certain state of knowledge it must appear, and ever retaining the moral elements that give it vitality? As in advancing life the lower form ever retains its place as the form of life at that stage.

And do not the lower forms persist as monuments of the progress?

Men distrust analogical arguments, because they do not know how to use them. They are aware there is no force in them as they themselves employ them, therefore they have no confidence in them however used. They cannot distinguish between good and bad, and so distrust all alike. The difficulty about arguments from analogy depends upon whether a man can see what constitutes such arguments at all.

The embracing *all* that ever was thought would be a beautiful position, and how fruitful! It links itself with other views as to the nature of the mental operations; viz. suggests the thought that all man's thought is in, and comes out of, Nature. It is *there*: it cannot therefore be false, it can only be not enough; it is in man's mind only by its *being*. One has a clue whence to trace thought; how to understand what it is, and whence it comes: it *is* Nature.

All opinions are true, *under their conditions;* and no opinion is true, otherwise. So nothing has ever been thought of or said which is not right and necessary; only the conditions must be fulfilled—this is the great work of the world. A true and right instinct guides to all assertions; there is not one too many; only they are defective, and then there are different assertions, expressing differents parts of man. These furnish the conditions for each other—the problem is to *unite* them. May one say that all are right, not because there is anything in man that is so, but because they come into man from without, and are not from him? Each of those opinions

The Art of Thinking.

expresses, not self, but Nature : it is the limitations, the excludings, express the self.

Whatever has been an old notion we shall come to again ; not being conscious of turning, but to our surprise finding ourselves again at it. It is like going away from a spot round the world; we go straight on, but infallibly return to it. But we return with the gathered fruits of our experience ; like a man returning to the home he left as a child :—the place is the same, but he is different; and he sees it quite different too. So God put man in Eden, and drove him out; and he goes round the globe back to it; but it will be a different Eden to him when he returns.

Very interesting it is to note how errors are *exactly* related to truth, and so how significant. Errors are so many sign-posts saying : The truth lies out there !

The road to the heavenly city lay *through* the Slough of Despond. It was not to be reached by turning back, cowardly, and keeping on *terra firma* (as Christian philosophers seek to teach us to do). A man walking across a chasm on a narrow plank—all seems to reel to him ; but it is only that he is giddy. Go on steadily, and you are safe; the only danger is in fear.

The way in which some writers dispose of scepticism, viz. by the instincts, is very well for certain purposes. But the road to true knowledge lies *through* those doubts, not skirting the edge of them. That slough must be fairly crossed, or the journey's end will never be reached. It is easy to put the questions off, but we remain wanderers and guessers until we cease to do so, and *solve* them.

Those who do not use rigid logic are as if they used a flexible pole to push a boat; they do not *get on*. They do not see that the fact of logic being against their thought, and its repudiation by a portion of mankind, mean that there is something radically false in their conceptions. This is an evil result of acquiescence in mysteries; they think there is no need we should have clear understanding. This is it: some, influenced by the understanding, accept moral mysteries; others, influenced by the heart, accept intellectual mysteries. The reconciliation here is evident: get better premisses, which, with logic, will allow the now non-logical results.

It is evident there must be some premisses which will allow *any* results; and since men agree that premisses are not to be proved, nor ought to be provable by reason, it would seem that fresh ones are ever open to us. The obstacle to advance is evidently the clinging to premisses.

And the beauty is, that these improved premisses will ever give better results than the best obtained by force, against logic.

We cut off our hands and then complain of want of power; we refuse to be guided by sound reason, and then complain how little we know. Logic is of boundless power if we would not mistrust it so. For example, when it is demonstrated that, in believing "matter," we clearly believe in that which *is* not and cannot be, we say: "Ah, those things are beyond the scope of our reason; we must not subject them to such examination; must acquiesce in the mystery and suppose that our faculties are too limited." Let us rather accept the fact, and see what comes of it. We are necessitated to believe in that which is not; why so? Here is a great fact, a glorious problem; we shall learn something from it if we will not be afraid and shut our eyes. (And in the name of religion too; fancying that anything can hurt *it*: faith in God is truly faith in ourselves.) Why are we compelled to think that which is "not" to be? Because we, in being, are *not*. There is infinite instruction here; the fact of being landed in a paradox is proof that we can understand that; for these things our reason does suffice.

The question of axioms wants more looking into. It does not do to have certain things laid down as true without proof, and all proving rest upon those assertions. I think I find axioms to be mere definitions, to be true because the words used express and embody certain relations, which the axioms only assert explicitly, but which are truly in the words; that they are true because of the meaning of the words, and may be proved by a reference to such meaning. For example, "the whole is greater than its part." This is proved by reference to the meaning of the words "whole" and "part." So "motion takes least resistance." "A child is younger than its father" is an axiom: it is provable by referring to the meaning of the word father.

Axioms are not unprovable; they are provable, just as it is provable that a child is younger than his father. There are no unprovable propositions; all truth rests not on unprovable propositions but on *ideas*. There is a great difference; of course ideas are not provable; for proof is not a thing appropriate to them. Here is a point to look to—to trace ideas from sensation. Then, having ideas, all reasoning (the mental life) becomes simple.

Propositions respect the relations of ideas to each other; and all of these are provable. There is no failing of the process of proof, no falling short, in the sphere to which it is applicable, viz. in relation to propositions. To prove an idea of course is absurd; but as soon as a *relation* of ideas or a proposition exists, then proof is available. Axioms are not unprovable in the sense usually meant.

Now farther: that which is the nature of the truth of axioms, must surely be the nature of universal proof: i.e. proof of all kinds must lie in the nature of the ideas themselves, and all proof must be matter of definition. An axiom is only a proposition proved in the same way as all others—but of the simplest nature. All processes of proof must be just bringing down the special proposition to some simple ideas, the definition of which is seen to involve the point to be proved.

I see how mistaken people are in their great diffidence in theorising, not venturing an opinion upon any points on which they have not special knowledge, and so on. They do not see the point at issue, which is not any fact in Nature, but only a relation of our ideas. A theory fixes nothing external to us, but only says: of these ideas or conceptions of ours this is the right relation: leaving the question open as to the ideas, and therefore as to the fact. We are bound to be bold and free in thus regarding our ideas. This modesty has for its fruits idle fancies, hypotheses, and retardation of all progress. We are bound to put our ideas in the right relation, or we pay the penalty; and the guide to this is simplicity; the simplest relation is the right. By this means it is, and this alone, that we discover the wrongness of the ideas themselves, and so advance; by doing this boldly. Not doing it hides from us our ignorance.

True interpretation ever not only shows that the phenomenon is not, but also that it must be the phenomenon (e.g. the earth's motion and sun's, Christianity and

Judaism); so only can the hypothesis be destroyed; by being "fulfilled" ("filled with the fullness of God"). Interpretation is so the fulfilment of hypothesis. The form is filled with the fact.

The grandeur of Newton, the interpretative character of his work, is shown in the rugged and unconcealed incompleteness of it, by the rough unravelled edges:—the centrifugal impulse altogether unaccounted for, merely postulated, and gravity itself to his own mind quite unconceived as to its manner and mode. He said: This much is so; but as for these other things I do not know them; they must wait. It is the true attitude of the interpreter; he did not fear paradoxes. (But he never meant his unknown elements to be left as they have been since.) A man that "makes a theory" does not leave things unfinished like this; he shows how all may be from beginning to end. The interpreter shows how a part must be, and leaves the rest. But men cannot now raise themselves to the height of Newton's mind; they do not appreciate his attitude; they suppose the thing perfect, and that nothing more is to be done, letting the postulates remain uninvestigated.

A man that cannot face a paradox is no good. The great requirement for good thinking surely is, not to be afraid. But then this depends upon a man's senses—whether he can *see* or not; a man who sees his way is not afraid; one who cannot is sure to be so. The greatest of all aids to good thinking is an absolute faith in the moral and spiritual; such as gives a firm conviction that nothing that can be thought can be attended with any danger to it, a faith entirely above the reach of doubt derived from things that are in time. This sets a man at liberty—not to disbelieve in the spiritual, but to avoid fancying that he has to guard religion against the assaults of Science.

It is essential to good thinking to be able to receive and admit and cling fast to that which is true, though it be only part; and though perceiving that there is not only another side, but much that is opposite. "Hold fast that which is true," and wait; being willing for the rest; but do not try to make up; do not relax and smooth down and accommodate. The opposite is exactly what you want; but before you can properly receive that you must perceive in its full and perfect force that to which it is opposite. Truth is not *between* opposites, but a *union* of opposites: if you will not have one of them first, you will never get the other. Be bold; the timidity may be added afterwards to make up the prudence, but if you will not be bold you will never be prudent; there cannot be prudence without the boldness in it. We must have the extremes.

We must get well familiar with the conception of the "not." It is essential to our thought; as much to us as to mathematics, which indeed exists by it. Our analytical thought must be by means of the "not." If you speak to a mathematician of minus twenty, he does not laugh and say it is "mere nothing;" he knows it is an element of calculation just as important as any other. So when we speak of the "not-being" of anything, we must learn to rise above the vulgar instinctive contempt, and recognise in that as essential a conception for knowledge as any affirmation can be. "Not-being" is a relative fact of the very utmost consequence, as we know practically well enough. There is nothing more real, more important to us in daily life than "not;" we must bring our intellect into accordance with it.

Surely this is the relation of the intellect to the moral or spiritual—the intellect is compelled to suppress the fact of the moral, just as it is all other facts, in order to see them rightly, or as necessary. Hence if the function of the intellect be misunderstood, a difficulty arises. Perhaps indeed it is natural and necessary to man to conceive of the intellect as determining belief, until by the development of the intellect itself he has learnt better. And therefore when the intellect comes to deal in its universal manner with moral, actual facts, difficulty and dispute arise: for these facts are vital to man; he cannot *be* without them. The intellect deals with them no otherwise than it does with all others; but our necessary clinging to them raises an embarrassment directly; the intellect is put in opposition to the very fact of humanity on the one hand, and on the other it is checked and distorted, not permitted to act freely, by those who try to maintain those facts which it cannot help suppressing. Here of course is the origin of all the talk about the "inability of the intellect to deal with spiritual matters," the necessity of "acquiescing in mystery," and so on. The intellect can deal as well with these matters as with any other questions; first suppressing the facts it will show them necessary. But it must first suppress the facts; if we will not let it do that, we simply prolong a strife which can have but one end; we oppose life, which is ever a futile attempt. The intellect will render an infinite service to religion, but she must do it in her own way, and we only need to understand her.

Consider how absolute that law of our mental life, of our advance of knowledge, seems to be; that we first invent hypotheses which are afterwards proved to be unnecessary, and which yet are essential to that knowledge which proves them unnecessary, as nutrition is to function. It seems impossible to us that they should not be true, inconceivable and ridiculous to suppose them not to be, until the farther knowledge comes. Consider, I say, how absolute this rule is; the hypothesis seems simply saying what we see, the only way of stating it. See the bearing of this on the hypothesis of real matter. This was truly necessary till now, I grant; yet not more so than every exploded hypothesis has been in its day. It is the nature of a hypothesis, a false, a phenomenal view, to be thus necessary and unavoidable. We cannot state a thing we have observed save in the form of a hypothesis; the theory is involved in the saying it. We assimilate it, that is, and must do so; we must express it according to our previous knowledge and mode of thought; i.e. according to our *not:* our ignorance, or not-knowing. Every hypothesis must be set aside; by this means comes the function. Apply this to the hypothesis of real matter. If it is not set aside, producing so a function, it fails of its object; it is a nutrition, a life, wasted. We must not cling to them; at least only until they effect their function; then let them go—all, *all*. They are evils, like the evils of society; they exist to be put an end to, effecting so a function, not arbitrarily, but necessarily, or rightly. The evils of society must be put an end to not arbitrarily, but because it is right; (this is the necessity here) from love; this is the function, the development. They must be not merely suppressed, but put aside by introducing something which was not there before. This is very important.

All error is defect, is a result of *want*. In thinking of philosophical and other systems, to regard them aright we should not look at the forms of the error, this misleads us, takes us away from the essential point. We should regard the negation, ignorance, or wanting fact, from which it arises. The mischief in respect to thought is this: we will not give up. Some self-sacrificing, earnest, deeply religious man, starting from our false assumptions —false because defective—*thinks*. With all his heart and soul he gives himself to this most needful of all human works; and it results in some doctrine, which, when fairly stated and tried by our assumptions, seems like atheism and blasphemy. This is the logical result of our premisses; and what is it for? Why, to make us alter them; to show us our ignorance. But we, clinging to our assumptions as if they were our life, say: "What a wicked man!" we raise an outcry against him, and banish and proscribe his works. Why, there is more piety in one half-hour of that earnest toil of his, than in all our ceremonious, rigid, self-satisfied, self-seeking life. Why has he arrived at such a bad conclusion, then? Because he reasoned *rightly*. You have made up something to suit yourself; he has given up himself to find what *is*, and takes it, when he seems to have it, be it what it may. *He* believes in God and trusts Him; *you*—not an inch farther than you think you can see Him. (Surely the wonders *faith* works at this day are not less than those it wrought of old.) These strange, intolerable results are the necessary means of opening our eyes to our wretched assumptions; these show us how ignorant we are; these are the fruits, natural and necessary, of *our* view of Nature and of God; the badness is not in them but in their cause.

The point of hypothesis is, that it is the statement of the fact, as if it were necessary, but without any true necessity shown. Arbitrariness is put for necessity: e.g. the doctrine of "specific tendency" *seems* to make the special forms of living things necessary, but does not truly do so. It is as if necessity were inferred instinctively from the fact of Being. The source of hypothesis is the demand of man (or Nature) to have every fact *necessary*. Again the spiritual is here; for this demand for necessity is a demand for *law*. It is because all true Being is necessary; i.e. it is action, one with law —i.e. is Love. Science can end nowhere but in the recognition of Love as the only true or absolute Being.

Gravitation is exactly a hypothesis in this sense, a fact supposed as its own cause. What we have to do is to find out *why* bodies attract each other; then we at once exclude the "hypothesis" and see it necessary. So chemical affinity, surely is just a hypothesis. But such hypotheses are good in their way; for they mark the perception of the fact; though they are absurd when supposed as *causes* of the facts. They necessarily arise with the perception of any fact: we may say that no fact is truly perceived save in and by means of such a hypothesis. Is not this a law of our intellectual life? So our hypothesis of an external world is simply our way of perceiving the fact of our passion. So, before the interpretation, the hypothesis cannot be discarded; to deny it is to deny the fact. (E.g. we must believe in gravitation, until we know *why* bodies approach; in specific tendency, until we know why all forms are; in chemical affinity, and chemical elements and compounds, until we know the "why" of the phenomena.) Is not this partly the intention of cause and effect? The hypothesis stands to us for a cause; and of course, as nothing can be without a cause, to deny this, which is to us the cause, is virtually to deny the effect or fact. This is both why we suppose the hypothesis and why we cannot give it up. Hypothesis *seems* to supply a cause without truly doing so ; it seems also to supply a *law.* It gives us something, or rather some "not," which is so intangible and obscure that we may fancy it (according as we are devout or undevout), either existing by itself, or immediately dependent upon God. It serves to hide the gap as it were ; it "conceals our ignorance."

The philosopher could not think of the individual *fact* (e.g. chemical union) as existing of itself ; nor the man of piety as being directly caused by God ; but each of them puts this fact as a hypothesis ; viz. supposes a "chemical affinity ; " and then they can think of it, each one as suits him best. So hypothesis lures us on, encourages us at first, making us think we know something. Then, by failing, it reveals to us the fact. I see better from this again how all observation is truly subjective, is our own sensations hypostatized.

There are no words expressing man's thought which do not answer to something. Words live, do not come by chance. It is ever a folly to deny anything that is embodied in the words of a people. We should show what fact the words mean, what the fact is by the non-recognition of which the necessity for inventing hypotheses has arisen ; show the negation. Something acted on men to make them invent : what was it ?

All advance in knowledge is the art of using words rightly ; " the difference of true and false is a question of expression." Words are first applied to the phenomenon, so they have a fixed and definite meaning ; then the art of using them is that of applying words having such phenomenal signification to the real : so it is in truth the fixing of the correspondence of the two. Here is the life ;

now one sees the bond, the organization; and how words lead us on, and necessitate our progress, prevent our stopping, because so long as our view is incomplete words are not rightly applied, and are felt not to be so. There is, in the meaning of the words we use, that which requires adjustment; the phenomenon does not receive its full interpretation by such use of them. So the words are necessarily truer than the thoughts, because larger; they assert, by the necessity of the case, more than we mean. They connote more than we think of; so if we use them aright, we must have affirmed (and truly) more than we meant. This is what I have seen when I said words had a meaning of their own—the very words by which we try to define our first and primary positions, contain *assumptions*. So I suppose a child rises from mere phenomenalness at first, and so language; though the words refer truly to the actual. Historically (as Fichte would say) they are accommodated from the material; but philosophically, it is the reverse—the accommodation is *to* the material. But though the world is at first merely the phenomenon to the child, yet it is not *natural* to have all our hypotheses. It is as in astronomy: to the child the sun moves; but the Copernican astronomy is immensely more natural to it than the Ptolemaic. The greatest violence is done to "natural conception" by these hypotheses introduced on the basis of the existence of the phenomenon. They never would be but for our rooted assumption.

Every word is tied, as it were, to a certain phenomenal meaning, and with these words we test the spiritual. So all metaphysics is necessarily the interpretation of the phenomenon. Now it is true, words are, in time, separated more or less from their first phenomenal meaning, but this takes place only according to the laws of the case, and virtually the union is ever maintained, for the phenomenal signification is embodied in the secondary meanings. So each generation finds its predecessor's statements wrong or imperfect; for observe, our increasing knowledge of the phenomenon itself, i.e. as phenomenon, and in its own mutual relations, must give larger, deeper meanings to the words. So metaphysics ever waits for Science, for the meaning of its words to be unfolded. Metaphysics and theology can be developed only through the medium of Science.

All good thinkers, so far as they are good, are characterized by indifference to results; they do not care what sacred doctrines they set aside.

As for the objects I set before myself in my thinking— I have none. Exactly this is what I have not: I refuse all objects. I simply *see*, and have no wish, no desire, no anticipation; nothing I want to maintain or enforce. I wish to see what *is*: this is all. I tend to no end; Nature uses me. I have faith: faith that that which *is* is better than that which I could devise; faith that if I say what I see, that will most contribute to the knowing of that which *is*, which is the only good in respect to knowing; in truth the only knowing.

I do not hold that I can construct a final system; mine is but a step not more truly right than that which has rightly preceded; only the present right. Dearest and most welcome of all men to me is the man who shall supersede me. His further and clearer vision is to me even as if it were my own. But it must be by a step forward that I am to be overthrown. I am not so foolish as to imagine that I, a mere channel for the surging tide of truth, can stop its ever advancing waves. It flows *through* me and goes on. Thank God! When I have done my work what can it be to me but joy that others also should do theirs.

Thinking ought to be recognised as an especial work, and an especial gift, attaining its real use only by assiduous culture. What most (even cultivated) men should seek and expect is the capacity—not to *do* it—but to enjoy and appreciate it. In fact it not unfrequently happens that what people set up as their reasons, for example, for disbelieving a particular doctrine are, in truth, the very reasons for accepting it. Thinking, indeed, includes both the attractions of art and the positive results of Science.

This art of thinking must have its principles founded on the nature of our faculties, and on the truth of Nature. It must act on all these things, and fulfil all their demands. It must embrace and express the facts of our total condition and of our environment.

Surely the parallel of thinking to art—especially to painting—will throw light upon both; upon each through the other. Shall we find a correspondence even in the details of their course? We have seen that thinking is like music, and in comparison with music how undeveloped and poor! Now, from both these parallels will not light and even guidance come; guidance in thinking, the hardest of the arts, from the easier and therefore sooner developed ones? There is a new value thus revealed in them. Nay, may it be that by serving as guides and servitors to thought the arts are to render their great service of interpreting Nature; by being the ministers of the interpreter of Nature—*thought?* They are its ministers, as well as the senses under the form of observation and experiment. Bacon then erred, and our recent philosophy has erred too, in using only one of its ministers to serve it; the consequence has been dissension and separation. The arts have erected themselves apart from thought, and there has been even strife. In truth, all art and all observation are one; members of one body, built into one Head—*Thought.*

The chief element in thinking is really the imagination; imagination either as the power of seeing the unseen, or of putting ourselves away from the centre, and taking a view including ourselves, and not projected from us; that is, of truly using our impressions. Surely there is no exercise of the imagination equal to that which is involved in interpreting the vision of that unseen which presents to us the phenomenal, interpreting Nature.

The imagination, then, being the true faculty which works in thinking, how comes it that logic, being simply a kind of skeleton in it, has been supposed the thought faculty? May we not say of logic that it is the condition or mode under which imagination works in thinking, as in other arts it works under other conditions?

The imagination in thought has been suppressed for perfecting. In Art there has been beauty, the ideal, as opposed to thought which possessed truth rather; each of these confessedly being by the negation of the other. True thought is the union of truth and beauty.

The art-feeling is the affirmation of joy. Joy dwells in that region, is its idea, its principle; but it is not so of the phenomenal; hence the separation. And that which shows the phenomenal as the true sphere of joy must be union with the actual, taking away the middle wall of partition.

What was added to the Gentile elements in Christianity is parallel to that which is added to the art-elements in true thought. The Gentile culture bears the same relation to Judaism as Art now does to Science, Judaism answering to the line of growth, to Science. As Christianity was presented in two phenomena, so the actual world is presented to us in two phenomena; the physical is the one, the ideal or spiritual is the other.

One may note here a reason for the observation that in order for true knowledge of anything, it must be presented to us under two forms. For when this is the case there is a possibility of the two uniting, by the exclusion of the negation, and presenting a fact that appeals to another kind, or mode, of knowing. (Two sensible apprehensions to one intellectual apprehension; two intellectual apprehensions to one spiritual knowledge.)

Recognising the part of imagination in true thinking we see another thing. Since logic in its development suppresses imagination, is not this very fact proof that they are two complementary lines? Is not the exercise of imagination which is thus suppressed the anticipation? Does not the suppression prove this, and prove that the interpretation will be its perfecting? Whenever one development of human tendencies especially suppresses any other, this is to be perfected and restored in the fulness of that other. Thus, those tendencies, those emotions of joy, free-liking, &c., to which religion in its progress is opposed, are emphatically the ones in which perfected religion consists; the opposition is the proof of it. (Even as the exhibition and play of the vital force is the very substance of life; that for which all opposition to it, and failure of it, in normal development, exists.) So the question is answered why logic especially was put as thinking. It is just as that which opposes and checks pleasure and freedom, activity and enjoyment, has been put down as religion. The intellectual process, referring all to general laws, sinking all individualities in abstract statements, must repel the imagination; even as the developing religion the strongly sensitive and joyful. And so the imagination and the pleasure, thus suppressed, barred and cut off, have been keeping up an isolated and in part despised life of their own. Their true relations have been misapprehended; they have to be grafted in again. *Then* will there not be "life from the dead"? Will it not be a renovation when pleasure becomes one with religion, and art with strictest thinking?

As Christianity came through the Jews, but turned to the Gentiles, and had its real kindred with them, with their liberty and spontaneity, so does not the true thinking, though coming indeed through the love of logic (or reason or science) have its true kindred and affinity with imagination, the line of liberty and joy? Think how image-making was forbidden to the Jews, and Art (with the exception of music) banished; and how Christianity has again recalled Art. So those devoted to thought proper, or to Science, turn away from its true significance. We have to appeal to the imagination-class, and say: "What you ignorantly worship is here; Nature *is* this."

Is it not beautiful to see the whole department of imaginative life as one of two imperfect lines coming by a negation? There is no more any mystery in it; its mystery is that it is not enough. Truth, true knowledge and thought is such—involves such seeing the unseen—that from it, by negation, *poetry* must emerge.

In this more perfect life of imagination in union with logic is exhibited the perfect human joy that is in sacrifice; the perfect having that is in giving. In what crushes down one person's spontaneity or imagination,

M

that of another finds a more perfect freedom and satisfation; but in no one is this latter primary and immediate; it is always a result of discipline and learning. "Thy statutes have *become* my song." Law crushes all men's spontaneity at first; hard fact crushes all men's imagination; but they may be made one at length, and the man may say: "These real and strict logical relations are *become* the very world of my imagination."

Thought can achieve such wonders for us, can do and give us so much; can elevate our life to the region of the actual; surely the need for the attainment of its fruits is immense. But this can only come in one way. We must recognise thinking as a special art, and cultivate the power of appreciating it, of criticism.

V.

THE SELF AND CONSCIOUSNESS.

Individuals are states of humanity—Individuals are separate because physical—Man as a parasite—The self is negation—Eternal life is deliverance from the self—Descartes perverted modern thought by starting from the self—The untrustworthiness of consciousness—True consciousness is the opposite of self-consciousness—Unsatisfactory nature of the doctrine of immortality—The desire for immortality is not man's highest aspiration—What absorption into God means—Love is not self-sacrifice—We want martyrs—To give love is to create—Men are sacrificed for man—How happiness is attained—Only love can satisfy—Happiness is a putting aside of consciousness—Pleasure comes from want—Personality is not highest—God is not personal—The Trinity—God is Being—No mind without body—God as light—The fact is love and is shown by Christ.

WHAT is that "I" that has consciousness? After all that question returns. Surely it is the same as: What is that thing that has weight? Take it away and leave the consciousness, and it is not missed. Now may not this individuality or personality be *states?* Since this *I* is in time it must be only a form, only a state; just as "things" are states. Now do I not get a clue to the relation of persons, i.e. of the physical humanity, to the actual? There is a succession of persons; they cease, and must therefore be states. Persons are states of humanity; they are forms or states from the actual, by a "not."

There cannot truly be a "not." We are forms, as I

have said; but then just as a *thing* cannot truly be because it is only a form, so cannot a *person*. We are forms of course; the *I*, the person, is a "state" of humanity. In that very axiom that only forms can be in time, it follows that persons are forms, or states. States or forms of what? Why, of humanity. This personal is the form of humanity from the "not." In saying our body and mind are part of God's act which is Nature, I have said all this before; personality goes with the mind.

Must we not look at this self, or consciousness (clearly they are one), in connection with the unity of humanity? There are now many selfs, in humanity, because it is fallen. It is as material that men are many or separate. Even mentally one sees how they are one. Without his material nature clearly man is one. First destroy this separateness of men and make one humanity again; then the separateness of man and God is destroyed: this is redemption. Yet what beauty and joy there are from this separating humanity; here is the demand for love, self-sacrifice. See how the demand for self-sacrifice, in respect to men, is only of the material or sensational; love is the doing away with the separateness; it is making our material powers another person's, his will, his demands, act through me. Let this be only perfected and man is no more many. The separate individuals are from the "not" in relation to man, as man is from the "not" in relation to God.

Are we not *parasites?* See how the parasite has not the life of that living body on and in which it is; it is part and yet not part.

So we are part of the physical universe, and yet distinct. We have an individual life which it does not share; yet all that is in us is from it; and all our power, all that by which we live, is its. Just so is the parasitic animal to its nidus, as we are to physical Nature.

Now the parasite has *individual* life, in which its nidus does not partake; yet is that nidus living, only its life is larger. From our point of view we might well see how its nidus should be to the parasite distinguished from itself as *not living*. The parasite might well seem a living or organic thing in an unliving "world."

Is not the universe thus *collectively* living; in relation to us being as the tissues of an animal are to the parasite in them.

This is the entire point of all I see; the root, heart, and being of my views—that *self is negation*: all is included in it.

But then, how can "negation" be conscious, intelligent, and sensational? This is just what proves it to be negation, this shows it in time. There must be a *not*; for being conscious, &c., as implying time, means the "not;" for that which is in time *is not*. So, except as being negation, there were not possibly self, or consciousness, or intelligence. Think how in a limb, e.g. so long as it is healthy there is no consciousness of it; when it is diseased then consciousness begins. The negation is not the consciousness, but the action of Being on the negation produces consciousness and all that is thus "personal." The "Being" is actual; all that *is* necessarily is actual.

Being redeemed is being delivered from ourself—not therefore necessarily from consciousness, or perception, of it, but from the illusion of thinking it the fact, or our true Being, i.e. from self-love or self-regard. We cannot believe but that we are all right in our views. But if we can give up ourselves, then we can see that perhaps we are subserving some much greater end than any benefit to ourselves; and may not feel so sure that we must know all these essential points. So we shall comprehend that God may permit us to be in error and darkness, to redeem the world. We think God loves our *self;* that self is of very little regard to the universe, of very little regard to God; of which the proof is, that we are only then right to the universe or one with God, when it is of very little regard to us. God hates it, and so should we, and never grow content with it. That is why God abhors self-righteousness; He hates self. He means to destroy it; that is His love. It is curious: our idea of heaven is *saving* our*self;* God's idea is destroying it. He will deliver us from it and utterly exclude it and do it away, so that it shall plague us no more. Now here is a contradiction: the *self* will be taken away from *us*. This is the eternal; therefore to the intellect it is a contradiction. To be thus delivered from self is eternal life.

Looking at the physical human race, we think it dies out and nothing comes of it; but this is not possible. See how false opinions die out, necessarily; but in this is the removal of the ignorance; they cannot possibly die out but by that. So the human race; it cannot possibly die out save by the removal of the death of man, by virtue of which it is.

To be without a self, to get rid of the self, is simply to have all things to us exactly as they *are*. Things are so to God; that is, He is not a self; an infinite self is not self. As with space and time, infinity excludes them;

space, time and self are correlative; space as inertness or limit, time as form.

Omniscience is this—*not being a self;* even as omnipresence is not being in space, and eternity not being in time. The negation necessitates our affirming by negation. Self-sacrifice perfected is no more self-sacrifice. He is in us, self is cast out; there is no other deliverance from self.

Who are we, what is the human race, that we should be right, that we should not be subject to an illusion? This self of ours is to be destroyed, and man freed; therefore this illusion. God has sent us a strong delusion that we should believe a lie; we are damned through it, as we know; from which damnation only Christ revealing the fact to us can save us. Is it not certain that this authority of consciousness is maintained through *fear.* And what good ever came of fear? Our idea of God as a "self" spoils the relation; we conceive Him as loving Himself; this as the best and highest for Him, but not for us; we are to love Him chiefly, He Himself. So perfect sympathy and oneness are impossible; as we see that in friendship the perfect sympathy is in loving each other. But seeing God as *Being,* the absolute Being, all is right. Now we see that our love and God's love are one; alike in Him and us it is love of Being; God's love is not love of self, but answering to ours, love of Being, love of us as Being is in us. It is thus the perfectness of love; love of self in love of others. God's self-love is love of the creatures and no other, for the "Being" is them. So in being alive or one with God, man's self-love also is one with love of others, i.e. of all; because it is God in Him. Here is the being a new creature; being one with God, all things are made *right* to us.

Has not Descartes given a perversion to modern thought by making his position this being of the self; though he only expressed it, of course? How utterly false a starting-point, the assertion of the self as Being. It is true, however, the "cogito" proves Being; there can be none of those predications without that. If it were, "I think, therefore there is Being," that would be good. In truth, is not the step direct from the "consciousness" to God? We may say of a shadow, "It is dark, therefore there is Being." Do not all these passive affections (thinking, among them) necessarily belong to the negation?

All this work about the authority and trustworthiness of consciousness means simply that man wants a fixed standing point, and cannot be content with a life which perpetually grows. It is unbelief, and it is fear. And here is another connection; unbelief is one with fear. But then love casts out fear; therefore that unbelief is not love. Love and faith so identify themselves, as indeed they must, being evidently one. If consciousness deceives us, why, from the illusions of consciousness, should we not learn true facts as we do in reference to the physical, from the illusions of the sense? This argument about consciousness is nothing different from an argument by which it should be maintained that the senses cannot deceive. We are striving, just so foolishly, and in just such foolish fear.

Consciousness of self is the true *opposite* to consciousness. Observe, in ordinary life, self-consciousness is ever disease; the right and proper consciousness is that of other things, of external objects. The right consciousness indeed is perception, consciousness of other than self; when we become *self*-conscious, then we are morbid

The Self and Consciousness. 169

at once. And see how Adam's change at the Fall is even most prominently seen as *self*-consciousness. So the true consciousness is consciousness of Nature. With this idea of a consciousness not of our own self, how beautifully benevolence and sympathy, and indeed all virtue, appears. Is it not, as it were, a consciousness of others? And again: is not this universal consciousness, in truth, an infinite, or rather *the* infinite, consciousness? There is no possibility of ceasing, nor of loss; it is the eternal. To it there can be no evil; change or loss is consciously of form only. Here is the perfect happiness; it is the utter loss of *self*.

I conceive our present doctrine of immortality is very unsatisfactory. Is it not like that of the matter and force not ceasing, though "things" do (which indeed is used as illustration and argument)? I fancy there is nothing more in the one case than in the other; it is abstractions merely. The *man* ceases, even as the thing; it is the fact only that does not cease; which, I take it, is not the mind, as we talk. That which is in time cannot be eternal; we are deluding ourselves with a vain fancy. And surely Socrates' argument applies only to the actual—if there be that in a man. If actualism seem to deny personal immortality, it denies nothing that is worth retaining.

Surely the desire of personal immortality is not truly a noble or worthy attitude of humanity. At least it is not the highest. Granted it was an advance in humanity to attain to it, but may it not be a greater to give it up? Man rose to it from less, from indifference; he should give it up for more, for self-sacrifice. We should lose this feeling of good and evil to ourselves apart from that of others. And is not this an instance of a law? Perhaps the "self-consciousness" is a rise from unconsciousness, but it is a greater rise to altruistic consciousness. From ignorance first to error, then to knowledge. And is it not the self ever first, self-desire, self-consciousness, self-knowing, i.e. the not-Divine, and then the Divine, or altruistic? What I would have is to have no joy or sorrow of my own apart from that of others, to escape this isolation and limit, and to be like God, whose joy and sorrow are in others; who *creates*. Is this creation—to be in others? So in our poor way we say of the creator, the artist, that he *is* in his work. This I mean by being Divine; it is being infinite, unlimited.

The dispute respecting "absorption into God" may be easily disposed of by the scriptural statement that we are one with God, even as Christ is. The perplexity arises altogether from our introducing physical, inert, or negative conceptions into our relations to God. There is certainly no absorption, because there is Being and life. It is not losing, but having; not ceasing to be, but being. We, having put the negation for fact, find the *giving* life a destruction. We *are* one with God, now. These physical relations, to which alone the idea of absorption applies, these negations which put us in time, have no bearing. Get to think rightly on the subject, and we see that the question of "absorption in God" (regarded as a ceasing to be—or indeed in any way) has no meaning. It is self, *death*, that we are delivered from; will it not content us to have God's Being? Must we stipulate for a sense of personal enjoyment? Let us be consistent, and bargain for perpetual youth, or that we may fare sumptuously every day.

Love in relation to consciousness, self, or time, is self-sacrifice; but this is an accident in our perception, not love in itself. It is absurd to make love self-sacrifice; even as it would be to define a fact as the destruction of its absence. Light is the destruction of darkness if there be darkness; but to define light as destruction of darkness is absurd; where light perfectly is there is no darkness; where love is perfectly there is no self. Love is positive; we do not know what it is—it is God, Being; but in respect to us, it is self-sacrifice. A Being with a "self" cannot know Love as it is, cannot know God. Love must be manifested in the flesh as self-sacrifice; to know God truly is to be in heaven, is to escape from this self, to be freed from consciousness, emancipated from time; that is, to be *eternal.*

Is not this, indeed, an excellent definition of the self—the way we feel the absence of God?

Men are not truly less prejudiced than they were; nor are the feelings which prompted persecution different; they are but of less intensity. The form is changed, not the fact: we are glad for those to suffer, to have no opportunity of influencing men, who seem to us to be putting forth injurious doctrines. And in those days, if there were martyr-making flames, there was also the flame of martyrdom in the human heart; and that was a considerable counterpoise. People could see men carried unflinchingly to the stake, and not be utterly puzzled to imagine why; they might execrate the impiety of the man, but they did not lift up their hands in pious amazement at his folly. It would not have been altogether out of their comprehension how a man should possibly find anything better than a large income. We want the spirit of martyrdom again, and nothing will kindle it but martyrs.

If we were self-sacrificing, we should see that nature is self-sacrifice; it is because we are self-seeking that we see God as such. It is ever so; that which we see must be that which we are. So we cannot be "saved" by nature, because we see in nature our own death; cannot be saved by being like a God whom, because of our own death, we see as self-seeking. We are shut out from the possibility of salvation save as God manifests Himself as self-sacrificing; which can only be in the self-sacrifice of a man, because it is only in a man that we can see self-sacrifice to be such. He cannot show us His self-sacrifice in Nature, because Nature is that very fact, and we cannot see it.

We cannot get Being for ourselves; we must have it given us; we must be created. Here is the necessity for Christ, for God's self-sacrifice; it gives us life. Giving love is the true creating, not the making of substance. We cannot create ourselves; practically we know we cannot make ourselves love.

We ought to look at humanity, and be content for its sake. We find it so difficult to look beyond the I; we think if all *men* be not saved there is so much loss of humanity; but it is for the sake of *man* that men must be destroyed. So, too, we put the "not" for the fact. God will destroy *men*, body and mind, that *man* may be. Humanity is the Being, the object of love.

Is it not one humanity in many forms, in many individuals; and this succession of individuals or forms goes on until humanity is redeemed? This redemption of humanity is the end, the function of the human race. This series of men is the fact under various forms; is not this what Nature represents? God saves man; i.e. man *is*; for us to be saved it is only necessary that we should be man, should *be*. God takes care of all that *is*; only the "not" He destroys. But to be man we must be united to Christ; for He is *man*, and all true humanity is one with Him.

This only is to be happy, not to pursue it. Self-sacrifice is eternal happiness. To give up the pursuit of physical happiness, to seek for heaven as not physical, is, in that very fact, to sacrifice self to love. It is to be in heaven. The eternal cannot be *pursued*, it *is*. Therefore he who is " pursuing happiness" cannot be on the road to heaven. And necessarily the pursuit of happiness must fail; it is exactly grasping at a shadow, a "not." Yes, our position is precisely that, throughout, of taking a shadow for the fact. To be happy means to love; if we are to be happy at all, it is now in this very present fact; for this is the eternal fact; there is no other fact for us. If we cannot be happy in sacrifice now, we never shall be; for there never will be ought else—never—it is the eternal.

He who pursues happiness must be miserable; as he who seeks comfort must be uncomfortable. And that we, thus miserable, do not know it, think ourselves happy if we can only succeed in our incessant pursuit; what does this show but that we do not know what it is to be happy? See how a person born with skin disease is content to pursue comfort, never having had it; finds his pleasure in this miserable temporary relief; does not know (at least for a time) how wretched he is. So are we; so engaged in seeking relief for this disease that we do not know, have no idea or imagination of what the true powers, capacities, happiness, of manhood are. We do not believe that there is anything else better for man than to scratch himself. (It is Plato's illustration, not mine.) The only way to have happiness is to be freed from this disease. And our self-indulgence, our getting, does but aggravate that disease of not-happiness. There is no attaining happiness so. We must be cured.

And see with what an eagerness of passion these things are pursued; we must do and enjoy such things; we are overpowered, are not ourselves. That not-happiness, that discomfort, overpowers all things. All truly valuable and great objects and pleasures are nothing to such a poor man; he *must* scratch himself. So are we with our imperious passions, our necessity for pursuing happiness, in spite of all considerations.

And clearly there is but one relief for such a poor wretch; no philosophy, no talking, is of any avail. He may abstain from scratching; but if the desire continues he is miserable. This is self-righteousness, asceticism. But *cure* him, give him comfort, and he no longer pursues comfort; give us happiness and we no longer pursue it. Yes, cure us, give us happiness, that is, *make us love*. Take away that inertia. All this comes because we do not love. Not-loving is our disease. Make us to love, and we shall pursue happiness no more so madly; we shall have it. Make sacrifice to be in us *self*-sacrifice, give us the life we cannot give ourselves.

Man is miserable because he wants to love, must love, and does not know. Man is seeking what he may love; and cannot find it. This is what these passions are; they are blind yearnings to love, wasted on the form, hurrying us into loving vice, and every abuse. Better so, than resting, contented with the form. Exhaust it, scorn it, cast it aside; behold the very fact of God awaits us.

Consciousness, being a regard to and thought of self, is certainly not love, not happiness. In fact, when we think of ourselves, that is *not* loving, *not* being happy. Does it not show a *failure* of happiness, if a person thinks: Now I am happy? It strikes me as true, even now, that perfect happiness means just a *putting aside* of consciousness. All physical pleasure seems to aim at this; but this is only transient, only in the passing from consciousness to not-consciousness. I do not mean the absence of consciousness as in sleep; but the swallowing it up in love. Surely pleasure is just the thinking of something else than ourselves; when we think of it lovingly so much that we entirely forget all else, especially ourselves, then we are, in that sense, perfectly happy. But to us now such a state never lasts; it passes away, and consciousness returns; we only remember that we were happy. But conceive such a state prolonged indefinitely; then would be no consciousness, no time; such is eternity. There can surely be no time where there is no thought of self, no not-love.

It has not been clear to me how all pleasures could be from a want, or discomfort; because at first they are quite new and unconceived. But I see now; the idea of eating as pleasurable only from hunger, applies to all. If we did not know about eating, hunger would be to us only a state of discomfort, not foretelling to us the pleasure of eating. So with all pleasures. That all are preceded by a want is shown in the fact of the instinct which leads to the procuring of them. It must have been a musical hunger that first lead to inventing music, and so on. And that the arts have attained to so great perfection and beauty is nothing more than the great perfection of cookery; it does not any more affect the question of whether all pleasure be not from *want*. And no doubt, before there was such wonderful advance, the pleasure from these sources of enjoyment was not at all less. Think, e.g., how much more is reported of the early music than we find it capable of effecting now?

The absence of appetite is disease; defective wants of all kinds are such. Physical being and well-being consists in abundant wants. Also with regard to having more or less physical good; I think we mistake in thinking that the less possession means the less enjoyment. An infant is perfectly happy with the milk; a man, with every conceivable luxury, has no more, nor so much enjoyment; not to speak of the depravation of appetite and health from luxury. Doubtless people suffer from the wishing for things they have not got; but this is quite different from the rich man *enjoying* more than the poor. We know it is not so; simplicity is the greatest enjoyment. So that this development of material good is not, and cannot be, for increase of enjoyment as its end. This perpetually increasing want is a means to quite other ends; to the understanding and interpreting of Nature; that by investigating her as material we may learn that the fact is actual; and that this perpetual getting, by its failure and the intolerable evils which result from it, may redeem us from selfishness and teach us to love. These two are correspondent; the latter is the actual, of which the former is the representation in the intellectual or formal.

Brinvilliers, when led to the rack, asked what that great pail of water was for, and was told it was for her to drink. Is there not, in this, a light on our physical life? Is it not *by torture*, as it were, that we have such intense need and desire for what otherwise we should not desire nor enjoy? The things which give us pleasure, and the withholding of which we cannot tolerate, are in no way to be accounted for according to our normal life; even as the intense thirst produced by torture was not. Christ says, "shall never *thirst*"; He gives relief from torture. Not so much that we, being physical, are surrounded by physical suffering, as that the being physical is the very receiving this unnatural pleasure; implies the "tortured" state, as making possible such enjoyment. And so the feeling that the physical existence is a matter of pleasure—a "filling the heart with joy and gladness"—is included also. The feeling of gratitude in respect to it has its place. The two opposite feelings are justified and united so.

That all pleasure must be from pain, must mean relief, seems certain. With respect to those cases when a pleasure is enjoyed for the first time, comes unexpectedly and unforeseen—first hearing music, &c.—such pleasure is no pleasure unless there be susceptibility. And this susceptibility surely means previous want; for it ceases with the enjoyment. The discomfort, or want, is not conscious; yet I think it clearly exists, and manifests itself in the dissatisfied, wrong condition of a person who has such susceptibilities which have never been gratified. This is like instinct, like genius; the pleasure or relief is not known nor consciously desired; but the necessity spoils the life, and when very strong works its own gratification. All pleasures, all arts, must have arisen so. The discontent and inability to rest or be comfortable of a person with an ungratified susceptibility proves the dependence of pleasure on pain; and after being once gratified, the want or discomfort becomes conscious enough. So capacity for pleasure means want.

Does this unconscious want answer to the unconscious love of God that our passions are? Our consciousness is illusion; Christ reveals the fact of God and Man. What distinguishes man but a capacity, unfilled, for better things? He knows not for what; nothing satisfies it; he is restless, he must attain, give himself to, Being; and this he knows not. So our passions, this love for good which knows not a true object, this capacity, this want, are not evil, though they produce sin, dissatisfaction, restlessness, and disappointment. See the susceptibility, the *fact* to which they have relation. And see, too, the gratification, the end; how the satisfaction comes is given, from without, and then the meaning of them is revealed. How many have testified this! We think we want enjoyment, when in truth we want love; we think we want to get, when in truth we want to give, to Be.

As the unconscious want of music is satisfied by music —given as from heaven, revealed to the longing but unknowing soul—so this longing for God is satisfied by God revealing Himself. Not from within but from without comes the answer to these inarticulate demands. Thus (as Maurice says), the Gospel says what all philosophers, all the longings of humanity, meant, but did not succeed in expressing or attaining. It does not oppose or suppress, but fulfils; and only by fulfilling puts away. It embraces all in a kingdom, revealing the kingdom in which all are. It affirms consciously as it were what they unconsciously, reveals what the want, the striving, meant; *satisfies*, as we know so many have testified. (That it does not satisfy now, is it because we have lost the *fact* which alone should satisfy?) And all these strivings, all these passions which waste themselves on that which satisfies not, all must predict and imply a satisfaction; all mean that man shall be redeemed. This is the prophecy of the passions; they are nutrition for that; they are God's love acting on man.

This confuses us: that as mind, consciousness, self-action, in a word *personality*, is the greatest thing to us, we assume that it is truly the greatest. So we put it into Nature and God, making ourselves the measures of all things. Do those who maintain this mean to say that God is truly such as we can think? Or if they grant He is above our thought, is it not clear that this is just what appears so evil in my doctrine; viz. that if God is necessarily such to us, but is not truly so, then what basis is there for our affections, is it not a mockery? I say this evil is not in the nature of the case, but in the artificial and forced limit of our thoughts; and if we will be natural, and say: " Clearly God cannot be truly such; how is He truly and in Himself?" we can know better; can attain a sure resting place, a satisfaction not failing either our affections or our intellects; a God to love, more perfectly, more profoundly, more naturally, more elevatingly. This God is the infinite God, Love: the love of whom is love of Being, is eternal life. The God who is manifested in Christ, who dwells and works in us, who works all things by His own will, in whom we live and move and have our Being, who is our Father, who forgives our iniquities, who makes us one with Himself. We can see God thus, can know Him, if we will not be afraid. The heart of man knows Him, and the intellect retires from its idle toil confessing itself incompetent. We will have a God whom our intellect can grasp. We think we can know fact, Being, by the intellect, but we cannot any more than by sense; a higher faculty must "know" God. We have to know here that the "fact" is not the intellectual phenomenon, but the cause of our perceiving it. So this is simple enough. I say we can know God, but not intellectually, and that this personal God, who acts in time, of which theologians tell us, is not possibly the true God, but is phenomenal merely; that it will not do. I do not deny it is the right phenomenon, but I say we not only can, we *must*, know the fact which is not this. This personal God is a "state of consciousness" like other hypotheses or phenomena. Here again we see the phenomenon must not, may not, be given up until the fact is known; we want the negation excluded, not another form of it. To know God is more than we have made it; we have reckoned it a means of obtaining everlasting happiness, and it *is* eternal life.

There is a true beauty in this conception of the non-personality of God; in truth, there is more in the true *One* than can be in one person. The true and absolute God is so vast, so rich, that if He be brought into personality, as for our apprehension He must be, there must be three Persons, as it were, to contain Him; the Godhead cannot be in one person. Even as Humanity demands the dignity of man, the tenderness of woman, the trust and joy of infancy, and cannot be without all three, so the Godhead demands the Father, Son, and Holy Ghost, fully to contain and to express it. This elevates our thoughts of God; humanity is none the less, it loses none of its moral value and dignity or of its spirituality, or any attribute of delight and glory, because it needs three persons to constitute it. So neither does God. Those who take one person for their God instead of three, simply lose so much.

The Self and Consciousness. 181

It is the necessity for three Persons in the one God that we see in redemption; and that is the necessity for infinite love and self-sacrifice In the absolute one God all this exists together; but if it is to exist in the personal it demands three persons. Love is one, is absolute, infinite; but if it become *personal*, there must be three persons. We see that it must be so; this is in all Nature. So if we are to understand, to know anything about the true nature of that absolute infinite Love that is God, we must see God as three Persons. And see here, how in fact those that make their God one Person, do lose the Love. Save in three persons, Love cannot represent itself.

The God of theism is, in the strictest sense, the *shadow* of ourselves. It is magnified, but the substance left out; and especially the *heart*.

We also take quite a wrong view respecting the Trinity, as a revealed doctrine: we abuse it as if it gave us some knowledge respecting the essential Being of God, made us know the unknowable. We should be content; that is how God must be to our apprehension. This is the true intent and meaning of it; and so seen, how simple, nay how impossible a subject it is for controversy or dispute. God to man must be three personalities; even because man is three personalities; it is part of the axiom that God to man must be a man. Our error has been fancying that we could know God intellectually; not recognising that the intellect necessarily introduces elements not belonging to that which truly is apart from it. We cannot truly know even a *thing* that is without us as it truly is in itself; we can only know the *form*; so we can only know God, by the intellect, formally. There is no Father without the Son and Spirit; they are correlative, each involves the other; they are all the one actual; that which the actual becomes by the "not." So one sees there is no Being who created, or could have created, the material world, there being none to create.

With regard to the necessity of God's being personal to the heart, consider this also. Setting aside love towards God (as the question *sub judice*), the very strongest of man's non-religious natural passions, *loves*, have been and are for that which is not personal, nay even for abstractions. See man's love of truth, of justice, honor, courage and loyalty. These are the strongest passions of man, as has been often proved. But I do not put an abstraction for God, proved though it be that an abstraction will do for the heart. My God is the farthest possible from an abstraction: He is *the* Being, the only true actual Being, and all of it. He *is*, so intensely, so actually, that personality detracts from Him. That is why He can be loved; not temporally, not physically, but eternally, and actually, with such an infinite and all-absorbing intensity. Love of the Infinite, of Jehovah, may be so infinite as to exclude all not-love, all consciousness, which love of a person could scarcely do. Is it not the triumph of the love of God above all other loves, that it alone is perfect, and destroys consciousness even of self? Is not this why even Christ shall deliver up the kingdom, and God be all and in all? No "person" shall interpose between that love made perfect and its God.

Reflect how "infinite" is a merely negative term. We have come by familiarity to overlook this. It means inconceivable, the denial of everything by which we conceive. Saying God is not personal, not conscious, not

The Self and Consciousness.

moral, is simply carrying out into particulars this general statement that he not-finite. We cannot conceive God as He truly is; yet if He were a person, or moral, or conscious, we could conceive Him. It is strange the reluctance there is to admit this; we seem to feel that by giving up as true in respect to God that which arises from limitation or negation, we are giving up His Being. God is none the less *not* these things that we are, because He is not so by being *more* instead of less. To a man to whom shadow is reality to say that there is no darkness, is to deny. Thus is it with us; when the darkness, the self-ness, is denied of God, we tremble, as if our God were being taken from us. But in truth, He cannot be God that *can* be denied; God must be such, the denial of whom is a contradiction in terms; if we could rightly see the case, we should see it so.

Think, in connection with this, of what is shown by history; that the first denial of idolatry or of a material God has ever been felt as a denial, and not as an affirmation, which it truly is. This shows us what takes place in ourselves; explains our feeling of losing God altogether when consciousness, personality, moral Being are denied of Him; we cannot feel that this is in truth only the affirmation of a truer, fuller Being, the denial of darkness or limitation. It is partly this, and partly because our conceptions have been degraded altogether; for, think, does it not seem absurd to us, that when Paul said we ought not to think that God can be bodily, the proper inference is that therefore He is an abstraction merely? We feel how entirely it is the other way; that what is asserted is that God's Being is too intense and perfect to be material; just as an abstraction is less Being than a stone. And so when we say we ought not to think that God is personal and conscious, it is not less absurd to infer that therefore we make Him a mere unconscious "thing." It is clear what is affirmed is an ntenser, more perfect Being than can be consciousness or person. It is true we cannot conceive of it; we *mean* the inconceivable and infinite. And let us remark, too, that we cannot conceive an infinite mind, nor a mind at all without a body, in any legitimate sense of the word.

We have gone back to Judaism. If to deny *body* is to assert more emphatic intense Being—if we can see this—how much more to deny *mind*. Both alike are denying that which is alone the only known being to us. But we have faith. We see that our being involves negation, and that to Him who truly *is*, such being as ours in any form cannot be rightly attributed, whatever our weakness may demand. We see that God must be personal to us, only until we are better capable of understanding Him. In truth, personality involves body. An irrational idea is that of a mind without a body—or even the good of one. Without a body to act on, and be affected by, the matter it "perceives," mind would be very forlorn. So the instincts of men have always made ghosts poor miserable creatures, much inferior to embodied men. In truth, a mind without a body, or relation to the material world, is not a cheering idea. There *is* an utter dissonance in the ideas, and it is the sign of a profound discordance; that was a deep intuition. He that perceives matter is necessarily material.

See the goodness and rightness of our thought that we cannot know in our present state, that our knowledge is limited. Certainly we cannot know till we get rid of the inertia. The ancients thought they could know in spite of the inertia; we have found that under this inertia we cannot. Instinct tells us that some things are unknowable, and that we must know the limits of our powers; that "essences," "substances," are not to be known. Most true; we cannot know that which is not. We can never know what "substance," what "essence" is, we can only know how we come to "suppose," them. Can we know epicycles? Of course not; but we can know all that is to be known about them—that they are *not*. We think it is the very being, essence, and fact of things we cannot know; because, of course, we put the "not" for the fact. We cannot know while we think the "not" is the fact; but when we see that it is a "not," then we know, and feel that we know, all about it, and are content. So respecting God: He is unknown so long as we think He has a "substance," an inert Being; but when we know otherwise, then we feel that we do know and see Him in Christ, and are content. Nothing shows more strikingly how we put the "not" for the fact than our being unable to conceive of God except as having a "substance," as something besides Love. We lie under this necessity by the "not" that is in our intellect; or, as I should say, that constitutes intellect. Of course we must put the "not" for the fact, when only by virtue of that "not" can we think or conceive at all.

God is light: what a new meaning is in this now. God is one; and yet a trinity. A trinity by the "not;" a trinity to our perception at first. The trinity is from the unity, not the union made up by the trinity. Yes, God is light, and He exists in His creatures as colors. As colors are to light, so are all creatures to one Being; various "nots;" yet all determined by one law, all love.

So from all this phenomenal or physical we get at the

fact by excluding the "not" by adding. Yet then the physical will not remain as such, any more than the color, as such, in light. Take away the "not," and the physical is gone. "Not that I would be unclothed, but clothed upon." To be freed from the physical it only needs that *more* Being should be given us.

For the existence of color a peculiar "not" is necessary; not less light, but a "not" of that which is essential to the being of light. All the variety and relations of things are in the conception of color. And see the good and rightness. Would we have all white light and no color? We are in such a relation to light that we can see the "not" aright, can see how it is essential to the good. What were light without color, without this interference, this self-sacrifice, which produces color? Light were no longer light if there were no not-light. God would be no longer God if there were no not-God, no creature. In color nothing is but light; it is all light: so the creatures are nothing but God. Color is from light by interference, by itself causing itself not to be. So the creature is from God by His self-sacrifice; and it is essential to the very being of God that it should be so, even as color is essential to light. From interference of the various coloured rays come inexhaustible combinations and variety. So by self-sacrifice of creatures other creatures are. Also darkness, too, sometimes—*sin*. All creatures are imperfect, colored, have a "not" in them, in reference to the true actual.

God is not said to be sound. Sound is not *one*, as light is. Is not sound more a representation of the physical? It is one out of many; light, color is many out of one. A kind of inversion is here, the same fact seen oppositely. Is not sound most parallel to the physical, light most parallel to the spiritual? Is it thus indeed that, as physical, sound is most to us? The ear is the most perfect. Are the less developed senses still more related to the spiritual? We do not see the light, as we hear sound ; we only see *things* by it. And only that which is from the "not," only color, do we perceive, not light itself. That is nothing to us, like darkness. When the light is not present we cannot see; but we do not perceive the light itself.—"Whom no man can see, yet in whom we live." Is there something in the conditions under which light forms colors, illustrating God and the creature? God who sees all as one, sees love alone; the evil is not in the universe, as the color is not in the light.

We are selfish, but the Fact, which we have not and are not, is Love. Looking at Christ we see that it is so; He shows us the infinite, the one, the only absolute. It is this, and only this. With our eyes opened by Him we can see that it is so. With that damnation taken from our hearts the shadow of death is gone from the universe. Loving, we can see that it is Love; we know it, knowing God.

I cannot admit that God must be personal to the heart. To the intellect He must be; and this probably misleads us. We have not thought of Him as Love, as He is, but only as personal. The heart delights in Love too great and pure to be personal; in eternal Love, which when manifested to us in time is self-sacrifice.

"Mere reason" cannot be tolerated in religion, even as it cannot in the sanctities of home. For religion is truly the home-feeling of the universe. The Church is the Home. Here comes feeble, weary, jaded humanity, to seek its rest. Here, called back from the toil and glare and coldness of the outer life, it is gathered into a family. Can mere cold reason intrude here, and not find itself on a foreign shore, not be seen hateful? A higher faculty, a better and more human insight, even the insight of a true sympathy, reign there, and give the whole tone to the place.

VI.

THE BIBLE.

Nature interprets the Bible—The work of the Bible is to give man life —What death means—Inspiration—No need for inspiration—To have life is to be inspired—We must not be afraid of the Bible—The source of the Bible's power—We put the divine element away from the present—The difference between physical and spiritual is one of perception— Redemption cannot be partial—Religion must not appeal to the selfish emotions—The mistake of our Christianity— The supposition of a physical hell—Hell cannot be remorse—The world accounted for by God's act and man's death—Christ does not save from the punishment of sin—What God's hell is—Heaven is love—Christ's work will cease—" This is my body" shows the spiritual nature of all existence—Prayer changes, not the fact, but the phenomenon—Christianity is not a theology but a fact—Our Christianity is dead—How Christianity may be surpassed.

I HAVE found that the nearer I have arrived to the Bible, the nearer I have been to the truth. But also I note that it is not so much by studying the Bible directly as indirectly through Nature that I thus come into unison with it. The Bible needs interpreting by Nature, even as Nature by it. Having our minds filled with the spirit of the Bible, and looking so at Nature, we see a truth and significance in the Bible we should never otherwise have discerned. We can in fact see and understand nothing by itself; we must go beyond and away from everything in order to grasp it properly; we want a key to it; and with the Bible as with all other things.

Looking at it alone, we cannot *see* it, we take phenomenal views, and read passages over and over again which most distinctly declare facts, without seeing them, or seeing them as just the opposite. As the Bible is the interpreter of Nature, so is Nature the interpreter of the Bible.

I believe few people's minds have ever been more filled with the Bible than mine has been since I began to see the deep truth of Nature. It brought me, unconsciously, to the Bible and has held me to it ever since. Seeing the truths of Nature, my eyes were opened to truths plainly stated, yet hidden, in the Bible, and which I believe I might have read the Bible endlessly without seeing, had not my eyes been opened by Nature.

We entirely misconceive the Bible when we think it is of so much consequence to understand it aright, or wonder that it is so easy to misunderstand it; alike for essential points as we term them and unessential. The essential point is that it should give us eternal life, make us love God. This is its work; if it does this, it does all that is necessary—it saves us. The understanding it is a matter of development; it takes place gradually in the world's intellectual progress; man's salvation does not depend on that, but on his feeling that God sacrifices Himself for him, and giving himself thereby to God, which may be felt and done under very many different forms of thought. We have oneness with God in Christ by this mutual love. It is well to understand the Bible, even as to understand Nature, but it cannot be done at will; it is a life, and it takes time and means: but the drawing of life from the Bible is so plain that a fool cannot err therein, it is in loving. The God whose heart bleeds in our sorrow—He gives us life, in Him we *live*. But to a God who feels not, does not give Himself to us, we could but say, "Turn away those calm, cold eyes; mock us not with that unmoved beneficence; let us perish without Thy pity." Not so, oh God; not so art Thou. Alas, what would it avail that God should love us if He will not make us love. That we do not love is our misery; that is the death from which we must be delivered. Who will give us life? Who but a God that gives to us His own?

Consider how the word "die," though hardly ever used for mere physical death, is constantly, and almost solely, applied to the sacrifice of Christ. Adam died; Christ died; we are dead in sins. But when the body dies we do but cease to breathe. This is the idea of the death of Christ; it was that true death which subserves a new life. Ever the word death seems to be used in that sacred sense. It is a sacred word; ought we to profane it as we do, by making it a mere ceasing to breathe? We should learn from the Bible to speak of bodily dying as sleeping, or giving up the breath; and sanctify the word "death" which has so profound, yea, at once so glad and sorrowful a significance. We speak too lightly of death; there is no "death" worthy to be so called, that does not stretch out its hand and grasp the skirts of a higher life; save indeed that utter death wherein he lives who lives in pleasure.

With regard to inspiration, the wonder is, not that these men knew the things they have said, but that all men do not know them. Is humanity so utterly fallen that our admiration of, and delight in, the true perception of any man, must be turned into incredulity? There are no such believers in the fall of man as such philosophers. They take a vain trouble to deny the fall in words who passively acquiesce in it as a fact, and try to teach men so; holding the fall as that whereby alone the dignity of man can be maintained, I deny that he is so fallen as they would make out. I deny that he is forbidden ever to aspire to absolute knowledge, to truly loving, self-sacrificing action. I hold him dead indeed, but capable of life; blind, but having eyes wherewith he is destined yet to see. Dead I admit him to be; yet I demur to the burial which these men are in such haste to celebrate, and to eat thereafter the funeral feast. Let the meats wait, the viands be untasted yet a little longer, while Love and Hope kiss the pale cheeks and unreturning lips. I believe in the resurrection of the dead; that this still cold corpse of humanity shall live again.

Where is the need for inspiration when the Bible doctrines are seen to be a simple statement of the facts, the clear and certain facts, of our life; and plainly written in all Nature? Is not inspiration, as every true miracle, the act of humanity, and therefore divine? Because of this truth is it not that there are so many meanings and applications of the language of the Bible, that it is found to apply to so many things, and to be capable of so many references?

The true aspect of religion is not: "Things are bad, take care" (this is the self-idea); but: "Things are good—understand and know;" your not knowing makes the evil; things are better than they are *to you*.

And farther, respecting inspiration, I remember that all such act of God is moral act, and results in moral Being; God's direct inspiration is not of the intellect, but of the spirit, the love, the *man*. What God's direct inspiration gives, is holiness; and so we come back to the beauty and delight, that it was holiness that was the inspiration of the sacred writers. "Holy men of God spake as they were moved by the Holy Ghost;" were moved to holiness by the Holy Ghost, and so spake. Yes, it was moral purity, the direct inspiration of God, made these men see. Intellectual enlightenment is, by the very fact of its being intellectual, necessarily among those divine acts which are classed as indirect.

"Holy men (i.e. humanity) spake"; i.e. God spake. They were holy men, and saw the world as spiritual. Were they not indeed the chief true *mystics*, who have since sadly degenerated? The Bible is the great interpretative, i.e. mystical, book; a book written truly by man, with a true perception of the spiritual, excluding the "not." And consider again with reference to these men seeing the spiritual, that in those days men were not so immersed in hypotheses by Science as we have become; were not so blinded by materialistic science as we are; and might have a clearer vision, of less extent perhaps, but of greater exactitude and completeness. I do not see why the truths of the Bible should not have been seen by *holy* men all those ages ago; because they are true, and because of the absence of the hypotheses which have so complicated all "actual" questions for us. So many unknown and arbitrary symbols have been of late introduced into our knowledge by the progress of observational or theoretical science, that we find it hard to conceive how clear might have been the vision before. We are not hereby undervaluing the introduction of these unknown symbols, but seeing quite well that they are the essential means by which alone a higher and more perfect knowledge can be obtained.

The difficulty about present inspiration comes from putting the whole affair into a human mode; inspiration goes with the life; it is part of it; having life from Christ we must be inspired. And our inspiration is of course the same as that of the scriptural writers; their inspiration was that they were made alive; it was not intellectual, nor is ours. How simple it would have been if instead of beginning a long way off we had commenced from the present. We are inspired; but we know our inspiration does not guard us from error; i.e. is not intellectual; it is a fact of life in the actual Being; it belongs not to the physical or mental, but to the spiritual. Thence we know what was that old inspiration; it guided into truth—not correct opinions; but actual truth. Errors in matters of "opinion" or of physical relation in the Bible teach us what true inspiration is, and that it is not a matter of the relative but of the actual.

It is curious the way in which our divines speak of the "imperfect" theology of the early centuries. In the second century the Christian writers had not a full appreciation of the Pauline doctrine. Men speaking the same language, partaking the same modes of thought, men whose immediate predecessors had themselves conversed with him,—these men did not apprehend the true Pauline doctrine. And they confounded justification with being made holy. Strange; when we consider that the word means being made holy. Is it rather possible that *we* do not quite comprehend Paul? Christianity was a power then in the world. May not the reason be that they knew what it was better than we? Perhaps they did confound justification with being made holy; but might it not be some compensation if they were really made holy? Perhaps they did not see Christ's death as a price, an expiation, as we do; but what if they were made "conformable" to it? Which is the important thing—the understanding or the being?

The true key to the Bible is to read it quite simply and naturally, without any particular regard or reverence, but as common sense; we pervert our view, trying to find deep meanings. In two opposite ways are we perverted;—we leave out all the actual meaning; e.g. in those passages respecting Christ as being man, and those which say that God is in us; and then we fancy deep and obscure ideas in things which are so very simple. We need have no discomfort in studying the Bible; it is the simplest, most transparent, most friendly and familiar of all books.

We are so afraid of the Bible, handle it as if it was full of traps and pitfalls, and if we were not most cautious would let us into some great sin. Surely it is a friend; it came into the world not to condemn the world, but that through it it should be saved. And why cannot we be content not to understand it; just as we are in respect to Nature? And how monstrous it is that we should think ourselves bound to "justify" it all, and be able to show it all worthy of God, &c. Even at the utmost we should say that if we saw it rightly we should understand; as we say of Nature. In truth, the study of the Bible and of Nature have been prevented very much alike by this idea; it interferes with all proper exercise of thought, besides constraining us to insist on ascribing to God and maintaining to be worthy of Him the most wretched fancies of our own. It is making our intellect the judge of God, instead of our hearts. This is the vicious root from which our opinion-religion springs. We should study the Bible: its being the word of God just puts it where Nature is; and it should be studied in the same way; with the same freedom, pleasure, patience; feeling that any opinion may be erroneous: this is the true reverence. An "opinion-religion" is a monstrous perversion, yet it goes necessarily with a sensational-religion. We may say to men: "Fear not; God will not damn you for anything you think or do respecting this book; but if you *are* damned you will dislike or despise this book: thus there is a sort of test for you in it." The Bible does not want any believing; it may be seen to be true; like other things that are true, the idea of believing is not to the point. "To believe in Christ" is another thing; that God sacrificed Himself in Him for man; this is to love God so as to have eternal life, to be saved. The man who believes in Christ will certainly be saved.

I have noted the infinity of the Bible; how it is like Nature in that; different from all other books, which have a certain grasp and limit, and which one can wholly master. Now, is not this the cause of it; viz. that all things are treated absolutely, in relation to the spiritual or actual; everything entirely in subordination to that and as dependent upon it? So it grasps the fact, and all the form follows by mere necessity. Surely if one can enter fully into the spirit of the biblical writings, their virtue may imbue his writings too; that marvellous power which the scriptures have possessed be shared as it were. All human books look at the forms as existing in and for themselves more or less; put the form for the fact; are limited therefore, and transient necessarily; but to lay hold of the fact, and show all forms as from and in relation to it, is to rise to the level of the Bible. All mystics have attempted this, but as yet has not only the Bible succeeded ? It alone sees all the form to be mere form ; truly draws the line of " being." The key to the Bible is these two things, first it puts the " not " in us ; second it is speaking of eternal things, not temporal, i.e. not future; in futurity the eternity is lost. The eternal is that of which existence can be predicated, and therefore it is not in time, in which is only form. The eternal not only is but always was. It is the fact, the actual ; it is that which brings us into relation and oneness with the infinite fact. The things that are unseen *are* eternal.

The Bible is a miracle, *the* miracle ; the type and example of them. If we can learn how it was, then we know all miracles. Nothing can be more miraculous than that its writers said those things; the raising from the dead is less, it raises *us* from the dead. Here is the problem of miracle submitted practically to ourselves ; find out *how* the Bible came to be. It is of no use saying nothing can transcend the laws of Nature, and so on— here is the fact ; find the law of *it*. The law of *love* it is, this includes all alike. Shew that the fact of Nature is love, and we have miracles in their right place at once.

We are of course *obliged* to deal with the Bible as we do, ignoring all but those passages which agree with our particular " views." It is not from any irreverence, but the necessary result of confounding the actual and the intellectual ; thinking that to religion certain opinions are necessary. We cannot let the matter rest open ; saying : This means more than I can see : my views on these subjects may be quite wrong. We cling to that which we think, which has been the best opinion we could arrive at, and there remain; to let our opinion go is to us letting religion go.

Here is the difference between the Bible and the world. The world says, "We are as God made us"; the Bible, "You are not as God made you, but in a state in which your true God-given Being is in abeyance." The world says, "The world is good as it is to us, and we will make it better." "It is not good," replies the Bible, "and you must be delivered from it." The world says, "Man is a great and glorious being; it is a grand thing to be a man, with his free-will and his virtue.". The Bible says, "This being *man*, as you call it, is being merely dead and corrupt; there is no goodness in it or in him; God must be in him; that is the sole possible good in relation to him." This is the radical opposition between the two, and our Christianity has in it the virtue of neither, and spoils both. So we are perpetually, while professing Christianity, apt to use the language of the world; ever prone to speak of man as the world speaks of him, because, in truth, that way of regarding him is in our doctrines and in our hearts.

We have done one thing with reference to the two ends of the world, as it were: viz. put into them all the Divine and eternal. We have put all creation into the past, infinite ages ago; all salvation and damnation into the future. The present, we are determined, shall be a blank; there shall be nothing Divine while *we* live. But in truth, in what does the present differ from all other, but in respect *to us?* The actual or eternal is as much *now* as ever it can have been or can be. We think the biblical writers were speaking of things a long way off, whereas they spoke of the eternal, of which it is the property *to be*. We think it far off because we do not see it; but this is not because it is so, but because we are *dead*. So we invent hypotheses necessarily; the actual is present in the Bible as in Nature, and we use them both in one way.

It is said that the difference of the physical and spiritual is one of time; I say it is one of perception only. So it cannot depend on bodily death, which is an affair of time, but must depend on some change in us not material. We being the same, must still be bodily; death is only a change, not a ceasing, of the material conditions; the material can cease to us only by a change in us which is not material. What a strange conception that by a change merely material, we can be delivered from matter. What a superstition that is about a person going to die, and unprepared! Transmigration, a material existence of some sort after death, would seem to be involved here.

Think how there cannot be true and absolute Evil (and therefore not absolute Good), because evil is no evil if the subject be altered; that which is pain and therefore evil, may cease to be pain by alteration only in the subject; so it cannot be in itself evil. In truth, Being, that which *is*, cannot be either good or evil; it is above them; it *Is*. So there is a wisdom in that " knowing good and evil." This has a wide bearing. Think how God appearing to Adam after the transgression—the chief and greatest of all goods—was evil to him; made him afraid and hide himself; he tried to avoid God. Now here is simply what we do; in all these things we call evil, God comes to us, and we are afraid. To us it is evil, and we try to avoid Him. This is the explanation of all. When we are made alive again we shall rejoice to meet God; there will be no evil, for observe how there can be no fact but God coming to us. There is no other Being to come. The fact of all our experience must be that; all else is negation merely.

Try it even with a child; is it possible to make him loving save by love? If he even *think* that the fact which surrounds him is not love, will he not certainly grow up unloving? Is not this now the basis of all wise education—make a child feel that it is loved? So *man* was growing up, not feeling that he was loved, in such a blind state that he could not see that the entire fact of his experience was indeed that; and God had to show him that he was loved to "save" him. This was the revelation the world wanted; not duty, not immortality, not retribution, not a personal God—but *redemption*; that the fact of man's experience is that he is *loved*. Thinking otherwise, man must of course strive after good for himself. It is useless to talk against it; so useless that it is not even tried. Theologians even, and preachers, have embraced that very doctrine. What the world wants is some revelation, some knowledge or fact, that should make us not care about ourselves. Orthodoxy has this element, in part, and it is its life. Its argument is, that Christ's loving and saving us will make us love Him, and so we shall not care about ourselves; but this will not do; it must be saving *the world*, or the purpose is not answered. No, not even the saving of a single soul can be achieved, not one man can be saved, if *humanity* be not redeemed. Even practically we see this.

I cannot even *think* a partial redemption. *Man* is either redeemed or not redeemed; for in truth each man is what he is by virtue of all being what they are; the state of humanity determines that of each man. This is our interest in humanity; what is to *man* is everything to us. Here is a profound truth: the true life and well-being of man, of each man, is in that of humanity; but it seems not so to us. So in learning self-sacrifice for others, we are in truth regarding only our own true good; it is only getting right to the *fact*.

It is said: Does not trust in God make men neglectful in respect to business, &c.? Here is the difference; it is as darkness and light. That is a trust on behalf of the self, thinking God will take care of my*self*. It believes in "special providences"; and this world's business is trusted to accidents; God is not seen in the laws of Nature and of Life. It is in truth the profoundest mistrust, it is the essence of unbelief. True trust is trust in God *against* the self; it is recognizing Him in all law and necessity; it is seeing eternal fact in these human affairs. How miserable is this belief in God taking care of the particular self; instead of delivering from it and destroying it. What a perversion of the idea of faith, what a travestie of religion, and, above all, of that of Christ! Happily the feeling, the heart of the men who say these things, is constantly quite different from their words.

Religion cannot and ought not to compete with the world in its appeal to the selfish passions. Men are right in preferring this world to the next; this is not wickedness, but mere common sense and scripturalness. It is a perversion to make out that the Bible seeks to make men give the preference to the future over the present; it seeks to make them give preference to the eternal, the actual, the fact which is necessarily present, over the form, which alone can be the future. This is the very spirit of the Bible, to seek not the future but the present. Do not *get* (future), but *be* (now). "Now is the . . . day of salvation." This is its doctrine, this its precept, this its suasion of love: attend to the present, do not sacrifice it for the future; live now, do not seek to get. Passion is ever in reference not to that which is, but that which is to be; it is from want; its eye is necessarily on the future. Christ seeks to turn us from the future, which can be only form, to the present. So men in refusing to attend to the future and preferring the present (or that which is nearest to it) carry out the spirit of the Bible. And the world ever will and ought to carry the day until it is put quite otherwise than thus.

It is interesting to see how theology has been misled by accommodating itself to the phenomenon. The phenomenon is that men are led by self-interest; so preachers have thought that if they could convince men that it was to their interest to be religious, they would be so. But it is a great mistake; it is not the fact that men are most influenced by self-interest. That is not the *power* in the world. Our passions, the pursuit of pleasure, are not self-interest or self-regard; they are *giving* self, finding our satisfaction in the object. [Not to say that all that truly moves mankind must have in it an element of generosity; even money-getting is for wife and children.] Religion can only subdue and rule the passions by being a giving of self also, a truer, fuller self-giving. It must say: "Give yourself"—as the passions do—or they will utterly overbear it. But "Give yourself to God; not to these mere forms which are illusions and deceits, but to the very fact and reality of all. Religion is the fulfilment, not the restraint, of the passions; it is liberty, not enslavement; it absorbs the humanity, not sets it aside. It is that for which the heart cries out and longs; which the visions of youth prophecy, the weariness of disappointed age implores.

Our Christianity making men think more of damnation, necessarily makes us think so much of suffering; it puts that as the great fact before us, and so unmans us. Thus we are vastly worse than the ancients, who gave freer play to that most distinctively human of instincts, that of despising pain, almost the first demand in a true, strong, great character. First get over the fear of pain, then some good may come to you—this is the true philosophy of human nature. But we say, "Be afraid of pain; so you may save your soul." It is a miserable state we are in, between two fires. Truly to be redeemed is to be redeemed from fear of pain; for fear of pain and self-regard are one and the same thing. Fear of pain is the source of all temptation. Nor is it any better to say that it is the hope of happiness, rather; for the two are one. Desire of happiness (any other than utter self-sacrifice) is only fear of pain. I say this doctrine of ours of salvation, making us regard pain so much, makes temptation so strong; this which is cultivated in us is the very strength of sin. So life is such a toil and struggle for Christians; it must be hard for them to practice virtue, for they are afraid of pain. Their very light is turned to darkness; the medicine that is given them takes away their strength.

Men preach, how if we will *do*, *believe*, &c., all will be well. How can I believe that which will only be *if* I believe? To be believed, a fact must *first* be, not afterwards. It is not, "If you believe, you are redeemed," but, "You are redeemed—believe it and know the fact!" This is it: alike the wicked and the good, the dead and the living, the self-regarding and the loving, the deluded and the knowing, are channels; they are sacrificed for the good of the world. It only needs that I should know this, and love or be willing, and at once I am perfectly happy. What more could I wish? We thought there was something more to *get*, and now we are awake and find that we have all things, and can only half believe it for happiness and wonder. It is like an infant dreaming: in its dream it seems in a desolate dark place, where its mother is not, and it *wants*; it strives to stretch out its hands to seek, to *get*; it seems to wander here and there, and never finds. Until it wakes; and then it sees and knows again, and behold, its mother's bosom is its pillow, and its little hands, groping in the darkness, have been clasped in hers. It did not *want* anything; only to be waked.

It is strange, except that we learn by error, that ever a real (physical) fire should have been supposed as hell. Christ's words, "the fire is not quenched," seem expressly designed to deny it. For it is the essence of the real to cease. Christ says "hell, where there is fire," but not physical; a worm, corruption, but not physical. Is not this the exact meaning of the passage, to guard us against supposing it merely physical? We are told—by denying its special characteristic—that it is not physical. And I believe this would be understood so by the hearers; it is a refinement of philosophers that matter and motion do not cease. Again, a burning heart is the intensest symbol of love, burning but not consumed; a ceaseless fire that burns without consuming, is the very type of love. The sun, too, is burning, and the functions of the body are a true burning; Science calls them so. Function, which is love, is ever burning.

This world differs from heaven and hell in one way; viz. that God's full presence is not made manifest, but obscurely seen by physical images. The full manifestation constitutes at once heaven to the good, hell to the wicked.

Do we want to know *why* violence and cruelty and every vice exist? It is to teach us—yes, *us*—that we must love and not be selfish. These things come because man is dead, and they bid him live. He would never have known that he was dead without them. When we *so* love that we treat all wrong with love instead of punishment, as God does, then wrong will cease. Then Christ will be seen; and His words spoken in such darkness and so little heeded, so held up to ridicule by those who know Him not, so cautiously explained and limited by those who think they know Him, lest they should impede His cause, will appear, as in truth they are, the most striking proofs that He was indeed The Man, i.e. was God.

Comte's idea of ignoring the absolute is like accepting the Iliad simply as a fact, and not asking any questions about either Homer or humanity. Which indeed would have the justification that neither Homer as an arbitrary fact, nor the development of humanity without Homer, sufficiently accounts for it. So, neither the theological nor the metaphysical view accounts for the world. But surely God's act and man's death *together* do. The great point is that of man's actual death; it is the "not" which "matter," or the hypothesis, reveals. This the theological view does not recognise, and so makes death a special affair, and one of difficulty and embarrassment. It has excluded it from its proper place as the cause of the materiality, or inertia, of Nature, and of course finds it a constant difficulty. This puts theology wrong in relation to the Bible, which is based on that fact from first to last. This is the key to the embarrassments of theology; it has to introduce man's death, as a fact, into a system which truly rests upon that fact, and yet is considered to be independent of it. Just as if, having refused to admit Homer as author of the Iliad, men should still be trying to bring him in as in some mysterious way connected with it, as having—heaven knows what—deteriorated it, or something. Science on the other hand looks at the "not" as being itself the fact, and ignores the actual fact itself, altogether. The oneness of the two, in spite of their apparent hostility, is evident.

Think of a man utterly selfish; how is it possible that anything worse should happen to him? How can we want to punish him; he is already the most miserable of beings, suffering the greatest evil, enduring the greatest loss. One may think pain may be added, and so a punishment; but certainly not *remorse*. Moral pain cannot be added leaving the selfishness or death; it is itself a sign and means of life. To suppose Hell remorse, is to suppose it a *rise*, a making alive, and not death. A man who has been sunk in selfishness can only *rise* into remorse. This is our error, that we put pain and pleasure above the moral, and think more of being miserable than of being wicked. Pain is in its nature temporal; the moral sense exists not for our punishment but to save us.

There is no dealing with the facts of the world save on

the view that the sensational is nothing. This is not hard-hearted, it is the only way in which the heart can face the facts of the world; a true deep sympathy necessitates it, or drives mad. We require to get back (in a higher form) that old doctrine that the material is below the man and unworthy of regard; our habit of regarding it so much and tracing in it so especially God's glory, has perverted our hearts.

Our idea of this as man's probation—especially when we force the Bible into it; or rather force ourselves to graft the Bible upon it—leads us to a view of the world that is utter mystery and darkness. Nothing can be clearer than that it was quite otherwise with those who wrote the New Testament. They had a view, a revelation, that made all *light* to them; they saw the earth "full of the glory of God;" they had something to proclaim, which, if people only knew it, would make them full of happiness and perfect in rejoicing. They had, in fact, *redemption* to proclaim.

Men will and must maintain a vicarious punishment, a forensic proceeding such as is the essential tenet of orthodoxy, while they think they are not punished in this world. Make them see that this is the punishment, the eternal damnation from which Christ saves them; that it is not postponed, and not possibly remitted altogether, and then this substitution theory falls. And then as for the punishment of men's evil deeds and feelings, that for which we have consciousness of ill-desert, these, as temporal or physical, have also their punishment. This too is inflicted, and to the full; sinning does work misery. Christ does not relieve men from this punishment of sin; a man who sows evil reaps evil—just as much the best Christian as any other man. It is the eternal, the actual punishment, the damnation, from which Christ saves us, from which we must be saved or are utterly undone. The other sensational physical punishment we can—nay, must—bear; by that (in part) our salvation is made possible.

This is God's hell—the very means and fact of redemption; bright with beauty, thrilling with delight, the image of that Love which is His Being, which is all Being, the want of which is death. This is God's hell—this glorious phenomenon, this marvellous life within us and without: so tenderly inviting, so sternly warning, so inevitably avenging—that wakens us to fervour, moves us to tears, fills us with remorse and agony and shame; that will not let us rest nor have peace, until self be made hateful to us and utterly abandoned, and God's own life be in us. This, that by suffering draws to love; by pain and pleasure, by temptation and failure, teaches us to give and not to get. I say this is God's hell: what of *our* hell?

Our notion of damnation makes it the very worst sort of punishment, that which all jurists deprecate—very severe and very uncertain. We darken the whole earth with it, and yet are afraid to pronounce it upon any individual. It is a mockery, this "eternal misery;" it prevents our saying of any one boldly, "He is damned;" and of course no one believes he will be damned. Infinitely better, even on lowest grounds, is the other view.

Think of this: how can we foresee what God will do for us? Suppose a child should stipulate about what sort of happiness he should enjoy as a man, would he ever have invented *love?* Would he not have insisted upon all sorts of pleasures and enjoyments, on having things given to him, on being made comfortable? Would he ever have thought of utterly abandoning himself in absolute devotion to another? Could he have imagined that new extatic *life?* Alas! we are worse than children, and more foolish. How soon children learn the idea of love; how easily and naturally it comes to them; how soon they understand the subject when they see lovers; what an instinct draws them to the unknown life. But we—we see heavenly lovers, yet our hearts do not respond; we see men who count all pleasures vanity, all sufferings a joy, because they *love* and give themselves, but our hearts do not beat with prophetic throbs; and when our childish thoughts stretch out to imagine for ourselves the coming bliss, we cleave to our toys and sweets, and say: "But when I am a man I shall have plenty of nice things." No, thank God we shall not; but we shall *love.* There shall be no pleasure for us in heaven, save in infinite abandonment; no gain but in utter loss; no possession save in giving.

The joy of heaven is the joy of love. The key to it is in Christ, who for the *joy* that was set before Him endured all. Christ's was the joy of self-sacrifice, of loving, of saving, of giving up His life for another's. But this is no joy save to those who love. Heaven is not a happiness save as we love; only to those who have eternal life can there be happiness. We cannot attain love by seeking for joy; so men are not to be converted by holding out to them the joy of heaven; that cannot make them love, any more than the fear of hell. We can only love for love's own sake, in sacrificing self. Love is the actual, it is *Being*: in loving, man *is*. It is true that much of this is *said* (truth always is); it is said that heaven would be no heaven to a wicked man. But then, to be consistent, what of those intellectual pleasures, and of the rest, and no more sorrow and sighing—are not these an attraction to the unholy? It is here we are wrong; in not seeing that the joy of love is all, and that it is enough.

God's love is not exhausted in Christ, only brought down to us. It is just so much as we can see; not a great effort, as it were, the highest achievement of Divine goodness, just done once. It is love, appearing so small that we may see that it is love; as a father condescends to do little things for his child that he may see that he loves him. The father's love is constantly active in vastly greater spheres, which the child cannot appreciate or know of, but in that loving and dying we understand that it is love. So even Christ's work is to cease; the Mediator to be no more; God is to be all in all.

As our power of loving, and therefore of knowing love, increases, we shall come to see the love of God swallowing up our special connection of it with the sacrifice of Christ. "He shall deliver up the kingdom to His Father." And think again, how the world could not have seen the love of God in Christ until it had been educated by all the previous time.

Man only needs to know that the fact of these things that he loves is God, and he is redeemed. These passions have for their object, God, the fact. We seek for God, else we should be contented by what we get. It is because we love God, and do not *know*, do not see the fact, that we go to such excess, run so into sin. We go ever on and on, and must, till we find what we seek. Man's soul thirsts for God. All his passions are the heaving of his soul beneath that Infinite Beauty; he cannot be content until he has found Him.

This goodness and love of God in making creatures happy, which we dwell upon, is not true love were it ever so perfect, which it is not. If we want truly to see the love of God we must see it where Christ sought it; in sorrow, in sin, in agony; in the lowest, the vilest, the wretchedest. It is not in lovely landscapes, in splendid palaces, in forms of beauty, in the heaping up of delights: that is *man's* love—God's love is seen in sacrifice. So too we see better why Christ was crucified; for our blindness' sake, that we might not be able to close our eyes to the Divine self-sacrifice. Not that that was so much in itself, but it was needful for our dull material sense to learn: such as that is all Nature. And so seeing, we come to perceive that the true death, the true self-sacrifice of God for man, infinitely outshining any martyr's torture, was the *life* of Christ; His becoming the dead man; not dying as man, to rise the living God.

The meaning of "This is my body" is very large. God giving us food is giving Himself to us. The fact of eating food is that; because it is in such form does not affect it. It is entirely an abuse, our making it such a special ordinance; not that it is not such, but that all are such. All life is sacred when we become quite spiritual, and see all as actual; but why not therefore now? It is the very means of our becoming spiritual. How powerful a means of redemption it would be as often as we used food to do it in remembrance of Christ; to see the spiritual fact beneath the form; to remember that Christ has shown us what the fact is, and so not be deceived by the form, thinking that the mere pleasure of getting can be the fact; writing "*non sibi*" upon all. And indeed, who can say "*non sibi*" and *not* think of Christ?

So here we see the meaning and feel the appropriateness of the Lord's Supper. It is because our relation to God is so intimate that no other expression for it is adequate or truthful. The use of it proves the case so. For what other relationship would "eating flesh and drinking blood" be fit language, or that sacrament a fit emblem? That relationship, not to be described like others, demands that expression. As bread and wine are the very life and body of the man—as he is not, except by them—so is it that God *is* us, makes us, is our life and Being; we cannot be separated, we must live by Him. It is not that we live separately and by ourselves, and then come into relation with a Being apart from us, as we do with others; but we only live or *be* at all by Him; the relation to Him is not a result, but the source of the life.

With regard to prayer. True, God does not change; the fact, His act, changes not, but the *phenomenon* of it may change. That is change, not in God, but in man. "If that be all, why then pray for it?" Observe, is it not real to us? Is it not what we want? We must allow that prayer will not change what *is*, but it may change what is in time.

Although the phenomenal only is subject to the power of prayer, yet is not that all that it should be? Is it not to *that* our feelings cling, and about which our hopes, fears, and desires twine? Is it not the "actual" *to us?* and is not that all we would wish or desire to alter?

The Bible.

Would we alter the *fact* of the universe, alter what God does and wills? This is the scope and place of prayer.

We may own and reverence, and heartily consent to, prayer; but we must nevertheless protest against its being brought in as a kind of salve to make tolerable a theory of things that ought to be intolerable, and left in its naked hideousness in order that it might be felt so: viz. the idea that God has arranged a system in which evils, and bad and inexcusable things in themselves, may befall, by His *abstinence*, as it were, and permission. We must not call in prayer and Divine interference, to help us to swallow this camel; straining meanwhile at the gnat of him who says: "I see that God rules all, and I do not see how to pray." Of course, a seeing person cannot see how to pray, when prayer has been obscured, nay blotted out, by such representations.

Christianity is not a theology but a fact. We see men are fallen, *are* wicked, and are redeemed by Christ; words are vain, and nothing to the point; say it how we like, here it is. Wicked men, dead men, do receive life from Christ; are redeemed, are made holy; it matters not to talk. And there is "none other Name"—no other religion does it, attempts it, tends towards it.

Seeing the world perfectly right and good is the true basis of all earnest and energetic action; for it is as a *means* it is right, because of what is to be by it. A man who sees and approves a means as such, does not rest in it; he acts and uses it. Seeing the world thus right and good, necessarily we throw ourselves heart and soul into the great life; God's (Nature's) action absorbs and carries us away too. If *He* works in us, there is a necessarily unfailing source of activity and zeal that casts the self out of us, and makes us one with the course of Nature. All other action must be laborious and lifeless in comparison. So we see the meaning of the apostles' contentment with the world; their finding it full of God's glory; and at the same time their earnest, intense zeal to alter it. It is as God finds it, as He sees the world. His seeing the evil right and good, and not being a thing he cannot tolerate (or however we may like to say it) does not paralyse *His* activity, does not prevent His curing the evil.

Men will cling to the form, let what will come of the fact. We will have the believing in Christ, though there be nothing in it, it must be that form though it be nonentity. The fact, the life, or what is nearest to it, may be elsewhere; but this we utterly abjure, if there be not the Christian form. It is thus: once there was connected with Christ the very fact of man's Being; He gave life to men; now we have forgotten all about the life, and use Him more or less worthily merely as a means for getting something. And yet now more than ever we will have Him accepted and sworn by, though there be no longer any life connected with Him: this is our orthodoxy. But this is not the end; the stream does not flow through the channels where His Name is named; but it flows still, and none the less from Him. Christ is the sole life of this our modern world, the sole though unacknowledged source and spring of its love and self-sacrifice. In those ages when the Church was darkest, where were the saved? Why, out of the Church; among those who denied *that* Christ. Men are bound to deny *our* Christ, but that does not make them less Christians. If God be in them, and they true men, Christ is in them; they live by Him. It is monstrous to make believing in Christ the accepting of a name. We retain the name but have given up the fact. Never shall the world have true life until men see the fact of Christ again.

Surely it may be that there is a sense in which even Christianity is to be surpassed. Not, certainly, in the revelation of God to the heart and sight; not in the doctrine which shows Him as the giver of Life. In this, all thought apart from it has fallen infinitely short; nor can any advance do more than restore it, and place it in its true light. But in this sense such an advance may be destined: in the leaving behind the miraculous element— "greater works than these shall ye do"—which shall come through the perception of the spirituality of all our experience, truly, *through Science*. This is simply a corollary from the idea that miracle is by a negative. That *less*, that revelation by a minus, was needed then. The time may come when it will be thus understood, and no longer needed. Science faintly whispers about it now in the doctrine of God revealed in "law." Let us only see that this "law" is one with the revelation of self-sacrifice in Christ, and then, surely, this higher point is attained.

VII.

HOLINESS.

Nature is self-control—The moral life is parallel to the mental—To be moral is to act—Ago ergo ego—Misery only removed by removing selfishness—No action but right action—There is no true arbitrary action or free-will—Arbitrary action is sin—Freedom because necessity—Man cannot fail because he is a part of Nature—The only mystery is man's death—The moral lesson of Science—Our moral life is passion controlled—The phenomenal nature of evil—Sin as inaction—The analogy of disease to sin—Evil to the individual is good to the race—Life comes only from death—We are redeemed, not tempted, by matter—Creation is self-control—God has no physical power—"Creation out of nothing"—The creature is one with the Creator—Self-sacrifice is not loss—A selfish world is the necessary phenomenon of an altruistic world—No nutrition without a final function—The resurrection of the dead comes by Man.

NATURE is self-control, yet no restraint. It is perfect liberty; absolute, self-enjoying freedom. Oh wild luxuriance of beauty! forms of perfect loveliness in infinite diversity, wandering at your own sweet will, creeping over earth or towering to heaven, making space resonant with gentle laughter and radiant with smiles. Ye speak to my heart of passion wisely ruled, of affections directed to the right. Due self-control, ye testify ever to reluctant man, is life, is joy, is liberty. What gentle entreaties, what earnest admonitions, what solemn testimony, " God does thus," have ye uttered all the ages past, are ye uttering still. Ever ye say to man, " Be free like us; make not thyself a slave." I do believe that if I can show that this moral meaning is the true meaning of Nature; if I can connect these thoughts with natural objects, not as an arbitrary, ideal association, but as the reality of them; it will be a means in the hand of God of making men better.

In everything it seems to be one of the last achievements of Science and sound understanding, to let Nature alone. But in morals we cannot let Nature alone; it is for us, there, to create Nature, by introducing the resistance. We by control have to make the moral region natural and living which else by our default is unnatural and deathful.

Here again is a curious relation, parallel somewhat to the mental life: the moral control or suppression of our passion constitutes our own life: the suppression of the not-me, as it were, produces the me. Is not this as the suppression of the phenomenal or subjective, in Science, gives us the true? The ignorant man who lives in appearances is a type of the sinful man who yields to passion; as the phenomenon is to the reality, so is our "passion" to spiritual act. In truth both are one; the intellectual phenomenon, and the emotional phenomenon; the former called Nature, the latter passion; the former the subject of mental life, the latter of moral life: the "sense of right" operates in both.

We, as spirits, are placed among other spirits, and deriving from their passion, as it were, our own. Even as we see in respect to motion, that it is transmitted from particle to particle; each of which has its own vibratile passion, receives force, undergoes divergent passion, and approximation after, and then its passion ceases. It has had its life. Thus is passion transmitted to our spirits, forming our bodily and mental life. But—and here is our prerogative as spirits—this passion we may make our own, our spiritual moral life. We take for our own, permanently, our eternal life, the life thus wrought within us by self-control. This is our privilege, our power, our duty—to make the life of Nature our life.

When we see a man doing wrong, we should think: "This is inertia where there should be life. All this mischief is because he does not act, but is acted through merely, like an animal; the evil is, not that he does these things, but that he is not a man."

I see now how much there was in the emendation of Descartes' maxim, to *ago ergo ego*, for see what it comes to; the very statement of the not-being of humanity; I do not act, therefore not I. The thinking, the passion does not make the I: it is the not-acting which reveals the not I.

Refinement, progress, civilization, virtue even as it is called—all that leaves the selfishness, leaves *all* that is evil; makes not a single step towards holiness, towards life. The misery, horror, and degradation that are in the world are for the nutrition, for the life. Suppose there were this selfishness of man and *no* misery: what a hopeless state were that!

This misery from our passions is simply the ruin arising from the operation of Being (love) on the not-being (the absence of love) of man. This is not the evil; this is the remedy for it; it makes the nutrition, the life; without it there were no remedy for human death and ruin. The failure and suppression of humanity is necessary for its development as part of the infinite life. This curse is also a blessing, as all God's curses are. And so all plans for getting rid of suffering, misery and degradation, save by getting rid of not-being, destroying the selfishness by true spiritual redemption, must fail. It cannot be suppressed; it is the result of action. Destroy the not-being, give the love; only so is any progress made. If there were not misery where there is selfishness, there could be no action around, no love, no God. So surely as God is, there must be misery from selfishness, ruin and woe where there is sin; the passion ensures, must ensure, wretchedness. The proof (and necessary consequence) that God is, and that He is Love, is that inertia, or not-love, inevitably produces misery and discordance with Nature. If it were not so, the Infinity must be a mere blank void. It is the love of God inflicts our misery. *This* is Being giving itself to not-being.

So those who can truly see, see only the selfishness of man as death. The misery and wretchedness, the evil of all kinds that is not selfishness, they see as life, nutrition, redemption, a means of blessed function. And think: it is not the suffering, the miserable, who are truly to be pitied : "*blessed* are they that mourn"; but those that are *selfish;* those are the truly miserable ones, those for whom we should weep. "Weep not for me," said He who hung in death's extremity upon the cross; "weep for yourselves." So may you say, oh sons of penury, earth's most outcast and perishing sons and daughters—" weep not for us but for yourselves." Truly it is not to those whom God loves most, not to His favourites, that He gives peace, prosperity, affluence—with cold hard hearts.

Now does not our entire conception of a free will want rectifying? I think we must have been in error here. Surely we have been considering as belonging to our constitution, as moral Beings, that which is in truth only the result and sign of our sinfulness; viz. this power of *arbitrary* action. We think we have the power of doing as we choose. I see that this is altogether a false issue. It is not the point; nor is it true. What we have is the power of *acting*, i.e. of acting right; but when we act we must act right; the rightness consists in that fact of acting. If we have not acted *right* we have not acted. The question of moral freedom has been wholly misunderstood; the wonder is that it stands so well on such false ground.

There is and can be no such thing as arbitrary action; all true action is love, self-sacrifice; it is the only fact of law. There is no arbitrariness in all the universe, least of all in God; only love, which of all is most its opposite. Love, or be not; this is the only alternative.

See here a oneness of the actual and physical. Does not arbitrariness in this point of view answer to a state of absolute rest, which is not nor can be? Man thinks himself arbitrary, even as he thinks the earth is absolutely at rest. Not only is not the earth at rest, but nothing is or can be. Absolute rest were absolute inaction. Everything is necessarily moving, is in action, is *giving itself*. Even equilibrium is equivalent to motion, it is a giving self. The whole must be in equilibrium, mutual self-giving, or love; the parts in motion. Arbitrariness is supposed by man, as absolute mere self-rest is supposed of the earth; these are the parallels, and both alike impossible. Being can only be in self-giving, in action, not to act is not to be. We do not truly see Nature as inert in seeing her under law, that is a step out of inertia; the arbitrariness which we first put into her is the true inertia, the most absolute form of it. Law is only from love, and in introducing law we make a step towards love, towards freedom. Freedom is the true opposite to free-will.

It is beautiful that in all that is not directly moral, or actual, man is strictly a part of Nature; in all man's arbitrary doings that are not wrong it is Nature that works; it is all a part of the great physical and psychical passive necessity. This is beautiful, making man's works truly instincts, in mind as well as body; all mutually determined, each just such as all others demand, constituting a living organization; by means of nutrition effecting functions. So each man and each working of each man is an organ of the whole, subserving the universal life: and all an image of the great spiritual or actual organisation.

We act arbitrarily only when we sin. In all un-moral things we act necessarily, viz. by our physical necessity. In right action we also act necessarily, viz., by a moral necessity, the true actual necessity. This is our freedom, our power of action, our Being, our personalty. When we sin or do not act rightly, then only are we arbitrary; we *are* not. Arbitrariness is not-being. Here again logic, though appearing for a time to be opposed to religion, is yet found altogether on her side, with its proof that man has not free or arbitrary will, and that all he does is necessary. It is most true; logic is on the side of religion, now and for evermore. Man is free, is moral, *because* he acts necessarily; even as God.

We are made to enjoy, and therefore to have passion, in order that we may have *life*. This is the meaning of our love, our longing and passion for happiness. Had we not this, there would be no life, for life is passion controlled. Is it not beautiful; this passion or tendency, which is desire or love given to them to obtain life, eternal life? The passion in spirits is that force which will be life in them, if they will, by God acting in them; if they will not, then are they dead.

Thus I see, temptation is not so strictly to *sin*: Nature does not tempt us to sin, but it produces in us passion, which, if we rightly control it, is our life; if we do not, it is death. Nature is ever holy. Sin is not in the thing done, but in the refusal to control our passion; the refusal of God, in fact.

We are parts of Nature and share her perfection. To a man who thus acts with Nature, failure is not nor can be. He does not succeed in life; his life is success. Even as Nature is not moral, because it is morality. Success cannot have success, even as morality cannot have a moral. Success is yoked to his steps and cannot leave him; nothing can bring to him other than constant good. Nothing should disturb such a man's equanimity; for all wrongness and loss are nutritive, the means of higher ends. Whatever happens, my *Life* has been and is; Nature has accomplished her ends, God has accomplished his; and therein I mine. My will is done because and while it is one with *The Will*. This is success, to find, in all events, my Life. It lies not in the result but in the deed. Life ever succeeds and must succeed. It laughs to scorn opposition, failure, loss, for these are not her contraries, but her very being; they are the means of her progress, the willing instruments of her achievements. But that this may be true for us, we need to have life; and sin is death. To sin is to sacrifice and cast away this joy, this triumph. Sin has no part in life, nor he that sinneth. It is the right deed only that succeeds; wrong is death, despair, and horror, in itself,

Holiness.

not in its results. "What shall it profit a man if he gain the whole world and lose his own spirit?" Granted that the world is his: but if *he* be not? There is no earthly event that should have power to make a man unhappy. But this is not said of sin. He who sins is not above grief but below it, and should thank God that he may rise through grief again to holiness.

We must learn to see ourselves as part of a great life, to which we are absolutely subordinated; even as the elements of our bodies are to us. Human life is nothing more than any other form of passion to Nature. Cease to regard the bearing on ourselves of facts in Nature as of any real importance in relation to the things themselves; e.g. consider diseases as essential and absolutely good parts of the universal life, and cure by utilizing the force which causes. This is the practical lesson, that as we are parts of a living whole, we must be living, i.e. holy, accept our part, control our passion, do as God does; being part of Nature, be natural.

We must do right, to make our moral life; here is the fact; it is no matter how it is defined, let it be any way in theory; do the right: that is what remains when metaphysics is laid aside. Let thought be function of the brain, let moral right be operation of physical laws, or form of motion; it will all do. But do the right; *Live*: that is the lesson of the physical world; and this necessity returns upon us just the same after all our speculations: live. If it be physical, live; if it be spiritual, live. What matters it?

We should see in our inclinations as it were chemical attractions: a source of life if controlled, but death, decay and loathsomeness if uncontrolled; death to us, but still forming part of the great life of the universe. We do not call chemical attraction evil; the results are bad only in relation to the particular organisation; it is the result of that special relation only. This is the idea of evil being not real but only phenomenal, or from our relation. We should learn to understand that our tendencies, our natural inclinations, are not really evil (even when they produce unholiness or death in us), but only phenomenally, i.e. in their special relation to us.

There is but one mystery in all God's universe, and that lies in us. Not in gleaming suns or circling planets, not in the myriad forms and varied capacities of living things, nor in the mighty achievements of the intellect. Life is no mystery; it is an axiom; it all lies in a definition. The mystery is, not life, but *death*—not that Nature lives, but that man refuses to live. The mystery is the mystery of sin; not indeed as it affects God's universe; it casts no shadow there; but as it affects ourselves, the sinners. The dark cloud lies in our own breasts; the heavens and the earth afford no solution, as no parallel. All there is life. The death within us seeks in vain a fellow, save in hell. Our conscience testifies the fact; if a reason can be given our consciousness must give it. Let us search our own bosoms and say why sin is; answering at last the marvelling universe that calls to us in God's own loving words: *Why* will ye die? Let us give the reason now, dragging it forth from our deepest hearts. Let us say, *Therefore* we sin. That Nature may cease to be amazed, and life no longer shudder at the touch of death. Oh shame and sorrow infinite! we dare not tell it, not even to the gentle earth and placid stars; we dare not whisper it to the flowers, nor breathe it sighing to the sighing trees. Least of all to these, that love us with the trustful love of innocence; that smile upon us day by day, and stretch out gentle hands to greet us, bidding us welcome to their beauty, as if our hearts were pure and full of love like theirs. Not to these can we breathe the fell secret that haunts our memories, they would shrink from us in horror, and never again should we behold them free and unconstrained as now. Would to God we could hide it for ever! And yet, not so—that were indeed the worm that dieth not. Into God's ear will we pour it; He will listen and forgive; although for utter selfishness we have spurned His just authority and trampled on His law of perfect love; although we have disregarded conscience and been deaf to the voice of duty; though we have known the right and chosen the wrong, He will forgive.

There is no atom, no particle, no mass, no element throughout the physical and psychical universe, that does not willingly yield to the control which constitutes nutrition. We alone refuse. Let us be natural; let us take up the universal burden, and look on the attractive sins; feeling their strong temptation, and say: These are the elements of my life; the forces that shall nourish me, and give me vital power. For the resistance or control of passion constitutes the nutrition of the spiritual life. The holy acts we thus gain power to do are its functions. Much tried, much enduring man, who with firm heart withstandest the assaults of strong temptation and with resolute will controllest passion, blessed art thou! True image of the Deity, like Him creating life; sharer by thine own act, in the universal life. Thine own act indeed, for only so thy life; yet an act wrought in thee by God's free grace alone; taking for thy portion the life that flows eternally from God and making it thine own;

Q

life that is thus at once God's act and ours; God's holiness shared in by us.

We are so full of the wonder of the phenomenon of life, of its greatness, its glory, the skill of God in it, &c., that we will not let it go; we will not give up the shadow for the substance. We have to see that all that is *imaginary*, before we can see the true wonder. We need not fear; if there were not something great and grand in the fact, we should never have an image so glorious. Did our forefathers lose anything by giving up the phenomenon in their day? They were bolder, wiser, than we; they had no experience of their fathers to encourage them; cannot we take heart from theirs? Never fear to let go; it is the only means of getting better things; let go—let go; we are sure to have again. Thus how Science teaches the lesson of morals, which is ever give up—give up; deny yourself; not this everlasting getting; deny yourself and give, and infinitely more shall be yours; but *give*, not bargaining; give from love, because you must. And if the question will intrude: "What shall I have if I give up this?" relegate that question to faith, and answer: I shall have God:—yes, God gives Himself to me; my giving is my acceptance of God's act, God's act in me, which is myself. I live, I act, I create in giving. In my giving, in my love, God, who is love, gives Himself to me. Thus Science teaches the moral lesson of self-denial, self-control, and love.

The material is lowest; it is lost to the giver in being given. The intellectual is given, and not lost to the giver: the true or moral is not only not lost in giving, but *is* only in the giving. That this material is most to us, is just our death.

Holiness.

The phenomenon is ugly to us, as fireworks frighten children, while their parents go to gaze on them for their beauty. Sinai was the sunrise of one of the world's great days—a sun which set in blood when Jerusalem fell before the Romans. Fearful to us; but is it not heavenly beauty when seen aright? Was not the scene at Calvary the brighter dawn of a more glorious day, the loveliest sunrise within God's universe? Yet what was the phenomenon, but murderous malice and dying innocence?

If we do right, the passion so controlled becomes our spiritual, our real life; if not, it becomes the life of the universe. It is the same to God. The evil is but phenomenal evil; it is nutrition of the universal life. If we restrain the passion, that resisted tendency is our life; if we do not, the unrestrained passion is still resistance to tendency, is still life. It is our life, if we will take it; but if not, there is no loss.

The universe is necessarily as it is, because God is holy, and His act cannot be arbitrary. This physical and psychical necessity is, in reality, God's holiness. The necessity of the universe does not contravene, but reveals the holiness of God. Physical necessity is a phenomenon of which the reality is spiritual holiness; a theory of which the interpretation is moral rectitude.

Evil is life, and therefore we dare to look on it. "Ocean of life, whose waters of deep woe," says Shelley. The waters of life are woe; we need not be ashamed or afraid to own it. The perception of Nature as a spiritual reality, re-creates for us the world, and all that it contains; makes all new and of a higher order. Yet truly seen they are one. Rectitude, love, holiness, are expressed by, constitute, all these physical laws. We must learn to see holiness in them, and when we trace the working of material laws, or the results of physical passion, know and feel that the reality thus presented is one of infinitely vaster import, even the eternal rectitude of God.

To see that the phenomenal evil is not really evil, but only an effect on us produced by good, has this great advantage, that it enables us to face boldly the fact of the evil, and removes the disposition to regard the phenomenon as other than it is. Knowing that evil too, as evil, is really good, we are no longer afraid to do full justice to its proportions as evil, and to admit that, as seen, it is absolute evil, unredeemed by the least trace of good. With this faith of the absolute good (and it applies equally to beauty and ugliness) we can face the facts. It is just as in Science; men could not really see Nature, they could not bring themselves to look at her. so long as they thought she was really partly false. The experimental, inductive (phenomenal) Science arose necessarily from the faith (for it was strictly a faith), from the conviction as a self-evident fact, that Nature was absolutely and perfectly true. So will the same thing arise from the faith that she is really, absolutely, and entirely beautiful and good. A phenomenal art and philosophy will be the necessary fruits.

Knowing that the evil phenomenon is a real good, we can now, and now only, truly investigate the phenomenon itself. For investigation is, and means, comprehension, finding out the truth; but this means finding out the beauty and the good. So long as it is believed that any phenomenon is really ugly or evil, it can no more be investigated than if it be believed to be really false. There cannot be a phenomenal art or philosophy except upon the basis that all phenomena are really beautiful and good. This is clear enough of art. The phenomenon, as a whole, cannot be brought within its domain, save on

Holiness. 229

the assumption that it is (or will reveal) beauty. In philosophy this is less apparent, but equally true. Nothing comes within the domain of philosophy, except on the assumption that it is (or will reveal) good; to give a reason for anything is to show how and in what sense it is good:—save sin, the only account of which is that a being or spirit will not act, chooses death. Sin is not a fact or reality, but a negation; and, as such, needs only a negative account of it.

I love this idea of sin as not an act (or reality), but as inaction; a refusal to share in life. The mystery of the existence of moral evil is thus solved. Placing my eye right, I see something of the infinite wisdom with which this system of things is formed; the deep reality from which it flows. God has shown it to me. There is no blot on His creation that needs to be washed out, or compensated for. The idea has arisen from confounding the phenomenal with the real, thinking evil was really evil. So excellent is life, that not to live, is that foul and fearful fact of sin. What does the hatefulness of death prove to us, but the loveliness of life? It is so simple: first to see that Nature is God's act; that all God's act is absolutely good: this shows it all. It removes quite away that black pall that overlies the universe. It is God's hand wiping away our tears. The universe is a scene of absolute life and beauty and good; nothing is there that is not so. Only this sad fact which stains not its glory, that some spirits refuse to share in it, is the great mystery of sin.

This suggests to me, that we misinterpret what the Bible tells us of heaven. It says indeed that God will wipe away all tears, that sorrow and sighing shall flee away, even that there shall be no death; but it does not tell us that there shall be no phenomenal evil. That is quite another thing. Still shall there be life, yea, more life; still *therefore* evil. But not sorrow and sighing, not tears: everlasting joy and undiminished gladness, gladness for life, for evil seen to be good. We fancy if there be evil there must be sorrow, and sighing, and tears. But it is not so. To cure us of our grief, it needs not to take away the evil, but to show it us. Shall we grieve at the evil when we see it as God does? Let me only see the evil as it is, oh God, and my eyes shall weep no more, nor my heart know another pang.

The motion of the sun was a source of error to the men of former times; now God has removed for us that error; but He has not altered the phenomenon; still falsely, as falsely as when first Adam witnessed the illusion, rolls the sun around the earth. But God has shown it to us. The illusion remains, but the error is gone. So shall evil remain, but the grief shall be gone. The illusion shall not cease, but sorrow and sighing shall flee away. Not in the least jot will God alter His deed; it is eternal. In heaven there shall be all the evil there ever was on earth; nor shall we say it is too much. None shall gaze upon the life of heaven and say, "I will not live." So there shall be no sin there, no death.

The analogy of disease to sin is full of instruction. [I see this is the way to speak of analogy between the physical and the spiritual; not the spiritual analogous to the physical, but the physical to the spiritual.] The idea of the remedy for the moral disease by the annihilation of aught that truly is, is just on a par with the false therapeutics that seeks to cure disease by destroying something; considering inflammation to be excessive action, instead of the want of the right vital action. There is not too much action, but too little; all the force that is operative must and should be there; necessarily must be there, or there would not be the being at all, the organization, the possibility of life; but there ought to be there also another force, more action, a control, a life, that is wanting. To cure disease is to give life; to produce action is to destroy disease. Thus Christ gives life, and destroys not-life; the two are one. We have been deceived by the *phenomena* of sin, just as by those of disease; have alike considered that to be an action which is a mere want of action. Both we have to interpret; and to see the moral by the physical; for this end the physical exists indeed. But as disease if life be not restored destroys the body, the individuality, so surely sin does if life be not given by Christ.

The very things which are evil in individuals, are right and good and necessary in regard to the race. So that beings who should look on man as a whole would see no evil; nothing amiss, nothing wrong; a perfect, unmarred, and unboundedly lovely "instinctive" life; just as we see in Nature, of which man is part. And so in this perfect, this lovely Nature, as it is to us, so different from ourselves, may be this very *self-ness* which is in us; and sin and failure, and wrong, death and redemption; and yet we not see it at all.

That individual evil is right and good in respect to man, we see remarkably in Bacon. He regarded the material, and he moved men to do the same; and so Science is in one sense emphatically evil; it has deteriorated the world terribly. But in relation to man it is wholly good; it is simply that he gives up his ideal and takes God's; it is one of the most beautiful facts in his history. We may see it again in respect to religious thought. Our "spiritual" altogether being an invention from our not knowing the fact of the world, it is as necessary it should be denied as affirmed. So "matter" must be both affirmed and denied. This is necessary in respect to man, just as for right thinking it is necessary to hold both Being and negation. The sin of men works the purposes of God; it is necessary; it is involved in the true good, and to *Man* is only good.

Looking on the universal humanity thus, it must appear to other beings (of such a grade as to see it as one living thing) as a diseased body does to us. The elements which constitute it, partly or wholly dead; the body diseased by want of vital state of some of its elements. Christ heals humanity by restoring life to the individual spirits, the men that compose it. This is the only true cure of disease. To this we must attain before we are worthy of the name of physicians. To restore life to the elements that are dead, or dying in excess. Christ heals humanity by restoring holiness or life to the individual men; we attempt to heal the diseased body only by alleviating particular effects of the disease; checking the increased action, &c. What we must aim at is to restore the vital resistance, the due self-control. By virtue of Christ's healing of the diseased humanity, is achieved a result of a glory surpassing what would otherwise or could have been. Thus disease and nutrition come to be one: nutrition, in respect to the organization effected; disease, in respect to the elements themselves which constitute it. For what is disease but a living frame not attaining its ideal, not perfectly fulfilling its tendency? But this is life; there is a wonderful unification here. Disease is

Holiness. 233

ever life—life ever disease (i.e. using life for nutrition). Thus God uses sin, as it were; but does this cast sin on God? I think not. A spirit lives or not, as it chooses; but all the evil which it produces by refusing to live—all the disease—is not real evil, but nutrition or life. Thus, I think, we have attained the point from which the mystery of moral evil ceases; and we find it to be nothing but the simplest and most natural way of regarding the facts, that the true explanation is contained entire in the commonest physical phenomena. It is simply life, one instance of the relation of continuous and transitive vibration.

The decay of a human body is just so much nutrition to the physical universe, God counts it no less; we find it evil because of our relation to it. So, if a human spirit die, infinite is *its* loss (that is real death; spirit being reality); but it is no loss to the real or spiritual universe: God counts it no loss. But His love leads Him to redeem; not for His sake but for ours. And the very existence of medicine, the science of healing, among ourselves is proof and justification of redemption, makes it one with Nature. If the healing of disease be natural, so is redemption. Healing of disease, in fact, exists but as a type of redemption; that is the reality of it, as the reality of death is sin.

When we inflict pain upon each other we know it is not the part which feels, nor even the body at all though it looks like it, but the man whose body it is. So there would be nothing unreasonable in conceiving that when we inflict pain upon an animal, it is not the animal that feels it (though it looks like it), nor even the entire animal organization, but the being (the spirit) whose body that organization forms. And further, should we not conceive that all that we do in opposition to Nature inflicts pain upon the spirit whose organization Nature is; that by injury to any part of the external world we cause suffering to a spirit? I believe it. I have long had an instinctive feeling that all Nature was sensitive; and this is the truth of it. It is all sensitive, as our bodies are, viz. as being the organization of a spirit. The apparent sensation of animals, as animals, is designed to reveal that to us. Thus, the reason against cruelty to animals is not rendered less strong, but more so, and is extended.

Further; our sin, being disease in that organization of which we constitute elements, also occasions pain to that higher spirit whose organization or passion it is. Humanity is sick; and the spirit that "inhabits" it suffers. Sin produces pain (besides to ourselves and to our fellow creatures) also to a higher being — the "universal man," if we may name him so. But this disease and evil also are nutrition, forming yet a higher organization, of which these inclusive organizations are the elements.

There is a wonderful truth in those words, "without shedding of blood there is no remission of sins." Without death is no restoration of life, nor can be; for remission of sins must mean imparting again the lost spiritual life; death must yield the vital force.

Life comes only from death; the force only from the approximating passion. Nutrition is ever the result of function. Christ's death to give life to the world seems but a simple expression and instance of this universal fact, or more truly these phenomenal relations flow from the spiritual verities.

Christ's death restores the lost life; and, in restoring, effects an object higher than could otherwise have been.

The wrongness has been a nutrition, and redemption is its function. In Christ's sufferings there was more than the death of the body; a real spiritual life flows from His spiritual passion; He bore our iniquities, our death; from Him we thus derive new life.

It is a pitiful thought that we are sinful because we are in matter; that we are associated with the physical in order that we may be tempted as it were. It is not so; we are in a material world in order that we may be redeemed. A sinful spirit must be in a physical world in order to be redeemed; in a world of time where the deed once done may be undone again; where the eternal is diffused, as it were, into the temporal; where penitence may find scope, and repentance may avail; and where there are so many, not hindrances, but aids; where all things that live and rejoice say to us, "Live, control passion, and be happy!" and death, in its perpetual recurrence, warns us not to die; saying in tones that will not be denied: "Sin is destruction; he that soweth to the flesh shall of the flesh reap corruption: he that liveth in pleasure is dead while he liveth." Therefore it is we are in a world of things; that we may learn to live. The image of redemption, of being from not-being is around us, that we may be prevailed upon to accept our own.

To *be* is to be Divine. There can be nothing more than God. Creation is not an adding to Him, but rather (as we conceive it, introducing Time into that which is eternal), it is a making less, a taking from; God's self-suppression. The creative act of God is the very fact of self-control, of Holiness, of limit morally imposed upon Himself. My heart is overflowed with awe and glad amazement; the very fact and conception of holiness, even our holiness, stands thus as one with God's creative act. Divine self-control is creation, is life. Well does Nature present to us the one fact of self-control; well does that constitute our one action. It is *the act*, the act that constitutes the universe, the act of God. God's self-control is creation; and in this creation all that is consists.

We entirely think wrong when we attribute physical power to God, as if He could do physical things, move the earth, &c. The idea is not appropriate; of course He not only can do, but does it all; but not physically; it is by moral action that physical things are done in that higher, truer sense. How could the motion of the sun be stopped? In two ways: either by stopping the *earth*, or altering *man*. We see the sun's motion cannot be stopped, as such, there is nothing to stop; it is an image. Just so of physical things; God can alter them—or may be conceived as altering them—only in one of two ways: altering His own moral act, of which they are the image, or altering us who perceive His act so, by virtue of our being and relation to Him. God has not physical power in our sense; that is wholly phenomenal, belongs to matter; only that which has motion can produce or stop motion in that sense of physical force.

The view which assigns the doing of certain physical things to God, imparting original properties, moving planets, &c., is no more to be tolerated than any other mode of making God physical. The essence of idolatry is in it, which is a *limitation* of God; a denying Him to be Being. Doubtless idolators made images, and thought of God as bodily, for the very same reason as we think of Him as doing physical, material things; to realise Him better, that He might not be so far off. We have the strongest proof that the denying the materiality of God was felt by the nations of old as equivalent to atheism. They could not receive omni-presence any more than we can receive omni-action; and observe the identity of reason; if God be omni-present, He is present no where as bodily; so if God be omni-active, omni-agent, He does nothing as physical. We must give up this as our fathers, the idolators, gave up the other; in short we must give up the material as true Being, and see that all that truly is, or is actually done, is *spiritual*.

I make full admission of the moral excellence and rightness of these views during our ignorance; I reverence them and the men who have clung to them. Speaking of the moral history of man I would do them full justice, but now I speak of truth and reason, which is quite another matter. And also, doing justice to those views, I should claim justice for idolatry also. I doubt not men have loved and worshipped God under idolatry, who would not (and could not with the knowledge they had) have done it any other way; the denial of idols to them would have been atheism. As we find respecting our materially-acting God. Is it not strange that we should make such a distinction between material-being and material-acting? We have to learn that Being and acting are one. There is nothing at all that God does not do, in *every* sense of the word. I grant there is much we cannot so consider, but this is the point and good of the argument. All that appears to us, and must be considered as not strictly done by God (i.e. all that is in cause and effect), is the result of our not-seeing, our ignorance. It is not done by God because it is not the actual fact, but the fact in it is that which is done by God.

There is profoundness in that thought of "creation out

of nothing;" it is wrong, with an exquisite rightness. We must deny the "nothing," from which the creation is supposed, and hold the infiniteness of Being: but we can see the excellence of the idea—the *relation* is right. If the "nothing" cannot *be*, then of course that which is created out of it cannot *be*. The necessity which has driven men to this expression is beautiful; from the truth, and man's intellectual relation, how clearly it is necessitated! Material things "are," in the same sense as "nothing" can be. "Nothing" can be *to us*; it can be perceived as being. Here, then, is evidently the nature of the things so created.

This "mere motion" is what Life, Being, the divine and eternal, becomes to us, by us. By our negation Life is emptied, and made mere change in relation to space; we do not see it, nor what there is in it. So one understands the value of that strong feeling of the sacred mystery of life; this guarding it from any mere physical explanations. I do not go against that. I do not deny the sacred mystery; but I say that all this which we treat so lightly partakes of that sacredness. There is no more in life than in motion, only because in motion is all that is in life.

Is not all included in that doctrine of love, of creation as God's self-sacrifice; that is, that the creature is one with the Creator? Only so do we know God, because we *are* God. When God would show us Himself, He shows us—what but *ourself*, man? We recognise God in Christ, *because* we recognise humanity. God does in Christ what we would do, what alone would constitute us men. He cannot be God if He be not man; nor the Creator if He be not one with the creature. Are we not "children of

God" only as one with Christ, as bearing the same relation to the Father as Christ does? This gives a new conception of our sonship to God; and throws a light on Christ's sonship too. If we are sons as He is, then surely is He the Son even as we are; He one with God as we are. See how we can interpret these mysteries from simple and familiar things—that Christ is at once God and man; the Son of God and one with God; a distinct Person, and yet He in the Father, and the Father in Him, and all one God. All this is no mystery, but the fact of our own Being; we too are in the Father and He in us. We may say: "The works I do, I do not of myself, but the Father who dwelleth in me." Again, our bodies are "the temples of the Holy Ghost." Interpreted thus from within, starting from the *known*, these divine mysteries become plain and happy truths.

"God sacrifices Himself utterly," even to become the creature—it is so that we are. And does He not emphatically sacrifice Himself in all this misery and sin and evil, that as we say He *permits*, so calmly as we think; all for His own glory, that He may *get* thereby! Does not its agony, its hideousness, go to His heart infinitely more than to ours? How could this great "not" be, that is sin and sorrow, save by His self-sacrifice? That there is sin and woe is not a contradiction to God's love, it is the very fact of it; because He loves and sacrifices Himself, it must be. It is thou, oh God, who art the martyred one, the anguished, the oppressed. It is Thou that bearest all this sin and agony, that there may be living, loving man, to share thy joy! So that passage: "Heaven and earth are full of Thy Glory," stands out in full and simple majesty. The glory of God being the fact of His love, of His self-sacrifice, earth too, in all its sin and sadness, is full of

God's glory. It needs not that God's glory be educed from sin; in the fact of it His glory is made perfect, even as it is in the Cross of His Son. The mystery of sin is blotted out; all must be that great fact of self-sacrifice.

What a delusion this passion is, this desire for having or acquiring, as if happiness were in *that*. This desire is given to us in order that from it we may make our life, by controlling it; that we may have the happiness of giving. It is the source of our moral life, the force which becomes the vital force. It is just as the phenomenon (or impression) is in the mental life—a delusion; but because so, the source of our mental life. It is given us to be assimilated by sense of right and made to constitute our life.

Give up and you shall have; cast out self and all is yours, even God; we are heirs of God. The universe is the very best for you; give up that self-will and you will find it so. It is as good to you as to God; because the world *is* redeemed. So all men's good is in the destruction of the evil. The casting out of self—not-God—from us, is our life. Genius proves that men have their true life, their Being, in being one with Nature. In men of genius Nature, God speaks. Yet are they the typical "men." So in inspiration. Are not the inspired men the true *men?* Are not they the truly individual, the personal? We need not fear to be divine.

How interesting it will be, with these views of the physical as the image of the spiritual, to trace the meaning of the incarnation, and other events in Christian history. They cannot lose anything of their value; a phenomenon cannot be made less. Because the body is an image of a spiritual fact it is not therefore less a body; it is a body because it is such an image. That is the meaning of the word body. Consider, too, the symbols of the Old Testament; just so is the universe a symbol; and as the great fact of all the Scriptural symbols is that of sacrifice, so is the great fact of the symbol-universe, of Nature, sacrifice.

Spiritual self-sacrifice is not (like the phenomenal) a ceasing to be, a less; it is the very being; it is the act that constitutes the being and the life. In giving ourselves, emphatically we have ourselves, we are: so Christ's self-sacrifice for us; so God's self-sacrifice in creation. It is no loss. The self-sacrificer—the Creator, the Redeemer—*is* in the creature, in the redeemed; is and lives in, and by virtue of, His self-sacrifice. Even we say: "I live in that which I love;" that to which I have given my being, my soul.

Wonderful is this world; every one having as it were to seek his own good at another's loss; this "competition," each one taking for himself instead of another having. It is evidently the necessary phenomenon *to the self* of an altruistic world. It is only the converse of that constitution of the world, a necessary opposite view of it. Being constructed on the truly good plan—that of sacrifice, the self given up to others—necessarily from the self-view, according to the self-action, it is this opposite of the self-getting at the expense of others. This latter is involved phenomenally in the former; that best good implies it. It is we trying to reverse it, reading it backwards; but if it had not this backward construction the truth could not be so good. This is what comes when the self is in an altruistic world. And so the world is good, if we put our standard high enough, and include the sacrifice of the self; but from this of course comes the effort to reverse it on the part of the self. But observe, this does not succeed, that is the point; if it did it would be bad. The self *is* sacrificed in spite of all its efforts; the world *is* altruistic, even when most of the self seems to succeed; it still fails utterly, perhaps *then* most utterly. Is here the truth in the representation of future punishment in the sense of suffering, phenomenal evil, or evil to the self succeeding selfish enjoyment; so that the most successful self-attempt fails in the long run even from the self-point of view? But then there is a great perversion here. People do not see that it is the *self* cannot succeed at all, and so comes the notion of making the best of both worlds, which perhaps is exactly the greatest mistake the self ever made: though it has done nothing else from the first. This sacrifice of self is martyrdom, is the destiny of man, whether he will or not, and the glory is that he is to will it. There is beauty even in Calvinism here; it represents the destiny of the lost strictly as a *martyrdom;* they suffer for God's glory, for the good of the universe. It is this gives it its power, and is its charm. It is true: man can accept that—only each ought first to accept it for himself.

God does not let the smallest atom be placed in opposition to its affinities or tendencies but to effect a higher function; not one is allowed to suffer but for a vastly higher end. And so with man. Not one pang is inflicted upon him, not one felicity withheld, one tendency restrained, but for the purpose of nutrition and subservience to a function. We must liberate ourselves from the thraldom of thinking that we are the object of creation. We are part of it; elements forming part of the universal life; we must be content to bear our share of nutrition, and offer up ourselves willing instruments in the production of the function; yield gladly our bodies to suffering, our hearts to sorrow, our desires to disappointment; bear our part in the great life, ennobling and exalting it by willing subservience.

In life there is no particle that has not at last its tendencies and affinities fully gratified, carried completely out. But by the violence done to them, the restraint imposed upon them, it is made to form part of an organism; and by obeying its affinities, by carrying out its tendencies, it effects the function. So, surely, in respect to the nutrition effected by violence done to human affections, restraint on human tendencies, all shall come right at last.

Let us rejoice that God uses us and our troubles and resentment and intolerance of the evil, to bring about the good. Also He does the best for us, for each one; our trials are the only best for us. What a wonder it is: the best for the world, the best for each one also. And yet not a wonder, for only by being best for each one could it be best for the whole. We think individual welfare is sacrificed for the welfare of the whole: it is a mean mistaken thought. The good of the whole comprises and consists in the good of each part. We think God does like us, who are obliged to manage, and contrive, and choose, and sacrifice some objects for others: God attains the perfect good of the universe by, and with, and not without my perfect good.

We admire this nutrition and development by limit and excess and resistance in nature; we sympathise not with her toil and long-suffering and patient endurance. But when it comes to ourselves and we have to live also, bear the wrongness, resist the passion, then we complain sadly, and even doubt if God can be good; or we think He has much to do in the future to make it up. This doctrine of the future has utterly perverted our faith; at least it has made a great nutrition, and we will have a glorious function from it by and by. It is the poor sacrificed working people we should feel for; they are the martyrs sacrificed for earth's good. It is too much glory to share with them the work of developing the earth's life. For that is what this suffering and wrong is doing. I extend the idea of martyrdom, of suffering for the progress of the right and good, to all innocent suffering. When I say the noble army of martyrs, I think of more than martyrs at the stake and holy confessors. I think of the pale downcast operative, the degraded outcast, the tortured slave. All these are martyrs, sacrificed for the world.

Is there not something beautiful in the thought that sin pertains to the individual and exclusively so—not to man? Only so deep as the isolated individuality extends can sin extend. And thus it is that sin can be "washed away;" because it is superficial; because into the actual fact of man's being it does not enter. The sin has stained the self, not the *man*.

And an entirely new thought of the world comes with this. Amid all this sin is the sinless Man; and we who are sinful are to be brought into one with Him. "By Man came also the resurrection of the dead."

VIII.

ETHICS.

The practical problem is to unite work for man with the devotion connected with work for God—How to keep up the enthusiasm of religion—Not imagination but faith—Stoicism and actualism—The world is altruistic—Man's business is with the present—The practical as existing for the sake of the reflective—The evil of exalting individual over general regards—The self as the devil—Genius is a sufferer, not a doer—Our Christianity cannot give the enthusiasm which only can raise men above selfishness—Self-sacrifice is extended politeness—Poverty does not involve loss of refinement—A return to Nature—Good manners in the sphere of morals—The child state of humanity—The value of good manners as showing the pattern for life—The world goes best by being let alone—Mill's argument for liberty—What martyrdom is—The eternal necessity of martyrdom—Sociology—Social evil is nutrition—The life of society—Trade should be made a profession—The world was never worse than now—The evil of our modern life of refinement—Good is determined by its relations—Woman, like religion, needs to be liberated—Egoism is not the true basis of man's life—To be heroic we must advance—Future times will owe to this age the culture of the heart.

THIS is the problem:—to unite, with working for our fellow-men, the zeal, absorption and devotion which went with, and naturally go with, the idea of working directly for *God*. And how clearly, too, it is this which the actual view of life, and the world, solves. Is not the ethical doctrine exactly expressed thus : "Act for man, as men of old acted (superstitiously) for God"? Here is the proposition, implicitly, of martyrdom for the Christian *life;* of taking the lowest place. All the feelings, all the practice, which that "serving God" excited, are re-awakened and restored, and engaged in the service of man. See how that devotion and intensity are necessarily suppressed in the changing direction of men's thoughts and deeds; necessarily suppressed while they are in ignorance of what man's state is, and what life is for; and yet, from larger experience and knowledge, that change of direction necessarily comes. It must have been; the old God-serving, apart from serving man, could not have stood (it involved, too, a radical misconception of the relation of God and the creature). And so, too, how naturally and necessarily (how *vitally*, as by an organic life), that practical law arises from the "actual" doctrine. It must come; it is simply its flower and expression. It gives free scope again, in human channels, to that devotion and surrender, that entire using and spending and surrender of oneself, that man ever, and of necessity, aspires to pay to God. Wonderful (and yet necessary), that in directing this stream towards man, its strength and intensity should have been so weakened; and infinitely beautiful too, that in receiving this direction, the condition is fulfilled for its rising to its highest intensity, and developing its greatest strength. Stronger and more intense than ever it is to be; uniting thus *all* our nature.

All daily life and human intercourse is by this knowledge of what it is raised up to that level on which the old "worshipper" stood; and it rises, not by thought or effort, but naturally, up to the same level of heroism. Nay, above it; it is universalised by being perfected. In fact, it is that *part* of the old life taken and made the *whole* of life.

And so again one sees how asceticism—the devoted

Ethics. 247

isolated life—was an "anticipation" in another form; it was an attempt to make the whole life—what it *is!* Right was the thought and desire to have the whole world on the actual level; but this is to be a work of seeing, not of doing. So it is grand to see this in the ascetic life; a prophecy that *all* life is to be known as, and practically made, a religious devotion.

The practical problem in religion is to attain a means of keeping the enthusiasm and vigour of the religious feelings. Many doctrines, many means, excite it for a time, but how is it to be made permanent, and this not in a favoured few but in all? The ascetic life, the life of constant meditation, the exclusive devotion to religious works, has been tried for this; sometimes successfully, though often worse than failing; but, besides its other obvious objections, it is inapplicable to all. What then? Is not the exact thing we want this very result, which comes from seeing the present as the *phenomenon* of the eternal; viz. that of making our constant occupation consciously a religious occupation? This is to make the ordinary life of all the very same as the life of the devotee, and perfected too; it is a simple union of two opposites, the two imperfect halves, the two phenomena of the true religious life (each a + and a —), related as physical and spiritual. And see, this is an instance of that law of partial opposites and why there must have been both. The necessity is to have our thought continually exercised on that which is religious, then let all ordinary things be religious; and let religion be reinforced by all that comes before us, so that the flame of Divine affection is continually re-illumed. All that the devotee seeks by shutting out the world, all that, and all he fails of, are gained *from* the world. Thus one sees how the spiritual and the physical have been two opposing things; each opposing the other, and alternately, and in different individuals, triumphing; but neither gaining permanent victory.

By what *imagination*, then, shall we make common life romantic and heroic? By no imagination; but by *faith*. "This is the victory that overcometh the world"; the realization of the not-seen. So here surely is the interpretation of that seeking the romantic; its truth is universal; the error is in not recognizing the fact, and so seeking it in partial and unreal forms. Just as in respect to "good": men seek good so vainly and wrongly, not seeing the actual goodness that *is*. So here is a meaning in the expressions, "lift Thou up the light of Thy countenance," "in Thy light we shall see light." May not this be a thought well ever to associate with them—that of making us *see?* When we perceive how good it is to "see," how much that is, may we not find this thought worthy of the terms?

So far from coinciding, stoicism and the actualist ethics are at the extremes of oppositeness; they are to each other as plus and minus. Paul expresses it perfectly:
Not that I would be unclothed, but clothed upon, that mortality might be swallowed up of life." Stoicism is the not regarding these things, finding them little and of no account. Actualism is the regarding them *more*, finding them great and full of an infinite value and worth. The one is crushing, the other is expanding; emptying, and filling to overflowing; despairing, and being overwhelmed with wonder and delight. The "actual" doctrine fills us so with joy, makes us see such an infinite glory and worth in the pettiest, paltriest

Ethics.

things, that it does away with selfish feelings; makes us feel these earthly passions no more, or feel them but to despise and loathe; it raises us above ourselves. Stoicism, fixing its gaze upon itself, wraps itself in contemptuous disregard. It is the difference between ice and fire. Think of the apostles and martyrs.

Is not here a parallel:—as, in respect to science, the perfect seeing of its *religiousness*, the recognition of the spiritual in all (i.e. of the phenomenal character of the physical) gives the most perfect freedom in dealing with it, the most complete and unbiassed control of all phenomena and of all our own thoughts:—as it is in this so is it not in respect to practical life? Is not the perfect and entire spirituality that which gives freedom from the shackles of a false and partial one?

The world is altruistically good: in cases innumerable we may see it. Our loss or suffering is the good of others (the phenomenal good); and this besides the revealed, actual, altruistic good of the redemption of man, which is in all. What we want is, to introduce this as our conscious element of happiness, think of it, be happy in it. It is just as if a person were in a position to hear the best and most perfect music at will, a person too with the most exquisite ear, but not cultivated; and he did not care to go and hear it, ignored it; thought it was, or would be, or could be, nothing. Now we should say to him: " Here is a continual source of most exquisite gratification, and exactly adapted to you: attend to it—cultivate your ear—you will have pleasures that now you cannot conceive." Every now and then we taste an altruistic pleasure; but the pleasure in altruistic action is to be known, like all true pleasures, only in enjoying it; it cannot be described; we must avail ourselves of it. Here it is: we *are* sacrificed for others. The sweetest of all harmony is continually performed for us; nothing is wanted but that we should attend, and grow into the full appreciation — a joy-giving appreciation excelling all tasted or conceivable before. Here, in this natural capacity and disposition (like a sensitive but uncultivated ear) for altruistic pleasure, lies the truth that those see who insist that there is the germ of a Divine life in man, that the Divine image is not wholly effaced. May we not thus attain a more perfect sympathy with the beauty of this life?

Men who suffer reap small consolation from the good to others, even though to very many this is so familiar as to be even a proverb, and it is no blame to them. Then see here how wrong we are in our very constitution. This "no-blame," this naturalness of that feeling, is the very telling point; it is no blame to us that we feel so; then see how radical is the flaw. Those evils and wrongnesses for which we are not "to blame" are the deepest.

It is no objection to a thing that it will not work the wrong way. If the world is good for *giving* in, it is good for the best purpose. Every one knows that giving is better than getting; all this is perfectly simple. The mystery and difficulty is from there being something in us which perverts our feeling; and if not remembered and watched against, perverts our thinking and acting too. But then to be on our guard against it is perfectly simple and easy when once we know. There is something wanting in us. It is as if intellect were wanting, and that we did not *feel* that two and two must make four,

Ethics. 251

but only *learnt* it, and had to remember that it was so, although we had a feeling the other way. That is just what we have to do in religion; to learn and remember something true although we have a feeling the other way. But there is a deeper feeling that way also; the false feeling after all is superficial; and here is an interesting thought—that the "self"-ness in man truly is but superficial.

I hold that it is *knowledge* regulates action. I do not deny that the soul, the life, is the spring of good, or the entirely subordinate place of intellect; yet I affirm it necessary. It is a condition; it is as weeding and ploughing to a field; not the cause of the growth of corn, by any means, but it may be *the* thing that is wanted at a particular time. The other elements may be ready, and wanting *that*. Now this I take to be the present state of Christendom: there is power and life enough for the growth of a truly good, practical life; *the* condition now wanting is a truer knowledge—ploughing and weeding. Men do not know what the world is, nor what the Gospel, nor what is right. They are rather uninformed than unwilling. Was it not so in Luther's time? Was it not the thought that was altered then? It is a *permission* of the goodness rather than its producing, that is wanted; and error prevents. Let us have men as good as they are ready and willing to be; that would be enough.

It is true; noble things are done now; but what we want is to have these things not the exceptions; to have all our life made so, to have this the fundamental principle. It would work. And for this we want to *know*, to understand. There is the willingness: that is proved by these exceptions.

Men cannot get perpetual motion, because motion is perpetual, but it is *altruistic*. Is not this analogous to our trying to get, and not being able to get, happiness or good? Is it not because it *is*, but altruistic? It is our relation, our mode of feeling, deceives us; and we try to get that which is, because it is not *to us*. Observe, too, how much better even our purposes are answered truly by the altruistic perpetual motion than if we could get what we wanted. Is it not so also in respect to the other good? And as in respect to the former, so also to the latter, is it not our part to enlarge our knowledge and conform our action to the truth? As practically there is not perpetual motion, and yet practically there is, so is it in respect to good. See how the oppositeness in us is shown perfectly by Science also. Practically motion ceases, practically it does not; yet is the truth only one, and human life is itself only in knowing and acting so. We *are* related to nature (the phenomenal) in a false way. There cannot be that perpetual motion "to us"; it is against the nature of motion, altogether against itself; so there cannot be that "good" to us; it were against the nature of good.

Man is truly one; therefore the true objects refer to man as one; i.e. the world exists for universal objects; in using it we must regard universal objects, or we use it as it is not. Is not this the same as that the world exists for spiritual objects, is spiritual? Is not the universal truly spiritual, the physical individual? There is not oneness in the physical; this feeling of oneness is in truth of the not-physical. There is no physical "man"; "men" are physical; man, spiritual. Our feeling in respect to the individual objects is a wrong feeling; when we are right we shall be freed from it.

Ethics.

So the individual, and its end, are not good or valuable, and so are sacrificed. *Man's* ends only are regarded, and these are spiritual; we must learn to regard these only.

The only sufficient consolation in sorrow must be that it is salvation; that it makes man love, and sacrifice himself. Not a balancing of less happiness against greater, but of an illusion against a fact; of sorrow, not against enjoyment, but Love. Future enjoyment cannot repay present sorrow; we know it cannot. Convince a man that vice is against enjoyment in the long run, and you are as far as ever from making him virtuous. The present asserts its rightful supremacy in spite of all such barriers. Man's business, man's life, is in the present, because it is in the eternal, of which the present is to him the only representative. And that men have preferred, and do prefer, the future to the present—that martyrs, for the sake of the world to come, have endured and will endure again—this is not to the point. If it be supposed that there was a balance of present against future suffering or joy, it is a great mistake: *that* may well account for our seeing so little like martyrs now. It was for present love that they endured. And that future enjoyment cannot console for present suffering, we see—it is a clear fact of all our daily life. Do we not firmly believe in a future and everlasting happiness, unutterable and overwhelming? Yet does it console us for our sorrows? Do we not know, that in darkest ages, amidst least believing natures, there never was a time or place when sorrow was so ill-borne, and suffering so feared? It is right that it is so; it helps us, or should and will help us, to a truer consolation. Enjoyment is not the consolation for sorrow—least of all future enjoyment—but Love which waits no lapse of time, which flies no wretchedness, which alights with its soft pinions there first where anguish has worn the deepest scars.

This is what the heart requires to know: what *end* does our life answer? Can there be all this mass of hope, and aspiration, and toil, and strife, and misery, and nothing *done?* And if once we come to this question, is it not evident what is done? We must look fairly and see truly what is evil in the world; how the worst results come *necessarily*, come by the truest, best designed, sincerest efforts of men for right and good. See those old trials for witchcraft. Is it not the same with many of the evils now, which perhaps are quite as horrible as any past, only felt not so because we are familiar with them: are not they too unavoidable; coming out of our very efforts to do our best?

People think the reflective exists for the sake of the physical or "practical." "What is the good of moral reflections, unless they be carried out in act?" Now they may be mistaken here: it may be that the physical exists *for the reflective;* the end may be not the attaining of such material results, but the experience, the subjective state, which flows out of them. Now if so, it does not follow that the practical may be neglected, that the reflective should *not* be carried out into act. It is a wonderful instinct, a glorious illusion, that the use of the reflective is to be carried out in act. Only by that carrying out into act (which seems to us the end or object) can be attained the basis and materials for a higher, truer, larger reflection. This is the good of the practical; it carries on and develops that subjective for which it exists; this imperfect subjective only attains its perfection, its advance, by the being carried into action; each end produces a new means. Here is the right relation. Be practical; but be so in the right way; attend to these physical things, but understand for what reason and purpose; they are not an end, they are not of value in themselves, but are essential to the attainment of that which is. There is more in them than we have thought. For of course they lose no value that they have, by being seen to have an altogether new and higher value before unseen. Would he be thought to deny the reality of a pound, to be unpractical or visionary, who should say to an ignorant man: "Do not use that sovereign merely for your amusement, it has uses, 'meaning,' value much beyond any that are apparent in itself; it is not a mere piece of metal, it is a pound"? "As seeing that which is invisible"—how exactly that applies to a man who should speak so of a pound; he sees an invisible fact respecting it. Would he urge inattention to sovereigns, because he should say: "The value of it is not this mere pleasure it affords you; do not regard it so; see its relation to the great facts of life"? And observe how he would say: "Do not hold it and keep it; give it up; use it. This thing held by you is nothing—part with it, and see what you have instead." So is this physical: it is *our money* used by us as if it were mere metal, to please ourselves with till we are tired of it.

All that is evil to us is for remedy of something which is bad and needs remedying, and how therefore can that be truly evil? If we say that that which the evil exists to remedy must be truly evil, the same thing is true of that also—*that* is an evil to us, existing to remedy some other evil, therefore how can it be evil? We are here in an endless chain; we cannot get at that primary evil; it is not, it rises and rises, until it shows itself the love of God, the creation of man. Redemption resolves itself into creation at last. Here what we call real and imaginary sufferings become one. For imaginary sufferings are not less truly sufferings, not less evil to us. "But there is no reality in them;" true, and so of these physical sufferings; they are truly evil to us; but there is no reality in them; the sufferings we call imaginary are real to us until we know; the sufferings we call real are real to us only until we know. The world dreams: I would it might awake out of this weary dream to *know*. All is suffering which is painful to us; and this is all the evil—the relation to us which therefore is necessarily one. All has that element in it, which, when we recognise it, makes us call it imaginary; we only need to recognise the fact, to be aroused from our dream, to see that all we call real suffering is truly such as we term imaginary. The *reality to us* (while ignorant) of imaginary sufferings or evil, is most instructive. I suffer; but there is no evil, only an imaginary evil, because I do not know what is; a nightmare, in which one struggles and struggles to be free, and cannot get so. Why are our struggles vain? because we are directing our efforts to the *phenomena*. We cannot regain comfort so; there is no fact there to deal with; we only escape from the sufferings of a nightmare by waking up and directing our efforts according to the fact of the case. It is just so with reference to these evils of life; we cannot escape them, struggle as we may, because we direct our efforts to the phenomena. The only remedy is to wake up and act according to the fact of the case.

Is there not even something good in ignoring the distinction between virtue and vice? That idea of "virtue"

Ethics. 257

goes with the thought and feeling of self: "I am good." There should be no "I," no goodness; but just this: God shall act, not the self; here shall be man, man's true Being and action and life, not "I" at all. The only deliverance from self must be by feeling that we *have* all; that there is nothing to get, that God's love is perfect, and is wholly ours; that man *is* redeemed. This is how Christianity can make the world holy, free from self; because it reveals to men that they have all, that all is good; winning love by love.

People without strong "affections" and "sympathies" are not worse than other people: we want a virtue that shall appeal to and embrace both sorts. See how these strong lovings are compatible with the worst lives and qualities, and *vice versâ*. There are many men who scarcely have these, who yet rejoice in the utmost sacrifice for the purest most unselfish ends, who would lay down their lives, endure all agony, for the world's bettering. And these are often the "bad people;" they are sullen, restless, unsocial, even depraved. We want a truer calendar of virtue.

It is quite the established doctrine to exalt the individual personal attachments and sympathies over general (what are called "cosmopolitan") regards. Now it is just the question whether this is right. I say it is not. Doubtless the personal affection is incomparably better than mere selfishness. It is better than indifference also, which is what perhaps goes under the name of "cosmopolitanism." And it must be, I conceive, from having only these to compare with it, that the personal regard has come to be so lauded. But I say let us look calmly at this, and see if these personal affections and devotions

s

be not rather the forms and pretences of virtue than the fact, if the very essence of selfishness be not in them, if what we want be not a true self devotion; not personal, not for individuals; a devotion such as Christ's, to the world; a devotion having reference to the fact and not to the phenomenon, the eternal and not the temporal, the actual and not the physical. What can come of these acute personal devotions, but self-regard? A little wider indeed, but just as hostile to the universal good as the mere individual. The same principle is in them. Devotion to *my* wife, *my* child, what is it truly better than devotion to myself? It is formally, phenomenally, better, I admit—infinitely so, and a necessary step out of that intensest death. This is the use of the personal affections (people say it indeed); not to be final, or an end and perfect result themselves; but to be a means and help towards a true all-embracing Divine Love. Then let it be a means; let the end come; a means is good if it be used as a means; made an end, nothing is worse. As we see, nothing can be worse than that domestic love (so called) in England this day. Is this the universal imperfection which brings suppression, a necessary suppression, owing to the imperfection of the other, which was surely from its not including a seeing the invisible?

In those narratives of the casting out of devils, we see *self* as the devil and how it is cast out, and must be, if any life is to be in us. Also, the evil spirit goes back to the man from whom it is cast out, when the house remains empty. Is it not so, when by self-righteousness, self-effort, the self is cast out? This is no deliverance from the self; the house left empty will but be filled with self again, worse than before. God must cast it out, and live in us, and fill us; else is our last state worse than the first. Think of this passage: "When the evil spirit goeth out of the man;" as if it were quite simple and certain that there is one in man, and either he must be cast out, and another spirit enter into his place, or he will retain his hold. What can it mean, but the *self*? And that God must take its place? I have thought long that when we came to know better we should see that these accounts of demoniacs were quite right, and only wrong to us by our ignorance. The self cannot cast out the self; love cannot be from the self; it is a contradiction in terms. Love must come from without, be given, poured into us. It cannot but be, if we believe, and regard what God is doing. Of this we may be sure; if the world is in any sense wrong to us, it must be because we regard it wrongly; we regard it from the self; only so indeed can it possibly be evil.

I think we shall never get right until we do truly feel about the self as a personal enemy, trying to draw us into slavery and destroy us; and that all that is *man* in us is against it. So that we should ever recognise the voice of self as that of an enemy, as the temptation to death; all yielding to self as abnegation and denial of humanity. In every case we should feel: Now humanity shall be, man's life and Being shall be in me; no devil shall destroy it. "This self is a devil:" when we find that out, with what glad, yet awful amazement it strikes us—fearful indeed, and terrible, but yet replete with joy. What a sense of deliverance, of hope and relief, it brings with it. It is indeed glad tidings; it makes the world, and all our thoughts, hopes, desires, prospects, our very Being new; we see so differently; our whole conceptions of good and evil are altered; we are right to the universe; we are to it as God is.

How are we to be happy under vexations? Not by trying and resolving. We want something in our thoughts that shall take away the disposition to grief; we want to remember the redemption. But in order for this we must associate it with all things; it must be *the* thing we regard in all, or else we shall not think of it till too late (even as to behave well on special occasions, we must on all). The only art of associating the redemption of the world with our particular little troubles when we want it, is to associate it with *all* things; in order to which we must only believe it. Just so for glorifying God; we shall be sure to omit to think of doing it at the right time, unless we are thinking of it, doing it, in all things; for which end we must know that God's glory is in all things.

Our right relation to things, in respect to joy and sorrow, appears somewhat here in the fact that only *forms* change. Surely we ought to be equally glad in the *fact* under any form. But these changing forms involve such losses to us, such evils; we cannot be equally glad in the one fact. But now, what do we want for our perfected joy? That the forms should be petrified and not change? Surely not; but that their changing should not affect us as it does. We want to be made to have one joy in and regard to the fact; and then the promise of the eternal, where no change or sorrow comes, is at once fulfilled. And that is open to us now. Let our joy be in the spiritual, in redemption; that remains the same under all forms. Only our feeling of forms as realities is the secret of our grief.

Talent is doing, genius is suffering. This puts suffering in its right light. For see: it is genius does the work of the world; talent exists only for it, it is of no use save as laying a basis for the work of genius. So man's work is done, not by doing but by suffering. It is by what we bear the world is redeemed; our doing is very unimportant, in itself of no value. It is in our suffering God's work is fulfilled; for suffering the world exists; then we are *used*; God's work is done in us; in our suffering is the Being of the universe. Christ was a sufferer, not a doer. What He *did* was of little moment comparatively, and of little efficacy; its use was not for itself but to reveal the true meaning and value of His suffering.

Only enthusiasm can truly raise a man above enslavement to himself, and his wants and pleasures; can free him. And our Christianity, the individual saving from punishment and hope of felicity, will not, does not, cannot, give us enthusiasm lastingly; it may for a time, but it dies away. We want another salvation to set us truly free. This is in the absolute salvation; it is an unending, unfailing source of enthusiasm, worthier, larger, more inspiring, and ever new, ever growing, ever afresh revealed. Think what interest it must give to life, to all events great and small, pleasant and painful, near or remote, to see in them all God redeeming man. Everything imparts to us a new and burning zeal and joy. Enthusiasm *cannot* cool. The world is full of God's glory, and how can we be dull and unconcerned? The wonderful fact so grows upon our perception, we cannot but be overwhelmed with emotion. How could we have such dull meetings, with nothing to talk about, or only these paltry interests, or some things to lament and groan over? It could not be. We have no interest in life, and how should we? What an emphatic condemnation of our piety are our hymns of praise—all about how happy we *ought* to be.

Yet there is no reason, I think, why, even without being different or better, there should not be a much better practical life; a seeking of others' pleasure rather than of our own, which all experience proves to be the best and greatest happiness. To argue the contrary from man's present ways, is like arguing that children who are greedy can never become polite. Why should not man be polite in great things as well as little ones? If the sacrifice is greater so also is the reward. Self-sacrifice is but politeness in reference to great interests. (How often that goes with absence of politeness in little things and *vice versâ*). Phenomenal people, who cannot understand, and who blame sacrificing material interests for moral or social ends, are like people who, not being able to see anything beyond the mere sensual, should be astonished and confounded at a polite man, should charge him with neglect, and often not of himself only, but of his own family. The case simply being that the polite man has perceptions which the vulgar greedy man has not; he acts in reference to other objects; he has more life, more Being; he comes nearer to manhood. (The vulgar man is not necessarily the worse man of the two; he may be the better.) Between a polite and a vulgar man the case cannot be argued; the only thing is: Can you give the latter the new perceptions?

Would it not be better merely for men to know intellectually that the true object is not their enjoyment, their edification, but the redemption of man? Would it not make them wiser, truer, in their practical life? Are they not wiser for knowing that the bodily appetites are not for their mere pleasure, but for nutrition and preservation of the life? Do they not act more wisely than if they did not know it? Their appetites remain the same, and much abuse remains, but not such mere abuse as if they did not know, not such mere abuse as exists now in respect to other self-indulgence—grasping at wealth and means of enjoyment or power. Men treat these just as they would eating if they thought it was solely for enjoyment, and did not know that on wisely regulating it depended health; as if they merely ate and ate and ate, for the pleasure of it, regardless of digestion—and having a stomach-ache, ate again. Merely knowing the fact does improve practice somewhat.

One chief practical error is the idea that poverty (especially when voluntarily encountered) by truly refined people, would involve loss of refinement. This it would not do; nay surely it would elevate and perfect it; is indeed needed for its perfecting. The unrefined want wealth to refine them (or that which is now only to be obtained by wealth); the refined do not need to retain it; nay, perhaps rather need to get rid of it, in order not to sink. The mistake then is holding to wealth after it has done its work.

People do sacrifice themselves when they see it clearly right, and especially when they see it a religious duty (as in martyrdom for doctrines, &c.) Then is not what we want to extend the sphere of this perception? That we shall see it right to sacrifice ourselves where now we do not see it? And observe, how these views extend especially the *religious* element; they make duties that seem irreligious to be emphatically religious—make *all* so, in truth. And this also they accomplish: they bring that special religious feeling, which now attaches itself so exclusively to dogmatical things, into all the common affairs of life. Here we see again an instance of a law: a true thing misapplied, and therefore suppressed (in part). This very feeling of religious duty, misapplied to doctrinal things exclusively, is set aside by another class of men altogether. But this is for its perfect restoration, in application to all life.

And with this look at another thing:—is not our civilization *perfected* for a return to Nature? Is it not a lower thing, introduced by suppressing a superior, imperfect and failing? And it also by failure leading to restoration of the former, but now renewed? This links itself with the choice of poverty by those who have wealth, the going back to simplest life and common pleasures, but now truly and aright. This is the end of civilization.

Is not here a key to life: that these " real interests " of life are truly matters within the sphere of politeness of good manners? These are its true sphere; not what we call manners only. Made perfect so, and so universalized (for thus only can good manners be universalized; the mass will never deal one way in trifles, and another in important things), there would be no more inconsistency and insincerity. And if it is right to be polite about a trifle, can it be right to be unpolite, greedy, about an important thing? The more important the thing, the more necessary it must be to use politeness about it. This may seem absurd to us; but how does giving up a good place at a dinner seem to a boor? The question is simply of what we value most. May we not attain to the treating the whole of this life as a polite man treats a day or an hour?

There is something worth considering in the French Novels of the 18th century: the representation of a heroic nature, carrying the maxims of polished society into serious life; and the sway of women. Surely there is the nature of a real anticipation in this dream, something of a prophecy. Would it not at least be beautiful, and a vast progress intellectually, to be able to see real meaning, and roots going deep into human nature and society, in such facts as these? Is there not the most complete contrast between the way in which the facts of social life are treated, and the facts of external nature? See how the latter are used by Science: now it is such a hold, surely, we want to get of the former; such a clue to them, and habit of treating them.

The getting and keeping to ourselves is the *child state* of humanity; it is as the child is with reference to its little enjoyments. Men rise above that; politeness is the giving up of those; it is manhood in reference to trifles. Would not the true manhood, the true life of humanity, be the same thing carried out in reference to the greatest physical things; a perfect politeness in reference to *all* the interests of man; a giving up, and putting others before us, in reference to all? And even so, this would be done only with reference to phenomena, only with reference to things which are truly *trifles*. Is not this the fact; that the giving up and sacrificing is of phenomena only, that we do truly have and keep all the true, the good?

Is not this a reconcilement; a fulfilling through suppression of that feeling that we ought to attain and have? We do so in giving up phenomena. That which is phenomenally sacrificing is truly getting.

A polite man sees this in reference to trifles; that giving them up for others' sake is not truly sacrificing but gaining. He sees this through seeing *more* in life; he regards things in a different relation, and sees that his natural feeling about them is a wrong one. [He suppresses the child-feeling, yet has it interpreted and restored.] Observe, too, how well it works; how those very trifles and comforts are so most obtained, most enjoyed.

And then again, how beautiful it is to see why good manners exist, and what they have taught us; they are the type and pattern for our life. And especially they have proved this: that the plan is safe, and will work; the comfort of life is nowhere and by no means so secured and perfected, as where all act on the principle of giving up. Good manners have proved to us that the plan will answer; for this end they existed. *Lie* as they are, they have their root in a truth, and bear a truth as their fruit. So that which might seem the destruction of the well-being of life is in truth its very basis. One might say: "If we regard these things as trifles, will they not be neglected and ruined?" Not so; then, and then only, will they go right and well. But observe: to have a politeness extending to the *real* (physical) interests, demands quite a different motive from one affecting only manners. The difference is between a true and a false, a spiritual and a phenomenal.

We train up children as if it were true that "honesty is the best policy"; and then wonder because it is a failure. It is a case of palpable and most matter-of-fact misapprehension; the fact is not as our action implies. Of course few turn out truly honest, as the facts of business and daily life attest. We have not given children *the habit*, the only truly available habit for life, of doing duty against interest.

And surely in this too the socialist is right; in affirming that there is a generous faculty in man to draw upon.

Ethics.

How constantly it is the case; the youth is full of enthusiasm for the world, longing even for a martyrdom. Would not this continue, and grow into a vigorous practical reality, if the child were taught that life *is* this longed-for martyrdom? But as it is, taught that he must live a life of self-interest, what wonder that he plunges into all extremes?

To give up interest for duty is the alphabet of morals, and it should be learnt when a child; or, like the other alphabet, the chances are it will not be learnt at all.

And here is an illustration of that beauty which is in truth in all the rest of Nature. See the compensation, the opposites united. Duty against pleasure is to be taught to children. How? Why, by letting them *have* pleasures, even to repletion. So God gives the thing He means us to give up. He gives men enjoyments and pleasures; lets them have them even at the expense of right—but for what? Surely that they may learn to give them up. It is a " condition " of the giving up.

Men believe that all they bear is God's will, is necessary for His work to be accomplished. But that is not Christianity; philosophy gets so far; but it is not enough. It does not *save* to know only so vaguely; does not content or make happy; we do not know that that will is anything that we should be glad at, or could be; feeling the phenomenon as fact, and feeling it evil. Christ shows what it is. This is the very point of Christianity; revealing what God is, and His work. That makes us truly willing to bear annoyances—*saves* us—makes us happy and truly content in knowing God. There is a radical defect in every religion that will not do this.

The feeling that we ought to secure certain objects inevitably depraves all things. We only can be right by treating all things as the phenomenon of a good fact. The lesson which all the experience of the world teaches is to do right in spite of all things, to suffer any evil or mischief to come—but to do right. But men do not read it so; they fix their eye on the particulars; they learn to understand that it will not answer to seek *certain* results by violation of principle; but do not see the true teaching—that it will not do to seek *any* results so. When a new case comes they go the same old way again, they try to avoid the evil. But we learn at last to seek no results, but only do right.

What if the world be so arranged by God that it goes best by being *let alone*; not being continually interfered with by us, to make it as we like it [as we find this the tendency of politics, certainly, and medicine]? May this be the truth: that man, having his interest devoted mainly to the spiritual, and suffering the phenomenal to go with less devotion of thought and labour, would find it go better by that very letting alone? One great part of our mischief is, that we continually alter (or try to) all phenomena to please ourselves, and so spoil things; our whole interest and thought is *to them*, and it is the wrong attitude of man to them; they go wrong by that very activity; and the remedy for this evil is the devotion of our thoughts to the spiritual, the phenomenal therefore going better. May not this be in part the meaning of "Seek ye first the kingdom of God," &c.? Do not pay so much heed to make these things go as you like them, and they will go the better; for it spoils even the phenomenon to make it as man likes it to be.

Mill's argument respecting liberty is simply an argument for *not-doing*. (It is as in medicine; ever the real advance is *not to do* something. True, something else is substituted; but this is only better in so far as it is simpler. The true gain is the abstaining from doing.) But his position is very interesting. He says, do not control for any good to the individual, only for self-protection. Will not the next step be not to control others, even for self-protection? Mill assumes that injury to self is a reason for such control; but it is not. Shall we not come to see this? And on Mill's own principles, is not this feeling about self, at its basis, a liking merely, one of those things against the authority of which he so emphatically contends? In the intellectual and moral he contends against the authority of feelings, and seeks to substitute only belief grounded on reason.

How essential to the martyrs must have been faith, true trust in God, that it was not necessary for them to *do* any good. Is not the want of that in us a chief reason why we are so conscious we could hardly be martyrs, and why we cannot take up the martyrdom that is even now waiting us? It is not that we are not good enough, but that we have not faith enough. We take the responsibility of the world so much upon ourselves; see how this is displayed in that excellent characteristic of modern times—the missionary work.

The nature of martyrdom is, that goodness opposes goodness. The martyr is not necessarily good; but he *sees*. He has the sense of sight, the persecutor the sense of duty; so it is implacable war—the one cannot alter his sight, the other cannot give up his sense of duty. So it is the sense of duty to oppose new sight. Is not this universal? Observe, too, how this sense of duty of the persecutor is very likely to have more of what is called "goodness" in it than the "sight" of the martyr. Yet is it a sort of self-goodness; a feeling of what *I* must do; whereas the "sight" is altruistic.

Men say, we are not now called on to be martyrs. Never was there a greater mistake. Men never were called on to be anything else; nay, they never had, or shall have, the chance of being anything else. For God will save them, will be in them, and that *is* martyrdom. God has shown us what His glory is, what He will give us. Nay, this thought lurks even in the very idea of Hell—the martyrdom of the universe. Shall we not find that it is the sublime redeeming elements in the thought of Hell, and kindred thoughts, that has made it possible to man, and has kept it alive so long. Is not the world so wonderfully made, with such an essential and inherent grandeur and good, so obstinate a rightness, that there is and can be nothing, not even in man's imagination, which has not, amid its vileness, also its awfulness of grandeur or of beauty.

Does it not thrill our hearts to think of it? God's glory, the glory of martyrdom, the glory that shines feebly in the martyr's flame—*that* is what He will give to us. That is the promise; and if we think, "How shall that draw men?" this is the glory of the promise beyond: He will make us so that it shall be happiness to us. This it is to be infinite, to be eternal, to have *life*. And think of this as the history and consummation of the world, as the work God will do.

That the very pleasant and amiable and successful, the most "complete," should be those who find it hardest to see the ethics of self-sacrifice, is right enough. May it not be probable that those who do best, are best organized to the present system, may be even least fitted for the new? And especially were not this *good?* For now it is only the few who thus succeed; in the other way were it not the many? Might not the many be then as the few are now?

May we not say that our natural tendency indicates the thing that is to be done (or thought), but that there is necessary first a fulfilling of conditions; and that this is an opposite, a giving up of that desired? The instinct to pursue happiness is a right one, but we must fulfil the condition; it must be *altruistic;* and for this it must be first a giving up of the self-happiness. This is embodied in the saying: "Love, and then do what you like":—*love*, but altruistically; not, "love yourself." Again: in the case of children, the instinct is to make them obey; true; but fulfil the conditions, which involves the giving up this. The end is to be their obedience; the instinct guides to the end.

We first take a self-way, and have to acquire an altruistic; which involves, therefore, the giving up, the suppression, of the former; and, in ignorance of this law, of course the means seems like giving up the end.

So in metaphysics: giving up the intuitive certainty seems like giving up certainty; it is giving up phenomenal or apparent certainty for altruistic, or true.

What we want in life is some motive, some power, which shall grow stronger as temptation comes; not weaker, and disappear. And is there not such a power in these motives? Should not the true motives be such as are to be intensified and brought out into strength by the very existence and stress of their opposites? For is not our weakness just in this, that in temptation the motives which would help us, which we own and desire to obey, grow weak and are blotted out. But is not the world's redemption and our martyr's privilege then most potent and present when the temptation is strongest and most overwhelming? It is not a thing apart from that temptation (as even love to Christ is) but is *in* it, lives in and grows with it, feeds upon it, overtops and slays it and makes its life its own.

Vicarious suffering is the Law of God's world. He saves us so, but makes us also its instruments; from our own suffering he saves us, but gives us that of others to bear. "Bear ye one another's burdens, and so fulfil the law of Christ." And how beautiful it is: bearing our own sufferings is misery and loss and ruin; bearing those of others is life and joy and happiness. See here the interpretation of suffering; it is the self-form only that is bad; let it be altruistic and it becomes at once glorious and Divine.

The *real* is of no consequence; therefore the moral, the doing properly, being virtuous, is a small matter. Circumstances determine that. A man brought up in certain circumstances is sure to become thus depraved; this is not the fact, the actual. Thinking of these things, how clearly it is that this is a state of *redeeming*; that man is saved. Indeed God designs, the world being dead, that it shall not be good and moral, and well-conducted. Here one sees the instinct of referring religion to the future, representing it as having to do primarily with the world to come; a perverted instinct from our putting the eternal into the future. It is beautiful to see how man cannot be crushed down to a religion of morals. Observe; *man* cannot; some men are; but others will not be. So of all things; some take one view, but if it be deficient, others are sure to assert the contrary. It is a mechanical process; press on one part of water, and another part rises. There is a vibration in these opposite opinions; one denies by logic, but necessarily another affirms. The form may vary; the fact cannot change.

The accomplishment of human good is delayed and resisted in order that it may form part of an organization, and, when it comes, may produce a function, do something beyond itself. Nature would have been ashamed to make even an insect to do nothing more than it could design and conceive; shall she not use man also for higher purposes than his own? The social evils of the age are a nutrition, and exist for a function. Not only these evils to be put right, but a function inconceivable by us is to flow from them. We think the good of man in its highest sense is the great good, the end, but it is not; we cannot foresee the function.

The accumulation of facts about social life is a nutrition essential to a true theory; but now when this is just beginning, is not the theory of life discovered, that the nutrition of Sociology may be on a higher level? Before we knew what life was, we could have made no sound progress in an induction respecting Sociology. Just as it was impossible to have a science—even to observe the facts—of sidereal astronomy until the true theory of the solar system had been ascertained. Knowing that the social state is a *life*, and with the true theory of life in our hands, we can enter upon sociologic science with the certainty of a successful issue.

The solar system is among the stars as a man in society; and the social life of the heavens cannot be even attempted until the life of the solar system is understood; so neither can the social life of man be until the life (physiological and mental) of the individual man is understood. And may it not be that Sociology will present somewhat the same relation to physiology in its largest sense, as sidereal astronomy does to solar? We may discover therein not only facts accordant with those which have been traced in the smaller science (as the mutual revolutions of the double stars) but also some quite different and apparently irreconcileable, as the spiral forms of the galaxies. Facts not indeed really irreconcileable, but necessitating a larger view of physiology to reconcile them, than, from the study of physiology alone, we should have attained.

The impossibility of constructing a satisfactory Sociology has arisen hitherto from the want of a knowledge that it is a life, that evils are nutrition, that like other life it consists of nutrition and function, and developes. Isolated facts and connections have been traced, but no general adequate conception. It will reveal itself in due proportions as a life. Two errors arise from not knowing this:—(1) The disposition to acquiesce in evils as necessary. (2) The disposition to regard them as merely evil. Again, the tendency of philanthropic effort is merely to remove and prevent evils, not seeing that they constitute the nutrition for the function. Society, of course, lives, and its life developes without our understanding; but the science can be only on such understanding: and the science ever becomes necessary in process of time. The scientific life becomes linked with and essential to all other forms of life in course of development; and the true science is produced when required, for passion in least resistance truly is action in direction of most want. Everything comes in its time.

Evils can be prevented only by turning the force which produced them to good. Make the force produce a good;

Ethics. 275

not put down anything, but embrace. All evils are nutritions; even probably in relation to society, moral evils. But moral evil is not natural evil; it is not to be included as nutrition; it is want of the natural control, and is death. It is ever an exception and unnatural.

It is a radical error to attempt to represent the phenomena as not evil. Their evil as phenomena must be seen, or their good cannot be seen: it is only as real that they are good. Their goodness consists in their being evil, that is nutrition; and as phenomena they must be asserted to be evil in the most unqualified terms. Who does not see the evil cannot see the good. The evil is good, not *although* it is evil, but *because* it is evil.

The competitive commercial system is a theory (phenomenal), the co-operative an interpretation (true). But then the co-operative is the function which can result only from the nutrition of the competitive. This wrong is the necessary condition of that right. The putting right of the wrongnesses of the competitive will reveal the co-operative; the latter will interpret, show the truth of, the former. It cannot been seen before, obtained by effort or design. The facts must show it; it must develope. Previous attempts to achieve co-operation have failed, like *à priori* science. They have been like Berkeley's theory, perhaps even like Comte; attempts to attain function without nutrition, inorganic instead of organic. Such as Berkeley's perhaps have been the religious co-operative efforts; such as Comte's the socialistic. Surely social life has many stages yet to run. It is not yet in the stage of our present art, the ideal; but in that primary phenomenal stage which precedes even that.

"England exhausts every form of error before she arrives at the truth." That is, England *lives*, goes through the nutrition, attains the organization, and thus effects the function. Those immediate plans of arriving at the right result that other nations try, are like inorganic food; like Berkeley's science. This is England's strength; she goes through the natural course and lives, accepts and undergoes the evil, is willing to postpone the good; in a word, her Sociology is phenomenal. England is full of hope, the living portion of humanity. Her phenomenal naturalistic Sociology shall have its interpretation soon, shall produce its function; a function not less glorious than that of Science; a Sociology that shall truly interpret or "re-present" Nature.

It is England's living task, her function, to solve this problem of the position of the labouring class, the relation of employers and employed, the distribution of the products of industry. It is not hard; it only needs to be seen. We shall wonder at its simplicity when it is revealed. For this function she has now the nutrition, now a theory preparatory to an interpretation, and it is hopeful; it has been truly passion in least resistance, a real organization produced, a real functional power, of which many hopeful signs. And this is the glory; the more evil the nutrition, the more terrible the wrongness, the more excellent the function. The function shall justify the nutrition. This is our joy, our faith in God, and in His act, which is life.

The competitive system is theory, an arrangement of the elements of society by force, according to our ideas. We think (as ever of theories before the interpretation) that it must be so, that it is so in nature. True the phenomenon is so. But this competitive system has to reveal a true, based on holiness, or passion really in least resistance, and duly controlled. This revelation will come, when the former has grown intolerable; by letting the elements arrange themselves in the simplest common sense and natural manner. We must not use force to make it.

The idea that that only which is bad needs to be reformed, superseded, or done away with, is perhaps the greatest hindrance to our progress in every respect. We must learn to see that everything, the good and necessary just as much as any other, requires to be reformed and superseded by the opposite, when it has had its day; that in truth, everything that *is* is good and needs to be replaced by the opposite, because it is good, and has therefore prepared for the opposite; that progress is spiral and all things are unipolar and demand their opposite. To recognize this thoroughly and wisely would put a complete end, it appears to me, to all the intellectual errors that oppose progress. Nor should we say that as we have advanced blindly hitherto without knowing what or why, so we can go on. We have arrived at a higher stage, at which an intelligent progress is to take the place of a blind instinctive one. Do we not see this in animal life, in man, as compared with other parts of nature?

How shall the means of remedying social evils be found? By seeing the life of society. Does not society progress thus: the instinct is for self; this is suppressed more or less; thus nutrition. Then it is seen that this self-sacrifice is the very best means of attaining the good desired by self. This is a development.

Yes, love is the remedy, the only remedy, for the world's evils, not contrivance in any form. Love is God's remedy. To save the world He gives Himself, and so must we. Nor, in truth, does God's remedy fail; it seems indeed to do so; but this is seeming only. God saves the world by love, as we shall see when time no longer makes us blind, or rather when, being no longer blind, we no longer see time. God saves the world eternally; it is for us to save it temporally; but there is only one way, the way God has shown us—love. How long it seems to be before it comes. Yet it is not truly wanting. It is absolute, eternal, infinite; only we cannot see it because we have it not.

The fact of Nature is *non-sibi*, and so must be the fact of humanity. This is the only way to make trade honest. Trade must be carried on not primarily for personal advantage, but for the good of others, for the good of society; this is the only possible purification of it. And surely this is possible to our humanity. How beautiful a science is trade, thus considered; how natural to man to work thus as a true merchant, desiring his own advantage subordinately. Surely tradesmen should study sociology, and practise trade as a profession. Thus it would come to be above the medical or the legal professions, as being of a wider scope, and involving broader interests. This is the renovation of trade; and all trades or speculations which are not socially useful should be held dishonourable. This is only carrying out and affirming the universal instinct. It should be dishonourable, unnatural (as it emphatically is), to act for ourself.

The phases and processes of the social life are large, and take a long time; but they must be, essentially, the same as the physical. So that the physical may be seen, as it were, set out for our observation. We shall learn organic life from the social. It is as astronomy is on the other hand; from astronomy and sociology we shall learn organic life.

See how the world has starved or murdered its men of

Ethics. 279

genius. Why? In order that that evil, that *not*, in men, which made them do this, should be removed. It is for this they have suffered; and less than their sufferings could not suffice. Whether men of genius be starved or not is of no consequence; they would say so were they asked; but that man should be redeemed from starving them, that is something; for that, the loss of innumerable thousands were a small price.

All attempts to put a stop to crime (which is hypothesis, result of ignorance, or not-love) by punishment, to suppress it, without giving the love, are "anticipations." They will not do. Thank God, we cannot succeed; no crime and yet no love we cannot have: that were sad indeed. All this failure is nutrition; the interpretation, the function, will be curing crime by love.

It is the evil in the world that is the working, useful, part of it. The evil is the *good* of the world; it is the *idea* of it; not enjoyment, which is, in truth, but a delusion, a feeling good that which is not good, a little momentary relief. What can be stranger than the idea of men damned and in hell thinking that the idea of the place is enjoying themselves, and admiring!

Was the world ever worse than now? Were the evils we shudder at in former days worse than those of the present, or more affecting human life? Nay, is not now the worst of all, the devil's best, because his time is short? When the devil has his way, the world will not be miserable, but *bad*. See what there is now: commerce, the most selfish of all the forms of human activity and pursuit; and, with it, a self-religion. Christianity perverted to self and commerce—what should they give us, but what they do? Gin palaces at every corner, and miserable drunken women and worse men, and children reared and steeped in vice, and streets crowded with harlots: and, on the other hand, beautiful, refined, luxurious households—because these also must be, to make up the full blackness of the picture. If there were not these, the other were not so bad; these are the dark background on which the lurid colours of sin and wretchedness may be shown. It is not that there is any good in them; they intensify the badness of the other. A world *all that* were not bad; it is *this* with it makes it so. And yet, if the one is not truly good, so is the other not truly bad; the one is the remedy for the other. But how inverted is our view; we look on the comfortable and refined as the healthy part of man, and think if we could make the miserable and degraded all like *that*, then the world would be well. Not so; this comfort and content is the disease; the misery and vice the remedy.

It is interesting to think of the feeling there has been continually in man's mind—even not knowing the martyrdom—of the real evil of human pleasure; shown in asceticism and puritanism. This instinct has ever protested that there is a higher nature in man, and that his life is larger than he would have been content with.

Is it not true that what men call pleasure—the best and wisest self-happiness, the well-ordered home, the temperate luxury, the refinement—is it not true that all this is, to the true good, only as the pleasure of drunkenness is to the best and wisest phenomenal pleasure? We cannot *know* it is not so; all we know is that we like it, and the nature of our liking is the very point. See the instinct of asceticism, that has ever broken forth among men, and now is ready to do so again; the feeling is, that the right thing for man in this world is not pleasure, but its absence, or even pain. But the ascetic did not know *why*; he did not see the martyrdom; and could not, not seeing the redemption.

Good men now expect that God will solve the problems of the world for them; will bring it to some end, or sudden change, not of their doing. I doubt it; I expect Christian men will find the work of putting the world to rights *theirs*, and that they will do it; and that the prophecies of what God will do mean what He will make them do; implying a different sort of Christianity in them.

Seen by itself, a beautiful house is beautiful; seen in its relations with poverty, it is *not* beautiful. Beauty depends on harmony.

We want, in fact, an extension of the sphere of what are called *morals*. A thief does but regard a physically good thing as good apart from its relations. It is good to the sense; the question is, how is it to the soul? We do not sufficiently ask this question; the condition of our fellow men has a bearing upon it. If this seems unnatural and forced to us, that is no evidence that it is not true. Honesty is not to all men, or to all nations, a beautiful thing; to steal seems not beautiful only to those who have reached a certain stage of civilization; and so for us not to feel the bearing of the condition of others might only prove what our condition as men is.

Surely it is evident that men's feeling on this point of securing their own comfort although the masses are so ill off, rests only on not considering. Every one at once would admit there is a line here which it were utterly bad to pass; that there *is* a relation of others' state to our right of enjoyment. Now the only question is, where is that line? Observe: we could not suffer others to die from want—this we see at once. But how then can we suffer them to lead a life which is worse?

Surely we see, respecting the condition of women, that what they want is to have their hearts liberated. In our society they have no fair chance; they cannot show what they are; they are bound up like men of genius so often are; the entire bearing of society is hostile to them: this getting, negative, selfish state. Women are crushed and appear necessarily to disadvantage; they must appear lower than man while the physical is reckoned the highest. But their day is coming.

Not so much in social disabilities is woman ruined, but in this: that she is so petted; so *made*, against all her nature, to be a getter. We can hardly see the woman at all. She cannot shew herself—as religion cannot—beneath this established theory and practice of selfishness. Love is lost and bewildered; it thinks it must be wrong and mistaken; it puts on the garb of its enemy, and falls into a weak imitator, and of course, inferior. As a getter, religion cannot compete with the world; the mistake is that it ever tried. So woman cannot compete with man. She, too, must appear in her true colours, as the giver; so shall she be glorious and all-powerful.

Religion and woman are in like case; this is their suppression for a glorious function. The spirit of the world is profoundly opposite to both; necessarily so, and rightly, doubtless. They represent the *coerced* force. They have both, as it were, tried to throw themselves into the spirit of the world, and therefore have failed, and seemed so weak. Woman cannot compete with man in the physical, the selfish; even as religion cannot compete with the physical, in its appeals to the selfish feelings. Engaging in that contest both must suffer ignominious defeat. Woman has had a great nutrition-state of coercion, subordination, suppression, all these ages; and there is a glorious promise in it. And see how her unhappiness and discontent prove it.

In order to get rid of war we must make peace heroic. By not seeing the nature and significance of our common life, it is sordid; and with that there exist heroic forms of activity (war, &c.) which are mischievous. How evidently these are two halves, which need union; let the heroism be in the common life, and the mischievous forms of it will cease. The union here is in common life being noble; which it must be when it is seen what it is, and what it allows scope for, and demands.

How strangely men overlook the bearings of things on others. E.g., a man rejoices (legitimately, as he thinks) in having sold certain shares before they went down to a degree which would have ruined him had he held them—never thinking who was ruined by buying them. Is not this alone enough to explain the *failure* of life? What ignoring of the relations of things; how can they be right or successful so? There must be ceaseless deception and disappointment. Try this principle in reference to material things. Suppose a man laying hold of a rope or plank to save himself from drowning, and being satisfied with laying hold, with merely having it in his hands, regardless of its other connections; whether it were not broken off just above,—however much he might be satisfied with feeling it in his hands, it would not prevent him from sinking. This absurd disregard of the relations of things is like a drowning man catching at a straw; it not only does not save, but often prevents his being saved.

See how we pity a really refined and beautiful nature

in a child wearing the gauds and trinkets of the stage, and especially if proud of them. Now why may it not be that the real jewels and splendour men value are such as this, degrading, and most to those who do not feel them so? And then, are not those natures which, however darkly, revolt at them, and feel it better to be without them, truly like the higher nature revolting in such a child, though perhaps little able to feel what a truer, better life would be, never having known or seen it? She might throw them off, and *sulk*. Is not this asceticism?

"Every man of common understanding will endeavour to employ whatever stock he can command, in procuring either present enjoyment or future profit . . a man must be crazy who does not." (Adam Smith, *Wealth of Nations*.) And yet how well it may be argued, not only by the nature of life and of man, but from facts and from experience, that a human life founded upon the altruistic element, and throughout regulated by it, is that which is to be. For see how much *stronger* that altruistic power is; how it has been proved to be so. To take the other for a basis is to take the weaker. The self-element is not strong enough; it is seen not to be, in the presence of the other. *That* has made men, in all times and places, perform and bear what the other could not make them, and certainly never *has* approached.

And even in this alone, how beautiful it is to see how man truly is made; what his actual nature is, however it may seem other. The native metal shines out here and there, spite of the rust. And this suggests a simile for political economy; it is as if a chemist, taking up a piece of precious metal, or a precious stone, rusted, or encrusted with a foreign substance, should insist on that as *the thing*, and speak of the other as subordinate. And in truth, that is what would come first; would be what appeared.

And here is another proof that this strongest element in man is the rightful basis and orderer of the whole life —viz., that while it is capable of being made perfectly and consistently so, the other *cannot* be. It never does—save now and then, to the horror of the race—furnish the *entire* basis and rule even of an individual life. It is never proposed, save as something needing to be modified, added to, restrained. Harmony and unity, on that basis, are impossible. See, too, the weakness of the self-element in this; that it fails in doing even what its exponents claim for it, preserve and establish peace. Commercial relations do not prevent war.

Again, what seems an argument against the belief that the altruistic elements in man are the destined basis and ruler of his life—viz., that the power of the altruistic part has hitherto been exhibited only by *some* of the race —really becomes a proof on the other side, when the law of man's life is known. For it is a law that that which is to be universal shows itself first in imperfect forms, which are, and can only be, partial. This exhibition of altruistic life is the very proof that it is, made higher and more perfect, to be universal.

Might not political economy by recognizing the self-element in man to be by negation, even gain additional scope and definiteness, and fuller sway? Would not the relative place of the "self" and "human" elements in man then be capable of exact definition? So that we might say, of certain departments of life : "These should be regulated by the self-element."

This suggested itself after reading about the puritans. The good in their life was their earnestness, their devotion;

and what we want is to bring back that. But this cannot be, on their level of goodness; for the very reason that society has advanced; for surely our life is, easily (in externals, or in the kind of living aimed at), what theirs was heroically. And so, if the external aim continues the same, the only true good, the *heroism*, is left out.

Thus the advance of society affords scope for new advances. [Is not this, indeed, its best result?] We must not let the admiration we justly feel for those men, and such as they, limit us; make us fancy that to do the same things, apply the same motives as they did, will be good for us. And this, too, throws a light on the whole of history. Abraham lived heroically a life which would be a very poor life for us. Now we have to outgrow the puritans as we have outgrown Abraham. And it is so clear; the only good is the heroism—the mere external actions are nothing. There may be one same level of true goodness through the whole course of that advance. As the world advances, therefore, in external moralities, we must *go on;* the good must go on, so as to be kept at a constant heroism; this being the sole good. And this constant going on alone can do it; the law lies in human nature.

Future times, looking back on this as the morally dark age, will see that it is great, will see that they owe to it a debt as real as to any other, *the culture of the heart*. And they will feel, too, what was suffered and sacrificed for that work. It will appear as a sublime sacrifice. And this justifies and sanctifies it. Because sacrifice is the life; that makes this age, with all its evil, glorious. And the future will see, too, that the men of this age have not so much been morally bad, as crushed and hampered and unable to apply their moral instincts; even as in the scientifically dark age men were not really wanting or weak intellectually. And this agrees with what has been widely felt in regard to this age, that people are really quite good enough to live immensely better lives, that practice falls far short of willingness, that not only our habits, but our opinions, forbid us from worthy action.

The work of the present age is the preparation of the moral sense for its future place; just as the " dark ages " prepared intellect for its work in science, and as the Greeks developed the senses. The special work of each age has to be seen; and will not the whole constitute a chain like the zoological? And it suggests itself here that the two lines of growth and development go on separately in zoology though contemporaneously, as in reptiles and birds. Is it so in the mental life? For example, is there not organization, intension, in respect to the moral sense, and a corresponding growth, expansion, in science? Both are needed for the future. The growth of one, the organization of the other, progressing together, apparently most diverse, are yet subservient to, and to be swallowed up in, a third.

Think, in respect to this as the morally dark age, of the story of Lady Godiva. Whether true or merely legendary, it shows how different that age was. Could we *imagine* such a thing done by a lady now? Not on account of the greater delicacy of modern feeling (which, indeed, is not proved), but that any lady should for a moment think such a sacrifice might be made. There must have been a totally different thought of life then. And how profoundly, consenting to that which is as a moral degradation, her act was like Christ's. She did that which scarcely the most degraded woman would do; for always the highest good seems only possible in that which might also be utter evil.

And look at it another way. See how the "good" now do what, if seen differently, only the most utterly and profoundly selfish could do. They do it, really and truly though not with equal clearness of apprehension, as Godiva did what only a shameless woman otherwise could do. Is not the parallel clear?

These people do not act thus with their eyes open. They are *used* for that purpose; and with the good meaning do the thing that were else utterly bad. And our indignation is right, remember; as his would have been who should have witnessed Godiva, not understanding.

Is it not sublime to see this? The thing needed is done; sometimes consciously by us, sometimes not; but God takes care it is done.

And how glorious is the thought of this age subjecting us involuntarily to moral degradation; not sinfully, but by loss imposed upon us. It exactly parallels our life to Christ's.

A LIST OF
C. KEGAN PAUL AND CO.'S
PUBLICATIONS.

12.81.

1, *Paternoster Square, London.*

A LIST OF

C. KEGAN PAUL AND CO.'S PUBLICATIONS.

ADAMS (F. O.), F.R.G.S.
The History of Japan. From the Earliest Period to the Present Time. New Edition, revised. 2 volumes. With Maps and Plans. Demy 8vo. Cloth, price 21*s.* each.

ADAMS (W. D.).
Lyrics of Love, from Shakespeare to Tennyson. Selected and arranged by. Fcap. 8vo. Cloth extra, gilt edges, price 3*s.* 6*d.*

ADAMSON (H. T.), B.D.
The Truth as it is in Jesus. Crown 8vo. Cloth, price 8*s.* 6*d.*

The Three Sevens. Crown 8vo. Cloth, price 5*s.* 6*d.*

ADAM ST. VICTOR.
The Liturgical Poetry of Adam St. Victor. From the text of GAUTIER. With Translations into English in the Original Metres, and Short Explanatory Notes. By DIGBY S. WRANGHAM, M.A. 3 vols. Crown 8vo. Printed on hand-made paper. Cloth, price 21*s.*

A. K. H. B.
From a Quiet Place. A New Volume of Sermons. Crown 8vo. Cloth, price 5*s.*

ALBERT (Mary).
Holland and her Heroes to the year 1585. An Adaptation from Motley's "Rise of the Dutch Republic." Small crown 8vo. Cloth, price, 4*s.* 6*d.*

ALLEN (Rev. R.), M.A.
Abraham; his Life, Times, and Travels, 3,800 years ago. Second Edition. With Map. Post 8vo. Cloth, price 6*s.*

ALLEN (Grant), B.A.
Physiological Æsthetics. Large post 8vo. 9*s.*

ALLIES (T. W.), M.A.
Per Crucem ad Lucem. The Result of a Life. 2 vols. Demy 8vo. Cloth, price 25*s.*

A Life's Decision. Crown 8vo. Cloth, price 7*s.* 6*d.*

ANDERSON (Col. R. P.).
Victories and Defeats. An Attempt to explain the Causes which have led to them. An Officer's Manual. Demy 8vo. Cloth, price 14*s.*

ANDERSON (R. C.), C.E.
Tables for Facilitating the Calculation of every Detail in connection with Earthen and Masonry Dams. Royal 8vo. Cloth, price £2 2*s.*

ARCHER (Thomas).
About my Father's Business. Work amidst the Sick, the Sad, and the Sorrowing. Crown 8vo. Cloth, price 2*s.* 6*d.*

ARMSTRONG (Richard A.), B.A.
Latter-Day Teachers. Six Lectures. Small crown 8vo. Cloth, price 2*s.* 6*d.*

Army of the North German Confederation.
A Brief Description of its Organization, of the Different Branches of the Service and their *rôle* in War, of its Mode of Fighting, &c. &c. Translated from the Corrected Edition, by permission of the Author, by Colonel Edward Newdigate. Demy 8vo. Cloth, price 5*s.*

ARNOLD (Arthur).
Social Politics. Demy 8vo. Cloth, price 14*s.*

Free Land. Second Edition. Crown 8vo. Cloth, price 6*s.*

AUBERTIN (J. J.).
Camoens' Lusiads. Portuguese Text, with Translation by. With Map and Portraits. 2 vols. Demy 8vo. Price 30s.

Seventy Sonnets of Camoens'. Portuguese text and translation, with some original poems. Dedicated to Captain Richard F. Burton. Printed on hand-made paper. Cloth, bevelled boards, gilt top, price 7s. 6d.

Aunt Mary's Bran Pie.
By the author of "St. Olave's." Illustrated. Cloth, price 3s. 6d.

AVIA.
The Odyssey of Homer Done into English Verse. Fcap. 4to. Cloth, price 15s.

BADGER (George Perry), D.C.L.
An English-Arabic Lexicon. In which the equivalents for English words and idiomatic sentences are rendered into literary and colloquial Arabic. Royal 4to. Cloth, price £9 9s.

BAGEHOT (Walter).
Some Articles on the Depreciation of Silver, and Topics connected with it. Demy 8vo. Price 5s.

The English Constitution. A New Edition, Revised and Corrected, with an Introductory Dissertation on Recent Changes and Events. Crown 8vo. Cloth, price 7s. 6d.

Lombard Street. A Description of the Money Market. Seventh Edition. Crown 8vo. Cloth, price 7s. 6d.

BAGOT (Alan).
Accidents in Mines: their Causes and Prevention. Crown 8vo. Cloth, price 6s.

BAKER (Sir Sherston, Bart.).
Halleck's International Law; or Rules Regulating the Intercourse of States in Peace and War. A New Edition, Revised, with Notes and Cases. 2 vols. Demy 8vo. Cloth, price 38s.

BAKER (Sir Sherston, Bart.)—*continued.*
The Laws relating to Quarantine. Crown 8vo. Cloth, price 12s. 6d.

BALDWIN (Capt. J. H.), F.Z.S.
The Large and Small Game of Bengal and the North-Western Provinces of India. 4to. With numerous Illustrations. Second Edition. Cloth, price 21s.

BALLIN (Ada S. and F. L.).
A Hebrew Grammar. With Exercises selected from the Bible. Crown 8vo. Cloth, price 7s. 6d.

BANKS (Mrs. G. L.).
God's Providence House. New Edition. Crown 8vo. Cloth, price 3s. 6d.

Ripples and Breakers. Poems. Square 8vo. Cloth, price 5s.

BARCLAY (Edgar).
Mountain Life in Algeria. Crown 4to. With numerous Illustrations by Photogravure. Cloth, price 16s.

BARLEE (Ellen).
Locked Out: a Tale of the Strike. With a Frontispiece. Royal 16mo. Cloth, price 1s. 6d.

BARNES (William).
An Outline of English Speechcraft. Crown 8vo. Cloth, price 4s.

Poems of Rural Life, in the Dorset Dialect. New Edition, complete in 1 vol. Crown 8vo. Cloth, price 8s. 6d.

Outlines of Redecraft (Logic). With English Wording. Crown 8vo. Cloth, price 3s.

BARTLEY (George C. T.).
Domestic Economy: Thrift in Every Day Life. Taught in Dialogues suitable for Children of all ages. Small crown 8vo. Cloth, limp, 2s.

BAUR (Ferdinand), Dr. Ph.
A Philological Introduction to Greek and Latin for Students. Translated and adapted from the German of. By C. KEGAN PAUL, M.A. Oxon., and the Rev. E. D. STONE, M.A., late Fellow of King's College, Cambridge, and Assistant Master at Eton. Second and revised edition. Crown 8vo. Cloth, price 6s.

BAYNES (Rev. Canon R. H.).
At the Communion Time. A Manual for Holy Communion. With a preface by the Right Rev. the Lord Bishop of Derry and Raphoe. Cloth, price 1s. 6d.
*** Can also be had bound in French morocco, price 2s. 6d.; Persian morocco, price 3s.; Calf, or Turkey morocco, price 3s. 6d.
Home Songs for Quiet Hours. Fourth and Cheaper Edition. Fcap. 8vo. Cloth, price 2s. 6d.
This may also be had handsomely bound in morocco with gilt edges.

BELLINGHAM (Henry), Barrister-at-Law.
Social Aspects of Catholicism and Protestantism in their Civil Bearing upon Nations. Translated and adapted from the French of M. le Baron de Haulleville. With a Preface by His Eminence Cardinal Manning. Second and cheaper edition. Crown 8vo. Cloth, price 3s. 6d.

BENNETT (Dr. W. C.).
Narrative Poems & Ballads. Fcap. 8vo. Sewed in Coloured Wrapper, price 1s.
Songs for Sailors. Dedicated by Special Request to H.R.H. the Duke of Edinburgh. With Steel Portrait and Illustrations. Crown 8vo. Cloth, price 3s. 6d.
An Edition in Illustrated Paper Covers, price 1s.
Songs of a Song Writer. Crown 8vo. Cloth, price 6s.

BENT (J. Theodore).
Genoa. How the Republic Rose and Fell. With 18 Illustrations. Demy 8vo. Cloth, price 18s.

BETHAM - EDWARDS (Miss M.).
Kitty. With a Frontispiece. Crown 8vo. Cloth, price 6s.

BEVINGTON (L. S.).
Key Notes. Small crown 8vo. Cloth, price 5s.

Blue Roses; or, Helen Malinofska's Marriage. By the Author of "Véra." 2 vols. Fifth Edition. Cloth, gilt tops, 12s.
*** Also a Cheaper Edition in 1 vol. With Frontispiece. Crown 8vo. Cloth, price 6s.

BLUME (Major W.).
The Operations of the German Armies in France, from Sedan to the end of the war of 1870-71. With Map. From the Journals of the Head-quarters Staff. Translated by the late E. M. Jones, Maj. 20th Foot, Prof. of Mil. Hist., Sandhurst. Demy 8vo. Cloth, price 9s.

BOGUSLAWSKI (Capt. A. von).
Tactical Deductions from the War of 1870-71. Translated by Colonel Sir Lumley Graham, Bart., late 18th (Royal Irish) Regiment. Third Edition, Revised and Corrected. Demy 8vo. Cloth, price 7s.

BONWICK (J.), F.R.G.S.
Egyptian Belief and Modern Thought. Large post 8vo. Cloth, price 10s. 6d.
Pyramid Facts and Fancies. Crown 8vo. Cloth, price 5s.
The Tasmanian Lily. With Frontispiece. Crown 8vo. Cloth, price 5s.
Mike Howe, the Bushranger of Van Diemen's Land. With Frontispiece. New and cheaper edition. Crown 8vo. Cloth, price 3s. 6d.

BOWEN (H. C.), M.A.
English Grammar for Beginners. Fcap. 8vo. Cloth, price 1s.
Studies in English, for the use of Modern Schools. Small crown 8vo. Cloth, price 1s. 6d.
Simple English Poems. English Literature for Junior Classes. In Four Parts. Parts I. and II., price 6d. each, now ready.

BOWRING (Sir John).
Autobiographical Recollections. With Memoir by Lewin B. Bowring. Demy 8vo. Price 14s.

Brave Men's Footsteps.
By the Editor of "Men who have Risen." A Book of Example and Anecdote for Young People. With Four Illustrations by C. Doyle. Sixth Edition. Crown 8vo. Cloth, price 3s. 6d.

BRIALMONT (Col. A.).
Hasty Intrenchments. Translated by Lieut. Charles A. Empson, R.A. With Nine Plates. Demy 8vo. Cloth, price 6s.

BRIDGETT (Rev. J. E.).
History of the Holy Eucharist in Great Britain. 2 vols., demy 8vo. Cloth, price 18s.

BRODRICK (The Hon. G. C.).
Political Studies. Demy 8vo. Cloth, price 14s.

BROOKE (Rev. S. A.), M.A.
The Late Rev. F. W. Robertson, M.A., Life and Letters of. Edited by.
  I. Uniform with the Sermons. 2 vols. With Steel Portrait. Price 7s. 6d.
  II. Library Edition. 8vo. With Portrait. Price 12s.
  III. A Popular Edition, in 1 vol. 8vo. Price 6s.

Sermons. First Series. Twelfth and Cheaper Edition. Crown 8vo. Cloth, price 5s.

Sermons. Second Series. Fifth and Cheaper Edition. Crown 8vo. Cloth, price 5s.

Theology in the English Poets. — COWPER, COLERIDGE, WORDSWORTH, and BURNS. Fourth and Cheaper Edition. Post 8vo. Cloth, price 5s.

Christ in Modern Life. Fifteenth and Cheaper Edition. Crown 8vo. Cloth, price 5s.

The Spirit of the Christian Life. A New Volume of Sermons. Second Edition. Crown 8vo. Cloth, price 7s. 6d.

The Fight of Faith. Sermons preached on various occasions. Fifth Edition. Crown 8vo. Cloth, price 7s. 6d.

BROOKE (W. G.), M.A.
The Public Worship Regulation Act. With a Classified Statement of its Provisions, Notes, and Index. Third Edition, Revised and Corrected. Crown 8vo. Cloth, price 3s. 6d.

Six Privy Council Judgments—1850-1872. Annotated by. Third Edition. Crown 8vo. Cloth, price 9s.

BROUN (J. A.).
Magnetic Observations at Trevandrum and Augustia Malley. Vol. I. 4to. Cloth, price 63s.

The Report from above, separately sewed, price 21s.

BROWN (Rev. J. Baldwin).
The Higher Life. Its Reality, Experience, and Destiny. Fifth and Cheaper Edition. Crown 8vo. Cloth, price 5s.

Doctrine of Annihilation in the Light of the Gospel of Love. Five Discourses. Third Edition. Crown 8vo. Cloth, price 2s. 6d.

The Christian Policy of Life. A Book for Young Men of Business. New and Cheaper Edition. Crown 8vo. Cloth, price 3s. 6d.

BROWN (J. Croumbie), LL.D.
Reboisement in France; or, Records of the Replanting of the Alps, the Cevennes, and the Pyrenees with Trees, Herbage, and Bush. Demy 8vo. Cloth, price 12s. 6d.

The Hydrology of Southern Africa. Demy 8vo. Cloth, price 10s. 6d.

BROWNE (W. R.).
The Inspiration of the New Testament. With a Preface by the Rev. J. P. NORRIS, D.D. Fcap. 8vo. Cloth, price 2s. 6d.

BRYANT (W. C.)
Poems. Red-line Edition. With 24 Illustrations and Portrait of the Author. Crown 8vo. Cloth extra, price 7s. 6d.

A Cheaper Edition, with Frontispiece. Small crown 8vo. Cloth, price 3s. 6d.

BURCKHARDT (Jacob).
The Civilization of the Period of the Renaissance in Italy. Authorized translation, by S. G. C. Middlemore. 2 vols. Demy 8vo. Cloth, price 24s.

BURTON (Mrs. Richard).
The Inner Life of Syria, Palestine, and the Holy Land. With Maps, Photographs, and Coloured Plates. 2 vols. Second Edition. Demy 8vo. Cloth, price 24s.

*** Also a Cheaper Edition in one volume. Large post 8vo. Cloth, price 10s. 6d.

BURTON (Capt. Richard F.).
The Gold Mines of Midian and the Ruined Midianite Cities. A Fortnight's Tour in North Western Arabia. With numerous Illustrations. Second Edition. Demy 8vo. Cloth, price 18s.

The Land of Midian Revisited. With numerous illustrations on wood and by Chromolithography. 2 vols. Demy 8vo. Cloth, price 32s.

BUSBECQ (Ogier Ghiselin de).
His Life and Letters. By Charles Thornton Forster, M.D. and F. H. Blackburne Daniell, M.D. 2 vols. With Frontispieces. Demy 8vo. Cloth, price 24s.

BUTLER (Alfred J.).
Amaranth and Asphodel. Songs from the Greek Anthology.—I. Songs of the Love of Women. II. Songs of the Love of Nature. III. Songs of Death. IV. Songs of Hereafter. Small crown 8vo. Cloth, price 2s.

CALDERON.
Calderon's Dramas: The Wonder-Working Magician—Life is a Dream—The Purgatory of St. Patrick. Translated by Denis Florence MacCarthy. Post 8vo. Cloth, price 10s.

CANDLER (H.).
The Groundwork of Belief. Crown 8vo. Cloth, price 7s.

CARPENTER (W. B.), M.D.
The Principles of Mental Physiology. With their Applications to the Training and Discipline of the Mind, and the Study of its Morbid Conditions. Illustrated. Fifth Edition. 8vo. Cloth, price 12s.

CARPENTER (Dr. Philip P.).
His Life and Work. Edited by his brother, Russell Lant Carpenter. With portrait and vignette. Second Edition. Crown 8vo. Cloth, price 7s. 6d.

CAVALRY OFFICER.
Notes on Cavalry Tactics, Organization, &c. With Diagrams Demy 8vo. Cloth, price 12s.

CERVANTES.
The Ingenious Knight Don Quixote de la Mancha. A New Translation from the Originals of 1605 and 1608. By A. J. Duffield. With Notes. 3 vols. demy 8vo. Cloth, price 42s.

CHAPMAN (Hon. Mrs. E. W.).
A Constant Heart. A Story. 2 vols. Cloth, gilt tops, price 12s.

CHEYNE (Rev. T. K.).
The Prophecies of Isaiah. Translated, with Critical Notes and Dissertations by. Two vols., demy 8vo. Cloth, price 25s.

Children's Toys, and some Elementary Lessons in General Knowledge which they teach. Illustrated. Crown 8vo. Cloth, price 5s.

Clairaut's Elements of Geometry. Translated by Dr. Kaines, with 145 figures. Crown 8vo. Cloth, price 4s. 6d.

CLARKE (Mary Cowden).
Honey from the Weed. Crown 8vo. Cloth, price 7s.

CLAYDEN (P. W.).
England under Lord Beaconsfield. The Political History of the Last Six Years, from the end of 1873 to the beginning of 1880. Second Edition. With Index, and Continuation to March, 1880. Demy 8vo. Cloth, price 16s.

CLERY (C.), Lieut.-Col.
Minor Tactics. With 26 Maps and Plans. Fifth and Revised Edition. Demy 8vo. Cloth, price 16s.

CLODD (Edward), F.R.A.S.
The Childhood of the World: a Simple Account of Man in Early Times. Sixth Edition. Crown 8vo. Cloth, price 3s.
A Special Edition for Schools. Price 1s.

The Childhood of Religions. Including a Simple Account of the Birth and Growth of Myths and Legends. Third Thousand. Crown 8vo. Cloth, price 5s.
A Special Edition for Schools. Price 1s. 6d.

Jesus of Nazareth. With a brief Sketch of Jewish History to the Time of His Birth. Small crown 8vo. Cloth, price 6s.

COGHLAN (J. Cole), D.D.
The Modern Pharisee and other Sermons. Edited by the Very Rev. A. H. Dickinson, D.D., Dean of Chapel Royal, Dublin. New and cheaper edition. Crown 8vo. Cloth, price 7s. 6d.

COLERIDGE (Sara).
Pretty Lessons in Verse for Good Children, with some Lessons in Latin, in Easy Rhyme. A New Edition. Illustrated. Fcap. 8vo. Cloth, price 3s. 6d.

Phantasmion. A Fairy Tale. With an Introductory Preface by the Right Hon. Lord Coleridge, of Ottery St. Mary. A New Edition. Illustrated. Crown 8vo. Cloth, price 7s. 6d.

Memoir and Letters of Sara Coleridge. Edited by her Daughter. Cheap Edition. With one Portrait. Cloth, price 7s. 6d.

COLLINS (Mortimer).
The Secret of Long Life. Small crown 8vo. Cloth, price 3s. 6d.

Inn of Strange Meetings, and other Poems. Crown 8vo. Cloth, price 5s.

CONNELL (A. K.).
Discontent and Danger in India. Small crown 8vo. Cloth, price 3s. 6d.

COOKE (Prof. J. P.)
Scientific Culture. Crown 8vo. Cloth, price 1s.

COOPER (H. J.).
The Art of Furnishing on Rational and Æsthetic Principles. New and Cheaper Edition. Fcap. 8vo. Cloth, price 1s. 6d.

COPPÉE (François).
L'Exilée. Done into English Verse with the sanction of the Author by I. O. L. Crown 8vo. Vellum, price 5s.

CORFIELD (Prof.), M.D.
Health. Crown 8vo. Cloth, price 6s.

CORY (Col. Arthur).
The Eastern Menace. Crown 8vo. Cloth, price 7s. 6d.

CORY (William).
A Guide to Modern English History. Part I. MDCCCXV.—MDCCCXXX. Demy 8vo. Cloth, price 9s.

COURTNEY (W. L.).
The Metaphysics of John Stuart Mill. Crown 8vo. Cloth, price 5s. 6d.

COX (Rev. Sir G. W.), Bart.
A History of Greece from the Earliest Period to the end of the Persian War. New Edition. 2 vols. Demy 8vo. Cloth, price 36s.

A General History of Greece from the Earliest Period to the Death of Alexander the Great, with a sketch of the subsequent History to the present time. New Edition. Crown 8vo. Cloth, price 7s. 6d.

Tales of Ancient Greece. New Edition. Small crown 8vo Cloth, price 6s.

School History of Greece. With Maps. New Edition. Fcap. 8vo. Cloth, price 3s. 6d.

The Great Persian War from the Histories of Herodotus. New Edition. Fcap. 8vo. Cloth, price 3s. 6d.

A Manual of Mythology in the form of Question and Answer. New Edition. Fcap. 8vo. Cloth, price 3s.

COX (Rev. Sir G. W.), Bart.—*continued.*
An Introduction to the Science of Comparative Mythology and Folk-Lore. Large crown 8vo. Cloth, price 9s.

COX (Rev. Sir G. W.), Bart., M.A., and EUSTACE HINTON JONES.
Popular Romances of the Middle Ages. Second Edition in one volume. Crown 8vo. Cloth, price 6s.

COX (Rev. Samuel).
A Commentary on the Book of Job. With a Translation. Demy 8vo. Cloth, price 15s.

Salvator Mundi; or, Is Christ the Saviour of all Men? Sixth Edition. Crown 8vo. Cloth, price 5s.

The Genesis of Evil, and other Sermons, mainly Expository. Second Edition. Crown 8vo. Cloth, price 6s.

CRAUFURD (A. H.).
Seeking for Light: Sermons. Crown 8vo. Cloth, price 5s.

CRAVEN (Mrs.).
A Year's Meditations. Crown 8vo. Cloth, price 6s.

CRAWFURD (Oswald).
Portugal, Old and New. With Illustrations and Maps. New and Cheaper Edition. Crown 8vo. Cloth, price 6s.

CRESSWELL (Mrs. G.).
The King's Banner. Drama in Four Acts. Five Illustrations. 4to. Cloth, price 10s. 6d.

CROZIER (John Beattie), M.B.
The Religion of the Future. Crown 8vo. Cloth, price 6s.

Cyclopædia of Common Things. Edited by the Rev. Sir George W. Cox, Bart., M.A. With 500 Illustrations. Large post 8vo. Cloth, price 7s. 6d.

DALTON (John Neale), M.A., R.N.
Sermons to Naval Cadets. Preached on board H.M.S. "Britannia." Second Edition. Small crown 8vo. Cloth, price 3s. 6d.

D'ANVERS (N. R.).
Parted. A Tale of Clouds and Sunshine. With 4 Illustrations. Extra Fcap. 8vo. Cloth, price 3s. 6d.

Little Minnie's Troubles. An Every-day Chronicle. With Four Illustrations by W. H. Hughes. Fcap. Cloth, price 3s. 6d.

Pixie's Adventures; or, the Tale of a Terrier. With 21 Illustrations. 16mo. Cloth, price 4s. 6d.

Nanny's Adventures; or, the Tale of a Goat. With 12 Illustrations. 16mo. Cloth, price 4s. 6d.

DAVIDSON (Rev. Samuel), D.D., LL.D.
The New Testament, translated from the Latest Greek Text of Tischendorf. A New and thoroughly Revised Edition. Post 8vo. Cloth, price 10s. 6d.

Canon of the Bible: Its Formation, History, and Fluctuations. Third Edition, revised and enlarged. Small crown 8vo. Cloth, price 5s.

DAVIES (G. Christopher).
Rambles and Adventures of Our School Field Club. With Four Illustrations. New and Cheaper Edition. Crown 8vo. Cloth, price 3s. 6d.

DAVIES (Rev. J. L.), M.A.
Theology and Morality. Essays on Questions of Belief and Practice. Crown 8vo. Cloth, price 7s. 6d.

DAVIES (T. Hart.).
Catullus. Translated into English Verse. Crown 8vo. Cloth, price 6s.

DAWSON (George), M.A.
The Authentic Gospel. A New Volume of Sermons. Edited by George St. Clair. Crown 8vo. Cloth, price 6s.

Prayers, with a Discourse on Prayer. Edited by his Wife. Sixth Edition, Crown 8vo. Price 6s.

DAWSON (George), M.A.—*continued.*

Sermons on Disputed Points and Special Occasions. Edited by his Wife. Third Edition. Crown 8vo. Cloth, price 6s.

Sermons on Daily Life and Duty. Edited by his Wife. Third Edition. Crown 8vo. Cloth, price 6s.

DE L'HOSTE (Col. E. P.).

The Desert Pastor, Jean Jarousseau. Translated from the French of Eugène Pelletan. With a Frontispiece. New Edition. Fcap. 8vo. Cloth, price 3s. 6d.

DE REDCLIFFE (Viscount Stratford), P.C., K.G., G.C.B.

Why am I a Christian? Fifth Edition. Crown 8vo. Cloth, price 3s.

DESPREZ (Philip S.).

Daniel and John; or, the Apocalypse of the Old and that of the New Testament. Demy 8vo. Cloth, price 12s.

DE TOCQUEVILLE (A.).

Correspondence and Conversations of, with Nassau William Senior, from 1834 to 1859. Edited by M. C. M. Simpson. 2 vols. Post 8vo. Cloth, price 21s.

DE VERE (Aubrey).

Legends of the Saxon Saints. Small crown 8vo. Cloth, price 6s.

Alexander the Great. A Dramatic Poem. Small crown 8vo. Cloth, price 5s.

The Infant Bridal, and other Poems. A New and Enlarged Edition. Fcap. 8vo. Cloth, price 7s. 6d.

The Legends of St. Patrick, and other Poems. Small crown 8vo. Cloth, price 5s.

St. Thomas of Canterbury. A Dramatic Poem. Large fcap. 8vo. Cloth, price 5s.

Antar and Zara: an Eastern Romance. INISFAIL, and other Poems, Meditative and Lyrical. Fcap. 8vo. Price 6s.

DE VERE (Aubrey)—*continued.*

The Fall of Rora, the Search after Proserpine, and other Poems, Meditative and Lyrical. Fcap. 8vo. Price 6s.

DOBELL (Mrs. Horace).

Ethelstone, Eveline, and other Poems. Crown 8vo. Cloth, price 6s.

DOBSON (Austin).

Vignettes in Rhyme and Vers de Société. Third Edition. Fcap. 8vo. Cloth, price 5s.

Proverbs in Porcelain. By the Author of "Vignettes in Rhyme." Second Edition. Crown 8vo. 6s.

Dorothy. A Country Story in Elegiac Verse. With Preface. Demy 8vo. Cloth, price 5s.

DOWDEN (Edward), LL.D.

Shakspere: a Critical Study of his Mind and Art. Fifth Edition. Large post 8vo. Cloth, price 12s.

Studies in Literature, 1789-1877. Large post 8vo. Cloth, price 12s.

Poems. Second Edition. Fcap. 8vo. Cloth, price 5s.

DOWNTON (Rev. H.), M.A.

Hymns and Verses. Original and Translated. Small crown 8vo. Cloth, price 3s. 6d.

DREWRY (G. O.), M.D.

The Common-Sense Management of the Stomach. Fifth Edition. Fcap. 8vo. Cloth, price 2s. 6d.

DREWRY (G. O.), M.D., and BARTLETT (H. C.), Ph.D., F.C.S.

Cup and Platter: or, Notes on Food and its Effects. New and cheaper Edition. Small 8vo. Cloth, price 1s. 6d.

DRUMMOND (Miss).

Tripps Buildings. A Study from Life, with Frontispiece. Small crown 8vo. Cloth, price 3s. 6d.

A 2

DUFFIELD (A. J.).
Don Quixote. His Critics and Commentators. With a Brief Account of the Minor Works of Miguel de Cervantes Saavedra, and a statement of the end and aim of the greatest of them all. A Handy Book for General Readers. Crown 8vo. Cloth, price 3s. 6d.

DU MONCEL (Count).
The Telephone, the Microphone, and the Phonograph. With 74 Illustrations. Small crown 8vo. Cloth, price 5s.

DUTT (Toru).
A Sheaf Gleaned in French Fields. New Edition, with Portrait. Demy 8vo. Cloth, price 10s. 6d.

DU VERNOIS (Col. von Verdy).
Studies in leading Troops. An authorized and accurate Translation by Lieutenant H. J. T. Hildyard, 71st Foot. Parts I. and II. Demy 8vo. Cloth, price 7s.

EDEN (Frederick).
The Nile without a Dragoman. Second Edition. Crown 8vo. Cloth, price 7s. 6d.

EDGEWORTH (F. Y.).
Mathematical Psychics: an Essay on the Application of Mathematics to Social Science. Demy 8vo. Cloth, price 7s. 6d.

EDIS (Robert W.).
Decoration and Furniture of Town Houses. A series of Cantor Lectures delivered before the Society of Arts, 1880. Amplified and enlarged, with 29 full-page Illustrations and numerous sketches. Second Edition. Square 8vo. Cloth, price 12s. 6d.

EDMONDS (Herbert).
Well Spent Lives: a Series of Modern Biographies. New and Cheaper Edition. Crown 8vo. Price 3s. 6d.

Educational Code of the Prussian Nation, in its Present Form. In accordance with the Decisions of the Common Provincial Law, and with those of Recent Legislation. Crown 8vo. Cloth, price 2s. 6d.

THE EDUCATION LIBRARY (Edited by Philip Magnus).
An Introduction to the History of Educational Theories. By Oscar Browning, M.A. Cloth, price 3s. 6d.
John Amos Comenius: his Life and Educational Work. By Prof. S. S. Laurie, A.M. Cloth, price 3s. 6d.
Old Greek Education. By the Rev. Prof. Mahaffy, M.A. Cloth, price 3s. 6d.

EDWARDS (Rev. Basil).
Minor Chords; or, Songs for the Suffering: a Volume of Verse. Fcap. 8vo. Cloth, price 3s. 6d.; paper, price 2s. 6d.

ELLIOT (Lady Charlotte).
Medusa and other Poems. Crown 8vo. Cloth, price 6s.

ELLIOTT (Ebenezer), The Corn Law Rhymer.
Poems. Edited by his Son, the Rev. Edwin Elliott, of St. John's, Antigua. 2 vols. Crown 8vo. Cloth, price 18s.

ELSDALE (Henry).
Studies in Tennyson's Idylls. Crown 8vo. Cloth, price 5s.

ELYOT (Sir Thomas).
The Boke named the Gouernour. Edited from the First Edition of 1531 by Henry Herbert Stephen Croft, M.A., Barrister-at-Law. With Portraits of Sir Thomas and Lady Elyot, copied by permission of her Majesty from Holbein's Original Drawings at Windsor Castle. 2 vols. fcap. 4to. Cloth, price 50s.

Epic of Hades (The).
By the author of "Songs of Two Worlds." Twelfth Edition. Fcap. 8vo. Cloth, price 7s. 6d.
⁎ Also an Illustrated Edition with seventeen full-page designs in photo-mezzotint by George R. Chapman. 4to. Cloth, extra gilt leaves, price 25s., and a Large Paper Edition, with portrait, price 10s. 6d.

EVANS (Anne).
Poems and Music. With Memorial Preface by Ann Thackeray Ritchie. Large crown 8vo. Cloth, price 7s. 6d.

EVANS (Mark).
The Gospel of Home Life.
Crown 8vo. Cloth, price 4s. 6d.
The Story of our Father's Love, told to Children. Fourth and Cheaper Edition. With Four Illustrations. Fcap. 8vo. Cloth, price 1s. 6d.
A Book of Common Prayer and Worship for Household Use, compiled exclusively from the Holy Scriptures. New and Cheaper Edition. Fcap. 8vo. Cloth, price 1s.
The King's Story Book. In three parts. Fcap. 8vo. Cloth, price 1s. 6d. each.
*** Parts I. and II., with eight illustrations and two Picture Maps, now ready.

EX-CIVILIAN.
Life in the Mofussil; or, Civilian Life in Lower Bengal. 2 vols. Large post 8vo. Price 14s.

FARQUHARSON (M.).
I. **Elsie Dinsmore.** Crown 8vo. Cloth, price 3s. 6d.
II. **Elsie's Girlhood.** Crown 8vo. Cloth, price 3s. 6d.
III. **Elsie's Holidays at Roselands.** Crown 8vo. Cloth, price 3s. 6d.

FELKIN (H. M.).
Technical Education in a Saxon Town. Published for the City and Guilds of London Institute for the Advancement of Technical Education. Demy 8vo. Cloth, price 2s.

FIELD (Horace), B.A. Lond.
The Ultimate Triumph of Christianity. Small crown 8vo. Cloth, price 3s. 6d.

FINN (the late James), M.R.A.S.
Stirring Times; or, Records from Jerusalem Consular Chronicles of 1853 to 1856. Edited and Compiled by his Widow. With a Preface by the Viscountess STRANGFORD. 2 vols. Demy 8vo. Price 30s.

FLOREDICE (W. H.).
A Month among the Mere Irish. Small crown 8vo. Cloth, price 5s.

Folkestone Ritual Case (The). The Argument, Proceedings, Judgment, and Report, revised by the several Counsel engaged. Demy 8vo. Cloth, price 25s.

FORMBY (Rev. Henry).
Ancient Rome and its Connection with the Christian Religion: an Outline of the History of the City from its First Foundation down to the Erection of the Chair of St. Peter, A.D. 42-47. With numerous Illustrations of Ancient Monuments, Sculpture, and Coinage, and of the Antiquities of the Christian Catacombs. Royal 4to. Cloth extra, price 50s. Roxburgh, half-morocco, price 52s. 6d.

FOWLE (Rev. T. W.), M.A.
The Reconciliation of Religion and Science. Being Essays on Immortality, Inspiration, Miracles, and the Being of Christ. Demy 8vo. Cloth, price 10s. 6d.
The Divine Legation of Christ. Crown 8vo. Cloth, price 7s.

FRASER (Donald).
Exchange Tables of Sterling and Indian Rupee Currency, upon a new and extended system, embracing Values from One Farthing to One Hundred Thousand Pounds, and at Rates progressing, in Sixteenths of a Penny, from 1s. 9d. to 2s. 3d. per Rupee. Royal 8vo. Cloth, price 10s. 6d.

FRISWELL (J. Hain).
The Better Self. Essays for Home Life. Crown 8vo. Cloth, price 6s.
One of Two; or, **A Left-Handed Bride.** With a Frontispiece. Crown 8vo. Cloth, price 3s. 6d.

GARDINER (Samuel R.) and J. BASS MULLINGER, M.A.
Introduction to the Study of English History. Large crown 8vo. Cloth, price 9s.

GARDNER (J.), M.D.
Longevity: The Means of Prolonging Life after Middle Age. Fourth Edition, Revised and Enlarged. Small crown 8vo. Cloth, price 4s.

GARRETT (E.).
By Still Waters. A Story for Quiet Hours. With Seven Illustrations. Crown 8vo. Cloth, price 6s.

GEBLER (Karl Von).
Galileo Galilei and the Roman Curia, from Authentic Sources. Translated with the sanction of the Author, by Mrs. GEORGE STURGE. Demy 8vo. Cloth, price 12s.

GEDDES (James).
History of the Administration of John de Witt, Grand Pensionary of Holland. Vol. I. 1623—1654. Demy 8vo., with Portrait. Cloth, price 15s.

GENNA (E.).
Irresponsible Philanthropists. Being some Chapters on the Employment of Gentlewomen. Small crown 8vo. Cloth, price 2s. 6d.

GEORGE (Henry).
Progress and Poverty. An Inquiry into the Cause of Industrial Depressions and of Increase of Want with Increase of Wealth. The Remedy. Post 8vo. Cloth, price 7s. 6d.

GILBERT (Mrs.).
Autobiography and other Memorials. Edited by Josiah Gilbert. Third Edition. With Portrait and several Wood Engravings. Crown 8vo. Cloth, price 7s. 6d.

GLOVER (F.), M.A.
Exempla Latina. A First Construing Book with Short Notes, Lexicon, and an Introduction to the Analysis of Sentences. Fcap. 8vo. Cloth, price 2s.

GODWIN (William).
William Godwin: His Friends and Contemporaries. With Portraits and Facsimiles of the handwriting of Godwin and his Wife. By C. Kegan Paul. 2 vols. Demy 8vo. Cloth, price 28s.

The Genius of Christianity Unveiled. Being Essays never before published. Edited, with a Preface, by C. Kegan Paul. Crown 8vo. Cloth, price 7s. 6d.

GOETZE (Capt. A. von).
Operations of the German Engineers during the War of 1870-1871. Published by Authority, and in accordance with Official Documents. Translated from the German by Colonel G. Graham, V.C., C.B., R.E. With 6 large Maps. Demy 8vo. Cloth, price 21s.

GOLDSMID (Sir Francis Henry).
Memoir of. With Portrait. Crown 8vo. Cloth, price 5s.

GOODENOUGH (Commodore J. G.), R.N., C.B., C.M.G.
Memoir of, with Extracts from his Letters and Journals. Edited by his Widow. With Steel Engraved Portrait. Square 8vo. Cloth, 5s.
* Also a Library Edition with Maps, Woodcuts, and Steel Engraved Portrait. Square post 8vo. Cloth, price 14s.

GOSSE (Edmund W.).
Studies in the Literature of Northern Europe. With a Frontispiece designed and etched by Alma Tadema. Large post 8vo. Cloth, price 12s.

New Poems. Crown 8vo. Cloth, price 7s. 6d.

GOULD (Rev. S. Baring), M.A.
Germany, Present and Past. New and Cheaper Edition. Large crown 8vo. Cloth, price 7s. 6d.

The Vicar of Morwenstow: a Memoir of the Rev. R. S. Hawker. With Portrait. Third Edition, revised. Square post 8vo. Cloth, 10s. 6d.

GRAHAM (William), M.A.
The Creed of Science: Religious, Moral, and Social. Demy 8vo. Cloth, price 12s.

GRIFFITH (Thomas), A.M.
The Gospel of the Divine Life. A Study of the Fourth Evangelist. Demy 8vo. Cloth, price 14s.

GRIMLEY (Rev. H. N.), M.A.
Tremadoc Sermons, chiefly on the SPIRITUAL BODY, the UNSEEN WORLD, and the DIVINE HUMANITY. Second Edition. Crown 8vo. Cloth, price 6s.

GRÜNER (M. L.).
Studies of Blast Furnace Phenomena. Translated by L. D. B. Gordon, F.R.S.E., F.G.S. Demy 8vo. Cloth, price 7s. 6d.

GURNEY (Rev. Archer).
Words of Faith and Cheer. A Mission of Instruction and Suggestion. Crown 8vo. Cloth, price 6s.

Gwen: A Drama in Monologue. By the Author of the "Epic of Hades." Third Edition. Fcap. 8vo. Cloth, price 5s.

HAECKEL (Prof. Ernst).
The History of Creation. Translation revised by Professor E. Ray Lankester, M.A., F.R.S. With Coloured Plates and Genealogical Trees of the various groups of both plants and animals. 2 vols. Second Edition. Post 8vo. Cloth, price 32s.

The History of the Evolution of Man. With numerous Illustrations. 2 vols. Large post 8vo. Cloth, price 32s.

Freedom in Science and Teaching. From the German of Ernst Haeckel, with a Prefatory Note by T. H. Huxley, F.R.S. Crown 8vo. Cloth, price 5s.

HALF-CROWN SERIES.
Sister Dora: a Biography. By Margaret Lonsdale.
True Words for Brave Men. A Book for Soldiers and Sailors. By the late Charles Kingsley.
An Inland Voyage. By R. L. Stevenson.
Travels with a Donkey. By R. L. Stevenson.
A Nook in the Apennines. By Leader Scott.
Notes of Travel. Being Extracts from the Journals of Count Von Moltke.
Letters from Russia. By Count Von Moltke.
English Sonnets. Collected and Arranged by J. Dennis.
Lyrics of Love from Shakespeare to Tennyson. Selected and Arranged by W. D. Adams.
London Lyrics. By Frederick Locker.

HALF-CROWN SERIES—continued.
Home Songs for Quiet Hours. By the Rev. Canon R. H. Baynes.

Halleck's International Law; or, Rules Regulating the Intercourse of States in Peace and War. A New Edition, revised, with Notes and Cases. By Sir Sherston Baker, Bart. 2 vols. Demy 8vo. Cloth, price 38s.

HARDY (Thomas).
A Pair of Blue Eyes. New Edition. With Frontispiece. Crown 8vo. Cloth, price 6s.

The Return of the Native. New Edition. With Frontispiece. Crown 8vo. Cloth, price 6s.

HARRISON (Lieut.-Col. R.).
The Officer's Memorandum Book for Peace and War. Third Edition. Oblong 32mo. roan, with pencil. price 3s. 6d.

HARTINGTON (The Right Hon. the Marquis of), M.P.
Election Speeches in 1879 and 1880. With Address to the Electors of North-East Lancashire. Crown 8vo. Cloth, price 3s. 6d.

HAWEIS (Rev. H. R.), M.A.
Arrows in the Air. Crown 8vo. Fourth and Cheaper Edition. Cloth, price 5s.

Current Coin. Materialism—The Devil—Crime—Drunkenness—Pauperism—Emotion—Recreation—The Sabbath. Fourth and Cheaper Edition. Crown 8vo. Cloth, price 5s.

Speech in Season. Fifth and Cheaper Edition. Crown 8vo. Cloth, price 5s.

Thoughts for the Times. Twelfth and Cheaper Edition. Crown 8vo. Cloth, price 5s.

Unsectarian Family Prayers. New and Cheaper Edition. Fcap. 8vo. Cloth, price 1s. 6d.

HAWKER (Robert Stephen).
The Poetical Works of. Now first collected and arranged with a prefatory notice by J. G. Godwin. With Portrait. Crown 8vo. Cloth, price 12s.

HAWKINS (Edwards Comerford).
Spirit and Form. Sermons preached in the parish church of Leatherhead. Crown 8vo. Cloth, price 6s.

HAYES (A. H.).
New Colorado and the Santa Fé Trail. With map and 60 Illustrations. Crown 8vo. Cloth, price 9s.

HEIDENHAIN (Rudolf), M.D.
Animal Magnetism. Physiological Observations. Translated from the Fourth German Edition, by L. C. Wooldridge. With a Preface by G. R. Romanes, F.R.S. Crown 8vo. Cloth, price 2s. 6d.

HELLON (H. G.).
Daphnis. A Pastoral Poem. Small crown 8vo. Cloth.

HELLWALD (Baron F. von).
The Russians in Central Asia. A Critical Examination, down to the present time, of the Geography and History of Central Asia. Translated by Lieut.-Col. Theodore Wirgman, LL.B. Large post 8vo. With Map. Cloth, price 12s.

HELVIG (Major H.).
The Operations of the Bavarian Army Corps. Translated by Captain G. S. Schwabe. With Five large Maps. In 2 vols. Demy 8vo. Cloth, price 24s.

Tactical Examples: Vol. I. The Battalion, price 15s. Vol. II. The Regiment and Brigade, price 10s. 6d. Translated from the German by Col. Sir Lumley Graham. With numerous Diagrams. Demy 8vo. Cloth.

HERFORD (Brooke).
The Story of Religion in England. A Book for Young Folk. Crown 8vo. Cloth, price 5s.

HICKEY (E. H.).
A Sculptor and other Poems. Small crown 8vo. Cloth, price 5s.

HINTON (James).
Life and Letters of. Edited by Ellice Hopkins, with an Introduction by Sir W. W. Gull, Bart., and Portrait engraved on Steel by C. H. Jeens. Fourth Edition. Crown 8vo. Cloth, 8s. 6d.

Chapters on the Art of Thinking, and other Essays. With an Introduction by Shadworth Hodgson. Edited by C. H. Hinton. Crown 8vo. Cloth, price 8s. 6d.

The Place of the Physician. To which is added ESSAYS ON THE LAW OF HUMAN LIFE, AND ON THE RELATION BETWEEN ORGANIC AND INORGANIC WORLDS. Second Edition. Crown 8vo. Cloth, price 3s. 6d.

Physiology for Practical Use. By various Writers. With 50 Illustrations. Third and cheaper edition. Crown 8vo. Cloth, price 5s.

An Atlas of Diseases of the Membrana Tympani. With Descriptive Text. Post 8vo. Price £6 6s.

The Questions of Aural Surgery. With Illustrations. 2 vols. Post 8vo. Cloth, price 12s. 6d.

The Mystery of Pain. New Edition. Fcap. 8vo. Cloth limp, 1s.

HOCKLEY (W. B.).
Tales of the Zenana; or, A Nuwab's Leisure Hours. By the Author of "Pandurang Hari." With a Preface by Lord Stanley of Alderley. 2 vols. Crown 8vo. Cloth, price 21s.

Pandurang Hari; or, Memoirs of a Hindoo. A Tale of Mahratta Life sixty years ago. With a Preface by Sir H. Bartle E. Frere, G.C.S.I., &c. New and Cheaper Edition. Crown 8vo. Cloth, price 6s.

HOFFBAUER (Capt.).
The German Artillery in the Battles near Metz. Based on the official reports of the German Artillery. Translated by Capt. E. O. Hollist. With Map and Plans. Demy 8vo. Cloth, price 21s.

HOLMES (E. G. A.).
Poems. First and Second Series. Fcap. 8vo. Cloth, price 5s. each.

HOOPER (Mary).
Little Dinners: How to Serve them with Elegance and Economy. Thirteenth Edition. Crown 8vo. Cloth, price 5s.
Cookery for Invalids, Persons of Delicate Digestion, and Children. Crown 8vo. Cloth, price 3s. 6d.
Every-Day Meals. Being Economical and Wholesome Recipes for Breakfast, Luncheon, and Supper. Second Edition. Crown 8vo. Cloth, price 5s.

HOOPER (Mrs. G.).
The House of Raby. With a Frontispiece. Crown 8vo. Cloth, price 3s. 6d.

HORNER (The Misses).
Walks in Florence. A New and thoroughly Revised Edition. 2 vols. Crown 8vo. Cloth limp. With Illustrations.
Vol. I.—Churches, Streets, and Palaces. 10s. 6d. Vol. II.—Public Galleries and Museums. 5s.

Household Readings on Prophecy. By a Layman. Small crown 8vo. Cloth, price 3s. 6d.

HUGHES (Henry).
The Redemption of the World. Crown 8vo. Cloth, price 3s. 6d.

HULL (Edmund C. P.).
The European in India. With a MEDICAL GUIDE FOR ANGLO-INDIANS. By R. R. S. Mair, M.D., F.R.C.S.E. Third Edition, Revised and Corrected. Post 8vo. Cloth, price 6s.

HUTCHISON (Lieut.-Col. F. J.), and Capt. G. H. MACGREGOR.
Military Sketching and Reconnaissance. With Fifteen Plates. Second edition. Small 8vo. Cloth, price 6s.
The first Volume of Military Handbooks for Regimental Officers. Edited by Lieut.-Col. C. B. BRACKENBURY, R.A., A.A.G.

HUTTON (Arthur), M.A.
The Anglican Ministry. Its Nature and Value in relation to the Catholic Priesthood. With a Preface by his Eminence Cardinal Newman. Demy 8vo. Cloth, price 14s.

INCHBOLD (J. W.).
Annus Amoris. Sonnets. Fcap. 8vo. Cloth, price 4s. 6d.

INGELOW (Jean).
Off the Skelligs. A Novel. With Frontispiece. Second Edition. Crown 8vo. Cloth, price 6s.
The Little Wonder-horn. A Second Series of "Stories Told to a Child." With Fifteen Illustrations. Small 8vo. Cloth, price 2s. 6d.

International Scientific Series (The). Each book complete in one Volume. Crown 8vo. Cloth, price 5s. each, excepting those marked otherwise.

I. Forms of Water: A Familiar Exposition of the Origin and Phenomena of Glaciers. By J. Tyndall, LL.D., F.R.S. With 25 Illustrations. Eighth Edition.

II. Physics and Politics; or, Thoughts on the Application of the Principles of "Natural Selection" and "Inheritance" to Political Society. By Walter Bagehot. Fifth Edition. Crown 8vo. Cloth, price 4s.

III. Foods. By Edward Smith, M.D., &c. With numerous Illustrations. Seventh Edition.

IV. Mind and Body: The Theories of their Relation. By Alexander Bain, LL.D. With Four Illustrations. Tenth Edition. Crown 8vo. Cloth, price 4s.

V. The Study of Sociology. By Herbert Spencer. Tenth Edition.

VI. On the Conservation of Energy. By Balfour Stewart, LL.D., &c. With 14 Illustrations. Fifth Edition.

VII. Animal Locomotion; or, Walking, Swimming, and Flying. By J. B. Pettigrew, M.D., &c. With 130 Illustrations. Second Edition.

VIII. Responsibility in Mental Disease. By Henry Maudsley, M.D. Third Edition.

IX. The New Chemistry. By Professor J. P. Cooke. With 31 Illustrations. Fifth Edition.

X. The Science of Law. By Prof. Sheldon Amos. Fourth Edition.

International Scientific Series (The)—*continued.*

XI. **Animal Mechanism.** A Treatise on Terrestrial and Aerial Locomotion. By Prof. E. J. Marey. With 117 Illustrations. Second Edition.

XII. **The Doctrine of Descent and Darwinism.** By Prof. Osca Schmidt. With 26 Illustrations. Fourth Edition.

XIII. **The History of the Conflict between Religion and Science.** By J. W. Draper, M.D., LL.D. Fifteenth Edition.

XIV. **Fungi; their Nature, Influences, Uses, &c.** By M. C. Cooke, LL.D. Edited by the Rev. M. J. Berkeley, F.L.S. With numerous Illustrations. Second Edition.

XV. **The Chemical Effects of Light and Photography.** By Dr. Hermann Vogel. With 100 Illustrations. Third and Revised Edition.

XVI. **The Life and Growth of Language.** By Prof. William Dwight Whitney. Third Edition.

XVII. **Money and the Mechanism of Exchange.** By W. Stanley Jevons, F.R.S. Fourth Edition.

XVIII. **The Nature of Light:** With a General Account of Physical Optics. By Dr. Eugene Lommel. With 188 Illustrations and a table of Spectra in Chromo-lithography. Third Edition.

XIX. **Animal Parasites and Messmates.** By M. Van Beneden. With 83 Illustrations. Second Edition.

XX. **Fermentation.** By Prof. Schützenberger. With 28 Illustrations. Third Edition.

XXI. **The Five Senses of Man.** By Prof. Bernstein. With 91 Illustrations. Second Edition.

XXII. **The Theory of Sound in its Relation to Music.** By Prof. Pietro Blaserna. With numerous Illustrations. Second Edition.

XXIII. **Studies in Spectrum Analysis.** By J. Norman Lockyer. F.R.S. With six photographic Illustrations of Spectra, and numerous engravings on wood. Crown 8vo. Second Edition. 6s. 6d.

International Scientific Series (The)—*continued.*

XXIV. **A History of the Growth of the Steam Engine.** By Prof. R. H. Thurston. With numerous Illustrations. Second Edition. 6s. 6d.

XXV. **Education as a Science.** By Alexander Bain, LL.D. Third Edition.

XXVI. **The Human Species.** By Prof. A. de Quatrefages. Third Edition.

XXVII. **Modern Chromatics.** With Applications to Art and Industry, by Ogden N. Rood. With 130 original Illustrations. Second Edition.

XXVIII. **The Crayfish: an Introduction to the Study of Zoology.** By Prof. T. H. Huxley. With eighty-two Illustrations. Third edition.

XXIX. **The Brain as an Organ of Mind.** By H. Charlton Bastian, M.D. With numerous Illustrations. Second Edition.

XXX. **The Atomic Theory.** By Prof. Ad. Wurtz. Translated by E. Clemin-Shaw. Second Edition.

XXXI. **The Natural Conditions of Existence as they affect Animal Life.** By Karl Semper. Second Edition.

XXXII. **General Physiology of Muscles and Nerves.** By Prof. J. Rosenthal. With Illustrations. Second Edition.

XXXIII. **Sight: an Exposition of the Principles of Monocular and Binocular Vision.** By Joseph Le Conte, LL.D. With 132 illustrations.

XXXIV. **Illusions: A Psychological Study.** By James Sully.

XXXV. **Volcanoes: What they are and What they Teach.** By Prof. J. W. Judd, F.R.S. With 92 Illustrations on Wood.

XXXVI. **Suicide. An Essay in Comparative Mythology.** By Prof. E. Morselli, with Diagrams.

XXXVII. **The Brain and its Functions.** By J. Luys. With numerous illustrations.

JENKINS (E.) and RAYMOND (J.).
The Architect's Legal Handbook. Third Edition Revised. Crown 8vo. Cloth, price 6s.

JENKINS (Rev. R. C.), M.A.
The Privilege of Peter and the Claims of the Roman Church confronted with the Scriptures, the Councils, and the Testimony of the Popes themselves. Fcap. 8vo. Cloth, price 3s. 6d.

JENNINGS (Mrs. Vaughan).
Rahel: Her Life and Letters. With a Portrait from the Painting by Daffinger. Square post 8vo. Cloth, price 7s. 6d.

JOEL (L.).
A Consul's Manual and Shipowner's and Shipmaster's Practical Guide in their Transactions Abroad. With Definitions of Nautical, Mercantile, and Legal Terms; a Glossary of Mercantile Terms in English, French, German, Italian, and Spanish. Tables of the Money, Weights, and Measures of the Principal Commercial Nations and their Equivalents in British Standards; and Forms of Consular and Notarial Acts. Demy 8vo. Cloth, price 12s.

JOHNSON (Virginia W.).
The Catskill Fairies. Illustrated by Alfred Fredericks. Cloth, price 5s.

JOHNSTONE (C. F.), M.A.
Historical Abstracts. Being Outlines of the History of some of the less-known States of Europe. Crown 8vo. Cloth, price 7s. 6d.

JONES (Lucy).
Puddings and Sweets. Being Three Hundred and Sixty-Five Receipts approved by Experience. Crown 8vo., price 2s. 6d.

JOYCE (P. W.), LL.D., &c.
Old Celtic Romances. Translated from the Gaelic by. Crown 8vo. Cloth, price 7s. 6d.

KAUFMANN (Rev. M.), B.A.
Utopias; or, Schemes of Social Improvement, from Sir Thomas More to Karl Marx. Crown 8vo. Cloth, price 5s.

Socialism: Its Nature, its Dangers, and its Remedies considered. Crown 8vo. Cloth, price 7s. 6d.

KAY (Joseph), M.A., Q.C.
Free Trade in Land. Edited by his Widow. With Preface by the Right Hon. John Bright, M. P. Sixth Edition. Crown 8vo. Cloth, price 5s.

KEMPIS (Thomas à).
Of the Imitation of Christ. Parchment Library Edition, price 6s.; vellum, price 7s. 6d.
⁎ A Cabinet Edition is also published at 1s. 6d. and a Miniature Edition at 1s. These may also be had in various extra bindings.

KENT (Carolo).
Corona Catholica ad Petri successoris Pedes Oblata. De Summi Pontificis Leonis XIII. Assumptione Epiggramma. In Quinquaginta Linguis. Fcap. 4to. Cloth, price 15s.

KER (David).
The Boy Slave in Bokhara. A Tale of Central Asia. With Illustrations. Crown 8vo. Cloth, price 3s. 6d.
The Wild Horseman of the Pampas. Illustrated. Crown 8vo. Cloth, price 3s. 6d.

KERNER (Dr. A.), Professor of Botany in the University of Innsbruck.
Flowers and their Unbidden Guests. Translation edited by W. OGLE, M.A., M.D., and a prefatory letter by C. Darwin, F.R.S. With Illustrations. Sq. 8vo. Cloth, price 9s.

KIDD (Joseph), M.D.
The Laws of Therapeutics, or, the Science and Art of Medicine. Second Edition. Crown 8vo. Cloth, price 6s.

KINAHAN (G. Henry), M.R.I.A., &c., of her Majesty's Geological Survey.
Manual of the Geology of Ireland. With 8 Plates, 26 Woodcuts, and a Map of Ireland, geologically coloured. Square 8vo. Cloth, price 15s.

KING (Mrs. Hamilton).
The Disciples. Fourth Edition, with Portrait and Notes. Crown 8vo. Cloth, price 7s. 6d.
Aspromonte, and other Poems. Second Edition. Fcap. 8vo. Cloth, price 4s. 6d.

KINGSFORD (Anna), M.D.
The Perfect Way in Diet.
A Treatise advocating a Return to the Natural and Ancient Food of Race. Small crown 8vo. Cloth, price 2s.

KINGSLEY (Charles), M.A.
Letters and Memories of his Life. Edited by his WIFE. With 2 Steel engraved Portraits and numerous Illustrations on Wood, and a Facsimile of his Handwriting. Thirteenth Edition. 2 vols. Demy 8vo. Cloth, price 36s.
*** Also the eleventh Cabinet Edition in 2 vols. Crown 8vo. Cloth, price 12s.
All Saints' Day and other Sermons. Second Edition. Crown 8vo. Cloth, 7s. 6d.
True Words for Brave Men: a Book for Soldiers' and Sailors' Libraries. Eighth Edition. Crown 8vo. Cloth, price 2s. 6d.

KNIGHT (Professor W.).
Studies in Philosophy and Literature. Large post 8vo. Cloth, price 7s. 6d.

KNOX (Alexander A.).
The New Playground: or, Wanderings in Algeria. Large crown 8vo. Cloth, price 10s. 6d.

LAMONT (Martha MacDonald).
The Gladiator: A Life under the Roman Empire in the beginning of the Third Century. With four Illustrations by H. M. Paget. Extra fcap. 8vo. Cloth, price 3s. 6d.

LANG (A.).
XXXII Ballades in Blue China. Elzevir. 8vo. Parchment, price 5s.

LAYMANN (Capt.).
The Frontal Attack of Infantry. Translated by Colonel Edward Newdigate. Crown 8vo. Cloth, price 2s. 6d.

LEANDER (Richard).
Fantastic Stories. Translated from the German by Paulina B. Granville. With Eight full-page Illustrations by M. E. Fraser-Tytler. Crown 8vo. Cloth, price 5s.

LEE (Rev. F. G.), D.C.L.
The Other World; or, Glimpses of the Supernatural. 2 vols. A New Edition. Crown 8vo. Cloth, price 15s.

LEE (Holme).
Her Title of Honour. A Book for Girls. New Edition. With a Frontispiece. Crown 8vo. Cloth, price 5s.

LEWIS (Edward Dillon).
A Draft Code of Criminal Law and Procedure. Demy 8vo. Cloth, price 21s.

LEWIS (Mary A.).
A Rat with Three Tales. New and cheaper edition. With Four Illustrations by Catherine F. Frere. Crown 8vo. Cloth, price 3s. 6d.

LINDSAY (W. Lauder), M.D., &c.
Mind in the Lower Animals in Health and Disease. 2 vols. Demy 8vo. Cloth, price 32s.

LOCKER (F.).
London Lyrics. A New and Revised Edition, with Additions and a Portrait of the Author. Crown 8vo. Cloth, elegant, price 6s. Also a Cheap Edition, price 2s. 6d.

LOKI.
The New Werther. Small crown 8vo. Cloth, price 2s. 6d.

LORIMER (Peter), D.D.
John Knox and the Church of England: His Work in her Pulpit, and his Influence upon her Liturgy, Articles, and Parties. Demy 8vo. Cloth, price 12s.

John Wiclif and his English Precursors, by Gerhard Victor Lechler. Translated from the German, with additional Notes. New and Cheaper Edition. Demy 8vo. Cloth, price 10s. 6d.

Love Sonnets of Proteus. With frontispiece by the Author. Elzevir 8vo. Cloth, price 5s.

Lowder (Charles): a Biography. By the author of "St. Teresa." Large crown 8vo. With Portrait. Cloth, price 7s. 6d.

LOWNDES (Henry).
Poems and Translations.
Crown 8vo. Cloth, price 6s.

LUMSDEN (Lieut.-Col. H. W.).
Beowulf. An Old English Poem. Translated into modern rhymes. Small crown 8vo. Cloth, price 5s.

MAC CLINTOCK (L.).
Sir Spangle and the Dingy Hen. Illustrated. Square crown 8vo., price 2s. 6d.

MACDONALD (G.).
Malcolm. With Portrait of the Author engraved on Steel. Fourth Edition. Crown 8vo. Price 6s.
The Marquis of Lossie. Second Edition. Crown 8vo. Cloth, price 6s.
St. George and St. Michael. Second Edition. Crown 8vo. Cloth, 6s.

MACKENNA (S. J.).
Plucky Fellows. A Book for Boys. With Six Illustrations. Fourth Edition. Crown 8vo. Cloth, price 3s. 6d.
At School with an Old Dragoon. With Six Illustrations. Second Edition. Crown 8vo. Cloth, price 5s.

MACLACHLAN (Mrs.).
Notes and Extracts on Everlasting Punishment and Eternal Life, according to Literal Interpretation. Small crown 8vo. Cloth, price 3s. 6d.

MACLEAN (Charles Donald).
Latin and Greek Verse Translations. Small crown 8vo. Cloth, price 2s.

MACNAUGHT (Rev. John).
Cœna Domini: An Essay on the Lord's Supper, its Primitive Institution, Apostolic Uses, and Subsequent History. Demy 8vo. Cloth, price 14s.

MAGNUS (Mrs.).
About the Jews since Bible Times. From the Babylonian exile till the English Exodus. Small crown 8vo. Cloth, price 6s.

MAGNUSSON (Eirikr), M.A., and PALMER (E.H.), M.A.
Johan Ludvig Runeberg's Lyrical Songs, Idylls and Epigrams. Fcap. 8vo. Cloth, price 5s.

MAIR (R. S.), M.D., F.R.C.S.E.
The Medical Guide for Anglo-Indians. Being a Compendium of Advice to Europeans in India, relating to the Preservation and Regulation of Health. With a Supplement on the Management of Children in India. Second Edition. Crown 8vo. Limp cloth, price 3s. 6d.

MALDEN (H. E. and E. E.)
Princes and Princesses. Illustrated. Small crown 8vo. Cloth, price 2s. 6d.

MANNING (His Eminence Cardinal).
The True Story of the Vatican Council. Crown 8vo. Cloth, price 5s.

MARKHAM (Capt. Albert Hastings), R.N.
The Great Frozen Sea. A Personal Narrative of the Voyage of the "Alert" during the Arctic Expedition of 1875-6. With six full-page Illustrations, two Maps, and twenty-seven Woodcuts. Fourth and cheaper edition. Crown 8vo. Cloth, price 6s.
A Polar Reconnaissance: being the Voyage of the "Isbjorn" to Novaya Zemlya in 1879. With 10 Illustrations. Demy 8vo. Cloth, price 16s.

Marriage and Maternity; or, Scripture Wives and Mothers. Small crown 8vo. Cloth, price 4s. 6d.

MARTINEAU (Gertrude).
Outline Lessons on Morals. Small crown 8vo. Cloth, price 3s. 6d.

Master Bobby: a Tale. By the Author of "Christina North." With Illustrations by E. H. BELL. Extra fcap. 8vo. Cloth, price 3s. 6d.

MASTERMAN (J.).
Half-a-dozen Daughters. With a Frontispiece. Crown 8vo. Cloth, price 3s. 6d.

McGRATH (Terence).
Pictures from Ireland. New and cheaper edition. Crown 8vo. Cloth, price 2s.

MEREDITH (George).
The Egoist. A Comedy in Narrative. 3 vols. Crown 8vo. Cloth.
* Also a Cheaper Edition, with Frontispiece. Crown 8vo. Cloth, price 6s.

The Ordeal of Richard Feverel. A History of Father and Son. In one vol. with Frontispiece. Crown 8vo. Cloth, price 6s.

MEREDITH (Owen) [the Earl of Lytton].
Lucile. With 160 Illustrations. Crown 4to. cloth extra, gilt leaves, price 21s.

MERRITT (Henry).
Art - Criticism and Romance. With Recollections, and Twenty-three Illustrations in *eau-forte*, by Anna Lea Merritt. Two vols. Large post 8vo. Cloth, 25s.

MIDDLETON (The Lady).
Ballads. Square 16mo. Cloth, price 3s. 6d.

MILLER (Edward).
The History and Doctrines of Irvingism; or, the so-called Catholic and Apostolic Church. 2 vols. Large post 8vo. Cloth, price 25s.

The Church in Relation to the State. Crown 8vo. Cloth, price 7s. 6d.

MILNE (James).
Tables of Exchange for the Conversion of Sterling Money into Indian and Ceylon Currency, at Rates from 1s. 8d. to 2s. 3d. per Rupee. Second Edition. Demy 8vo. Cloth, price £2 2s.

MOCKLER (E.).
A Grammar of the Baloochee Language, as it is spoken in Makran (Ancient Gedrosia), in the Persia-Arabic and Roman characters. Fcap. 8vo. Cloth, price 5s.

MOFFAT (Robert Scott).
The Economy of Consumption; an Omitted Chapter in Political Economy, with special reference to the Questions of Commercial Crises and the Policy of Trades Unions; and with Reviews of the Theories of Adam Smith, Ricardo, J. S. Mill, Fawcett, &c. Demy 8vo. Cloth, price 18s.

The Principles of a Time Policy: being an Exposition of a Method of Settling Disputes between Employers and Employed in regard to Time and Wages, by a simple Process of Mercantile Barter, without recourse to Strikes or Locks-out. Demy 8vo. Cloth, price 3s. 6d.

MORELL (J. R.).
Euclid Simplified in Method and Language. Being a Manual of Geometry. Compiled from the most important French Works, approved by the University of Paris and the Minister of Public Instruction. Fcap. 8vo. Cloth, price 2s. 6d.

MORSE (E. S.), Ph.D.
First Book of Zoology. With numerous Illustrations. New and cheaper edition. Crown 8vo. Cloth, price 2s. 6d.

MORSHEAD (E. D. A.)
The House of Atreus. Being the Agamemnon Libation-Bearers and Furies of Æschylus Translated into English Verse. Crown 8vo. Cloth, price 7s.

MUNRO (Major-Gen. Sir Thomas), K.C.B., Governor of Madras.
Selections from His Minutes, and other Official Writings. Edited, with an Introductory Memoir, by Sir Alexander Arbuthnot, K.C.S.I., C.I.E. Two vols. Demy 8vo. Cloth, price 30s.

NAAKE (J. T.).
Slavonic Fairy Tales. From Russian, Servian, Polish, and Bohemian Sources. With Four Illustrations. Crown 8vo. Cloth, price 5s.

NELSON (J. H.).
A Prospectus of the Scientific Study of the Hindû Law. Demy 8vo. Cloth, price 9s.

NEWMAN (J. H.), D.D.
Characteristics from the Writings of. Being Selections from his various Works. Arranged with the Author's personal approval. Third Edition. With Portrait. Crown 8vo. Cloth, price 6s.
*** A Portrait of the Rev. Dr. J. H. Newman, mounted for framing, can be had, price 2s. 6d.

NICHOLAS (Thomas), Ph.D., F.G.S.
The Pedigree of the English People: an Argument, Historical and Scientific, on the Formation and Growth of the Nation, tracing Race-admixture in Britain from the earliest times, with especial reference to the incorporation of the Celtic Aborigines. Fifth Edition. Demy 8vo. Cloth, price 16s.

NICHOLSON (Edward Byron).
The Christ Child, and other Poems. Crown 8vo. Cloth, price 4s. 6d.

The Rights of an Animal. Crown 8vo. Cloth, price 3s. 6d.

The Gospel according to the Hebrews. Its Fragments translated and annotated, with a critical Analysis of the External and Internal Evidence relating to it. Demy 8vo. Cloth, price 9s. 6d.

A New Commentary on the Gospel according to Matthew. Demy 8vo. Cloth, price 12s.

NICOLS (Arthur), F.G.S., F.R.G.S.
Chapters from the Physical History of the Earth. An Introduction to Geology and Palæontology, with numerous illustrations. Crown 8vo. Cloth, price 5s.

NOAKE (Major R. Compton).
The Bivouac; or, Martial Lyrist, with an Appendix—Advice to the Soldier. Fcap. 8vo. Price 5s. 6d.

NOEL (The Hon. Roden).
A Little Child's Monument. Third Edition. Small crown 8vo. Cloth, price 3s. 6d.

NORMAN PEOPLE (The).
The Norman People, and their Existing Descendants in the British Dominions and the United States of America. Demy 8vo. Cloth, price 21s.

NORRIS (Rev. Alfred).
The Inner and Outer Life Poems. Fcap. 8vo. Cloth, price 6s.

Notes on Cavalry Tactics, Organization, &c. By a Cavalry Officer. With Diagrams. Demy 8vo. Cloth, price 12s.

Nuces: Exercises on the Syntax of the Public School Latin Primer. New Edition in Three Parts. Crown 8vo. Each 1s.
*** The Three Parts can also be had bound together in cloth, price 3s.

OATES (Frank), F.R.G.S.
Matabele Land and the Victoria Falls: A Naturalist's Wanderings in the Interior of South Africa. Edited by C. G. Oates, B.A., with numerous illustrations and four maps. Demy 8vo. Cloth, price 21s.

O'BRIEN (Charlotte G.).
Light and Shade. 2 vols. Crown 8vo. Cloth, gilt tops, price 12s.

Ode of Life (The).
Third Edition. Fcap. 8vo. Cloth, price 5s.

OF THE IMITATION OF CHRIST. Four Books. Cabinet Edition, price 1s. and 1s. 6d., cloth; Miniature Edition, price 1s.
*** Also in various bindings.

O'HAGAN (John).
The Song of Roland. Translated into English Verse. Large post 8vo. Parchment antique, price 10s. 6d.

O'MEARA (Kathleen).
Frederic Ozanam, Professor of the Sorbonne; His Life and Works. Second Edition. Crown 8vo. Cloth, price 7s. 6d.

Henri Perreyve and His Counsels to the Sick. Small crown 8vo. Cloth, price 5s.

OTTLEY (Henry Bickersteth).
The Great Dilemma: Christ His own Witness or His own Accuser. Six Lectures. Crown 8vo. Cloth, price 3s. 6d.

Our Public Schools. Eton, Harrow, Winchester, Rugby, Westminster, Marlborough, The Charterhouse. Crown 8vo. Cloth, price 6s.

OWEN (F. M.).
John Keats. A Study. Crown 8vo. Cloth, price 6s.

OWEN (Rev. Robert), B.D.
Sanctorale Catholicum; or Book of Saints. With Notes, Critical, Exegetical, and Historical. Demy 8vo. Cloth, price 18s.

An Essay on the Communion of Saints. Including an Examination of the "Cultus Sanctorum." Price 2s.

PALGRAVE (W. Gifford).
Hermann Agha; An Eastern Narrative. Third and Cheaper Edition. Crown 8vo. Cloth, price 6s.

PANDURANG HARI;
Or, Memoirs of a Hindoo. With an Introductory Preface by Sir H. Bartle E. Frere, G.C.S.I., C.B. Crown 8vo. Price 6s.

PARCHMENT LIBRARY (The).
Choicely printed on hand-made paper, limp parchment antique, price 6s. each; vellum, price 7s. 6d. each.

Edgar Allan Poe's Poems. With an Essay on his Poetry by ANDREW LANG and a frontispiece by Linley Sambourne.

Shakspere's Sonnets. Edited by Edward Dowden. With a Frontispiece, etched by Leopold Lowenstam, after the Death Mask.

English Odes. Selected by Edmund W. Gosse. With Frontispiece on India paper by Hamo Thornycroft, A.R.A.

OF THE IMITATION OF CHRIST. Four Books. A revised Translation. With Frontispiece on India paper, from a Design by W. B. Richmond.

PARCHMENT LIBRARY (The) —continued.

Tennyson's The Princess: a Medley. With a Miniature Frontispiece by H. M. Paget, and a Tailpiece in Outline by Gordon Browne.

Poems: Selected from Percy Bysshe Shelley. Dedicated to Lady Shelley. With Preface by Richard Garnet, and a Miniature Frontispiece.

Tennyson's "In Memoriam." With a Miniature Portrait in eau forte by Le Rat, after a Photograph by the late Mrs. Cameron.

PARKER (Joseph), D.D.
The Paraclete: An Essay on the Personality and Ministry of the Holy Ghost, with some reference to current discussions. Second Edition. Demy 8vo. Cloth, price 12s.

PARR (Capt. H. Hallam).
A Sketch of the Kafir and Zulu Wars: Guadana to Isandhlwana, with Maps. Small crown 8vo. Cloth, price 5s.

The Dress, Horses, and Equipment of Infantry and Staff Officers. Crown 8vo. Cloth, price 1s.

PARSLOE (Joseph).
Our Railways: Sketches, Historical and Descriptive. With Practical Information as to Fares, Rates, &c., and a Chapter on Railway Reform. Crown 8vo. Cloth, price 6s.

PATTISON (Mrs. Mark).
The Renaissance of Art in France. With Nineteen Steel Engravings. 2 vols. Demy 8vo. Cloth, price 32s.

PAUL (C. Kegan).
Mary Wollstonecraft. Letters to Imlay. With Prefatory Memoir by, and Two Portraits in eau forte, by Anna Lea Merritt. Crown 8vo. Cloth, price 6s.

Goethe's Faust. A New Translation in Rime. Crown 8vo. Cloth, price 6s.

PAUL (C. Kegan)—*continued.*
William Godwin: His Friends and Contemporaries. With Portraits and Facsimiles of the Handwriting of Godwin and his Wife. 2 vols. Square post 8vo. Cloth, price 28s.

The Genius of Christianity Unveiled. Being Essays by William Godwin never before published. Edited, with a Preface, by C. Kegan Paul. Crown 8vo. Cloth, price 7s. 6d.

PAUL (Margaret Agnes).
Gentle and Simple: A Story. 2 vols. Crown 8vo. Cloth, gilt tops, price 12s.
*** Also a Cheaper Edition in one vol. with Frontispiece. Crown 8vo. Cloth, price 6s.

PAYNE (John).
Songs of Life and Death. Crown 8vo. Cloth, price 5s.

PAYNE (Prof. J. F.).
Fröbel and the Kindergarten System. Second Edition.
A Visit to German Schools: Elementary Schools in Germany. Crown 8vo. Cloth, price 4s. 6d.

PELLETAN (E.).
The Desert Pastor, Jean Jarousseau. Translated from the French. By Colonel E. P. De L'Hoste. With a Frontispiece. New Edition. Fcap. 8vo. Cloth, price 3s. 6d.

PENNELL (H. Cholmondeley).
Pegasus Resaddled. By the Author of "Puck on Pegasus," &c. &c. With Ten Full-page Illustrations by George Du Maurier. Second Edition. Fcap. 4to. Cloth elegant, price 12s. 6d.

PENRICE (Maj. J.), B.A.
A Dictionary and Glossary of the Ko-ran. With copious Grammatical References and Explanations of the Text. 4to. Cloth, price 21s.

PESCHEL (Dr. Oscar).
The Races of Man and their Geographical Distribution. Large crown 8vo. Cloth, price 9s.

PETERS (F. H.).
The Nicomachean Ethics of Aristotle. Translated by. Crown 8vo. Cloth, price 6s.

PFEIFFER (Emily).
Under the Aspens. Lyrical and Dramatic. Crown 8vo. With Portrait. Cloth, price 6s.
Quarterman's Grace, and other Poems. Crown 8vo. Cloth, price 5s.
Glan Alarch: His Silence and Song. A Poem. Second Edition. Crown 8vo. price 6s.
Gerard's Monument, and other Poems. Second Edition. Crown 8vo. Cloth, price 6s.
Poems. Second Edition. Crown 8vo. Cloth, price 6s.
Sonnets and Songs. New Edition. 16mo, handsomely printed and bound in cloth, gilt edges, price 5s.

PIKE (Warburton).
The Inferno of Dante Alighieri. Demy 8vo. Cloth, price 5s.

PINCHES (Thomas), M.A.
Samuel Wilberforce: Faith —Service—Recompense. Three Sermons. With a Portrait of Bishop Wilberforce (after a Photograph by Charles Watkins). Crown 8vo. Cloth, price 4s. 6d.

PLAYFAIR (Lieut.-Col.), Her Britannic Majesty's Consul-General in Algiers.
Travels in the Footsteps of Bruce in Algeria and Tunis. Illustrated by facsimiles of Bruce's original Drawings, Photographs, Maps, &c. Royal 4to. Cloth, bevelled boards, gilt leaves, price £3 3s.

POLLOCK (Frederick).
Spinoza. His Life and Philosophy. Demy 8vo. Cloth, price 16s.

POLLOCK (W. H.).
Lectures on French Poets. Delivered at the Royal Institution. Small crown 8vo. Cloth, price 5s.

POOR (Laura E.).
Sanskrit and its kindred Literatures. Studies in Comparative Mythology. Small crown 8vo. Cloth, price 5s.

POUSHKIN (A. S.).
Russian Romance. Translated from the Tales of Belkin, &c. By Mrs. J. Buchan Telfer (*née* Mouravieff). Crown 8vo. Cloth, price 3s. 6d.

PRESBYTER.
Unfoldings of Christian Hope. An Essay showing that the Doctrine contained in the Damnatory Clauses of the Creed commonly called Athanasian is unscriptural. Small crown 8vo. Cloth, price 4s. 6d.

PRICE (Prof. Bonamy).
Currency and Banking. Crown 8vo. Cloth, price 6s.

Chapters on Practical Political Economy. Being the Substance of Lectures delivered before the University of Oxford. Large post 8vo. Cloth, price 12s.

Proteus and Amadeus. A Correspondence. Edited by Aubrey De Vere. Crown 8vo. Cloth, price 5s.

PUBLIC SCHOOLBOY.
The Volunteer, the Militiaman, and the Regular Soldier. Crown 8vo. Cloth, price 5s.

PULPIT COMMENTARY (The).
Edited by the Rev. J. S. EXELL and the Rev. Canon H. D. M. SPENCE.

Genesis. By Rev. T. Whitelaw, M.A.; with Homilies by the Very Rev. J. F. Montgomery, D.D., Rev. Prof. R. A. Redford, M.A., LL.B., Rev. F. Hastings, Rev. W. Roberts, M.A. An Introduction to the Study of the Old Testament by the Rev. Canon Farrar, D.D., F.R.S.; and Introductions to the Pentateuch by the Right Rev. H. Cotterill, D.D., and Rev. T. Whitelaw, M.A. Fifth Edition. Price 15s.

PULPIT COMMENTARY (The) —*continued.*

Numbers. By the Rev. R. Winterbotham, LL.B. With Homilies by the Rev. Prof. W. Binnie, D.D., Rev. E. S. Prout, M.A., Rev. D. Young, Rev. J. Waite, and an Introduction by the Rev. Thomas Whitelaw, M.A. Third Edition. Price 15s.

Joshua. By the Rev. J. J. Lias, M.A. With Homilies by the Rev. S. R. Aldridge, LL.B., Rev. R. Glover, Rev. E. de Pressensé, D.D., Rev. J. Waite, Rev. F. W. Adeney, and an Introduction by the Rev. A. Plummer, M.A. Third Edition. Price 12s. 6d.

Judges and Ruth. By Right Rev. Lord A. C. Hervey, D.D., and Rev. J. Morrison, D.D. With Homilies by Rev. A. F. Muir, M.A.; Rev. W. F. Adeney, M.A.; Rev. W. M. Statham; and Rev. Prof. J. R. Thomson, M.A. Third Edition. Cloth, price 15s.

1 Samuel. By the Very Rev. R. P. Smith, D.D. With Homilies by the Rev. Donald Fraser, D.D., Rev. Prof. Chapman, and Rev. B. Dale. Fourth Edition. Price 15s.

1 Kings. By the Rev. Joseph Hammond, LL.B. With Homilies by the Rev. E. de Pressensé, D.D., Rev. J. Waite, B A., Rev. A. Rowland, LL.B, Rev. J. A. Macdonald, and Rev. J. Urquhart.

Ezra, Nehemiah, and Esther. By Rev. Canon G. Rawlinson, M.A.; with Homilies by Rev. Prof. J. R. Thomson, M.A., Rev. Prof. R. A. Redford, LL.B., M.A., Rev. W. S. Lewis, M.A., Rev. J. A. Macdonald, Rev. A. Mackennal, B.A., Rev. W. Clarkson, B.A., Rev. F. Hastings, Rev. W. Dinwiddie, LL.B., Rev. Prof. Rowlands, B.A., Rev. G. Wood, B.A., Rev. Prof. P. C. Barker, LL.B., M.A., and Rev. J. S. Exell. Fifth Edition. Price 12s. 6d.

Punjaub (The) and North Western Frontier of India. By an old Punjaubee. Crown 8vo. Cloth, price 5s.

Rabbi Jeshua. An Eastern Story. Crown 8vo. Cloth, price 3s. 6d.

RADCLIFFE (Frank R. Y.).
The New Politicus. Small crown 8vo. Cloth, price 2s. 6d.

RAVENSHAW (John Henry), B.C.S.
Gaur: Its Ruins and Inscriptions. Edited with considerable additions and alterations by his Widow. With forty-four photographic illustrations and twenty-five fac-similes of Inscriptions. Super royal 4to. Cloth, 3l. 13s. 6d.

READ (Carveth).
On the Theory of Logic: An Essay. Crown 8vo. Cloth, price 6s.

Realities of the Future Life. Small crown 8vo. Cloth, price 1s. 6d.

REANEY (Mrs. G. S.).
Blessing and Blessed; a Sketch of Girl Life. New and cheaper Edition. With a frontispiece. Crown 8vo. Cloth, price 3s. 6d.

Waking and Working; or, from Girlhood to Womanhood. New and cheaper edition. With a Frontispiece. Crown 8vo. Cloth, price 3s. 6d.

Rose Gurney's Discovery. A Book for Girls, dedicated to their Mothers. Crown 8vo. Cloth, price 3s. 6d.

English Girls: their Place and Power. With a Preface by R. W. Dale, M.A., of Birmingham. Third Edition. Fcap. 8vo. Cloth, price 2s. 6d.

Just Anyone, and other Stories. Three Illustrations. Royal 16mo. Cloth, price 1s. 6d.

Sunshine Jenny and other Stories. Three Illustrations. Royal 16mo. Cloth, price 1s. 6d.

Sunbeam Willie, and other Stories. Three Illustrations. Royal 16mo. Cloth, price 1s. 6d.

RENDALL (J. M.).
Concise Handbook of the Island of Madeira. With plan of Funchal and map of the Island. Fcap. 8vo. Cloth, price 1s. 6d.

REYNOLDS (Rev. J. W.).
The Supernatural in Nature. A Verification by Free Use of Science. Second Edition, revised and enlarged. Demy 8vo. Cloth, price 14s.

Mystery of Miracles, The. By the Author of "The Supernatural in Nature." New and Enlarged Edition. Crown 8vo. Cloth, price 6s.

RHOADES (James).
The Georgics of Virgil. Translated into English Verse. Small crown 8vo. Cloth, price 5s.

RIBOT (Prof. Th.).
English Psychology. Second Edition. A Revised and Corrected Translation from the latest French Edition. Large post 8vo. Cloth, price 9s.

Heredity: A Psychological Study on its Phenomena, its Laws, its Causes, and its Consequences. Large crown 8vo. Cloth, price 9s.

RINK (Chevalier Dr. Henry).
Greenland: Its People and its Products. By the Chevalier Dr. HENRY RINK, President of the Greenland Board of Trade. With sixteen Illustrations, drawn by the Eskimo, and a Map. Edited by Dr. ROBERT BROWN. Crown 8vo. Price 10s. 6d.

ROBERTSON (The Late Rev. F. W.), M.A., of Brighton.
The Human Race, and other Sermons preached at Cheltenham, Oxford, and Brighton. Second Edition. Large post 8vo. Cloth, price 7s. 6d.

Notes on Genesis. New and cheaper Edition. Crown 8vo., price 3s. 6d.

Sermons. Four Series. Small crown 8vo. Cloth, price 3s. 6d. each.

Expository Lectures on St. Paul's Epistles to the Corinthians. A New Edition. Small crown 8vo. Cloth, price 5s.

Lectures and Addresses, with other literary remains. A New Edition. Crown 8vo. Cloth, price 5s.

ROBERTSON (The Late Rev. F. W.), M.A., of Brighton—*continued*.
An Analysis of Mr. Tennyson's "In Memoriam." (Dedicated by Permission to the Poet-Laureate.) Fcap. 8vo. Cloth, price 2s.
The Education of the Human Race. Translated from the German of Gotthold Ephraim Lessing. Fcap. 8vo. Cloth, price 2s. 6d.
Life and Letters. Edited by the Rev. Stopford Brooke, M.A., Chaplain in Ordinary to the Queen.
I. 2 vols., uniform with the Sermons. With Steel Portrait. Crown 8vo. Cloth, price 7s. 6d.
II. Library Edition, in Demy 8vo., with Portrait. Cloth, price 12s.
III. A Popular Edition, in one vol. Crown 8vo. Cloth, price 6s.
The above Works can also be had half-bound in morocco.
*** A Portrait of the late Rev. F. W. Robertson, mounted for framing, can be had, price 2s. 6d.

ROBINSON (A. Mary F.).
A Handful of Honeysuckle. Fcap. 8vo. Cloth, price 3s. 6d.
The Crowned Hippolytus. Translated from Euripides. With New Poems. Small crown 8vo. Cloth, price 5s.

RODWELL (G. F.), F.R.A.S., F.C.S.
Etna: a History of the Mountain and its Eruptions. With Maps and Illustrations. Square 8vo. Cloth, price 9s.

ROLLESTON (T. W. H.), B.A.
The Encheiridion of Epictetus. Translated from the Greek, with a Preface and Notes. Small crown 8vo. Cloth, price 3s. 6d.

ROSS (Mrs. E.), ("Nelsie Brook").
Daddy's Pet. A Sketch from Humble Life. With Six Illustrations. Royal 16mo. Cloth, price 1s.

SADLER (S. W.), R.N.
The African Cruiser. A Midshipman's Adventures on the West Coast. With Three Illustrations. Second Edition. Crown 8vo. Cloth, price 3s. 6d.

SALTS (Rev. Alfred), LL.D.
Godparents at Confirmation. With a Preface by the Bishop of Manchester. Small crown 8vo. Cloth, limp, price 2s.

SALVATOR (Archduke Ludwig).
Levkosia, the Capital of Cyprus. Crown 8vo. Cloth, price 10s. 6d.

SAMUEL (Sydney Montagu).
Jewish Life in the East. Small crown 8vo. Cloth, price 3s. 6d.

SAUNDERS (John).
Israel Mort, Overman: A Story of the Mine. Cr. 8vo. Price 6s.
Hirell. With Frontispiece. Crown 8vo. Cloth, price 3s. 6d.
Abel Drake's Wife. With Frontispiece. Crown 8vo. Cloth, price 3s. 6d.

SAYCE (Rev. Archibald Henry).
Introduction to the Science of Language. Two vols., large post 8vo. Cloth, price 25s.

SCHELL (Maj. von).
The Operations of the First Army under Gen. von Goeben. Translated by Col. C. H. von Wright. Four Maps. Demy 8vo. Cloth, price 9s.
The Operations of the First Army under Gen. von Steinmetz. Translated by Captain E. O. Hollist. Demy 8vo. Cloth, price 10s. 6d.

SCHELLENDORF (Maj.-Gen. B. von).
The Duties of the General Staff. Translated from the German by Lieutenant Hare. Vol. I. Demy 8vo. Cloth, 10s. 6d.

SCHERFF (Maj. W. von).
Studies in the New Infantry Tactics. Parts I. and II. Translated from the German by Colonel Lumley Graham. Demy 8vo. Cloth, price 7s. 6d.

Scientific Layman. The New Truth and the Old Faith: are they Incompatible? Demy 8vo. Cloth, price 10s. 6d.

SCOONES (W. Baptiste).
Four Centuries of English Letters. A Selection of 350 Letters by 150 Writers from the period of the Paston Letters to the Present Time. Edited and arranged by. Second Edition. Large crown 8vo. Cloth, price 9s.

SCOTT (Leader).
A Nook in the Apennines: A Summer beneath the Chestnuts. With Frontispiece, and 27 Illustrations in the Text, chiefly from Original Sketches. Crown 8vo. Cloth, price 7s. 6d. Also a Cheap Edition, price 2s. 6d.

SCOTT (Robert H.).
Weather Charts and Storm Warnings. Illustrated. Second Edition. Crown 8vo. Cloth, price 3s. 6d.

Seeking his Fortune, and other Stories. With Four Illustrations. New and cheaper Edition. Crown 8vo. Cloth, price 2s. 6d.

SENIOR (N. W.).
Alexis De Tocqueville. Correspondence and Conversations with Nassau W. Senior, from 1833 to 1859. Edited by M. C. M. Simpson. 2 vols. Large post 8vo. Cloth, price 21s.

Seven Autumn Leaves from Fairyland. Illustrated with Nine Etchings. Square crown 8vo. Cloth, price 3s. 6d.

SHADWELL (Maj.-Gen.), C.B.
Mountain Warfare. Illustrated by the Campaign of 1799 in Switzerland. Being a Translation of the Swiss Narrative compiled from the Works of the Archduke Charles, Jomini, and others. Also of Notes by General H. Dufour on the Campaign of the Valtelline in 1635. With Appendix, Maps, and Introductory Remarks. Demy 8vo. Cloth, price 16s.

SHAKSPEARE (Charles).
Saint Paul at Athens: Spiritual Christianity in Relation to some Aspects of Modern Thought. Nine Sermons preached at St. Stephen's Church, Westbourne Park. With Preface by the Rev. Canon FARRAR. Crown 8vo. Cloth, price 5s.

SHAW (Major Wilkinson).
The Elements of Modern Tactics. Practically applied to English Formations. With Twenty-five Plates and Maps. Second and cheaper Edition. Small crown 8vo. Cloth, price 9s.
⁎ The Second Volume of "Military Handbooks for Officers and Non-commissioned Officers." Edited by Lieut.-Col. C. B. Brackenbury, R.A., A.A.G.

SHAW (Flora L.).
Castle Blair: a Story of Youthful Lives. 2 vols. Crown 8vo. Cloth, gilt tops, price 12s. Also, an edition in one vol. Crown 8vo. 6s.

SHELLEY (Lady).
Shelley Memorials from Authentic Sources. With (now first printed) an Essay on Christianity by Percy Bysshe Shelley. With Portrait. Third Edition. Crown 8vo. Cloth, price 5s.

SHERMAN (Gen. W. T.).
Memoirs of General W. T. Sherman, Commander of the Federal Forces in the American Civil War. By Himself. 2 vols. With Map. Demy 8vo. Cloth, price 24s. *Copyright English Edition.*

SHILLITO (Rev. Joseph).
Womanhood: its Duties, Temptations, and Privileges. A Book for Young Women. Second Edition. Crown 8vo. Price 3s. 6d.

SHIPLEY (Rev. Orby), M.A.
Principles of the Faith in Relation to Sin. Topics for Thought in Times of Retreat. Eleven Addresses. With an Introduction on the neglect of Dogmatic Theology in the Church of England, and a Postscript on his leaving the Church of England. Demy 8vo. Cloth, price 12s.

Church Tracts, or Studies in Modern Problems. By various Writers. 2 vols. Crown 8vo. Cloth, price 5s. each.

Sister Augustine, Superior of the Sisters of Charity at the St. Johannis Hospital at Bonn. Authorized Translation by Hans Tharau from the German Memorials of Amalie von Lasaulx. Second edition. Large crown 8vo. Cloth, price 7s. 6d.

Six Ballads about King Arthur. Crown 8vo. Cloth extra, gilt edges, price 3s. 6d.

SKINNER (James).
Cœlestia: the Manual of St. Augustine. The Latin Text side by side with an English Interpretation, in 36 Odes, with Notes, *and* a plea *for the* Study *of* Mystic Theology. Large crown 8vo. Cloth, price 6s.

SMITH (Edward), M.D., LL.B., F.R.S.
Health and Disease, as Influenced by the Daily, Seasonal, and other Cyclical Changes in the Human System. A New Edition. Post 8vo. Cloth, price 7s. 6d.

Practical Dietary for Families, Schools, and the Labouring Classes. A New Edition. Post 8vo. Cloth, price 3s. 6d.

Tubercular Consumption in its Early and Remediable Stages. Second Edition. Crown 8vo. Cloth, price 6s.

Songs of Two Worlds. By the Author of "The Epic of Hades." Sixth Edition. Complete in one Volume, with Portrait. Fcap. 8vo. Cloth, price 7s. 6d.

Songs for Music.
By Four Friends. Square crown 8vo. Cloth, price 5s.
Containing songs by Reginald A. Gatty, Stephen H. Gatty, Greville J. Chester, and Juliana Ewing.

SPEDDING (James).
Evenings with a Reviewer; or, Bacon and Macaulay. With a Prefatory Notice by G. S. VENABLES, Q.C. 3 vols. Demy 8vo. Cloth, price 18s.

Reviews and Discussions, Literary, Political, and Historical, not relating to Bacon. Demy 8vo. Cloth, price 12s. 6d.

STAPFER (Paul).
Shakspeare and Classical Antiquity: Greek and Latin Anti-

STAPFER (Paul)—*continued.*
quity as presented in Shakspeare's Plays. Translated by Emily J. Carey. Large post 8vo. Cloth, price 12s.

St. Bernard on the Love of God. Translated by Marianne Caroline and Coventry Patmore. Cloth extra, gilt top, price 4s. 6d.

STEDMAN (Edmund Clarence).
Lyrics and Idylls. With other Poems. Crown 8vo. Cloth, price 7s. 6d.

STEPHENS (Archibald John), LL.D.
The Folkestone Ritual Case. The Substance of the Argument delivered before the Judicial Committee of the Privy Council. On behalf of the Respondents. Demy 8vo. Cloth, price 6s.

STEVENSON (Robert Louis).
Virginibus, Puerisque, and other Papers. Crown 8vo. Cloth, price 6s.

STEVENSON (Rev. W. F.).
Hymns for the Church and Home. Selected and Edited by the Rev. W. Fleming Stevenson.
The most complete Hymn Book published.
The Hymn Book consists of Three Parts:—I. For Public Worship.—II. For Family and Private Worship.—III. For Children.
** *Published in various forms and prices, the latter ranging from 8d. to 6s. Lists and full particulars will be furnished on application to the Publishers.*

STOCKTON (Frank R.).
A Jolly Fellowship. With 20 Illustrations. Crown 8vo. Cloth, price 5s.

STORR (Francis), and TURNER Hawes).
Canterbury Chimes; or, Chaucer Tales retold to Children. With Illustrations from the Ellesmere MS. Extra Fcap. 8vo. Cloth, price 3s. 6d.

Strecker-Wishcenus's Organic Chemistry. Translated and edited with extensive additions by W. R. HODGKINSON, Ph. D., and A. J. GREENWAY, F.I.C. Demy 8vo. Cloth, price 21s.

STRETTON (Hesba).
David Lloyd's Last Will. With Four Illustrations. Royal 16mo., price 2s. 6d.

The Wonderful Life. Thirteenth Thousand. Fcap. 8vo. Cloth, price 2s. 6d.

Through a Needle's Eye: a Story. Crown 8vo. Cloth, price 6s.

STUBBS (Lieut.-Colonel F. W.)
The Regiment of Bengal Artillery. The History of its Organization, Equipment, and War Services. Compiled from Published Works, Official Records, and various Private Sources. With numerous Maps and Illustrations. 2 vols. Demy 8vo. Cloth, price 32s.

STUMM (Lieut. Hugo), German Military Attaché to the Khivan Expedition.
Russia's advance Eastward. Based on the Official Reports of. Translated by Capt. C. E. H. VINCENT. With Map. Crown 8vo. Cloth, price 6s.

SULLY (James), M.A.
Sensation and Intuition. Demy 8vo. Second Edition. Cloth, price 10s. 6d.
Pessimism: a History and a Criticism. Demy 8vo. Price 14s.

Sunnyland Stories. By the Author of "Aunt Mary's Bran Pie." Illustrated. Small 8vo. Cloth, price 3s. 6d

Sweet Silvery Sayings of Shakespeare. Crown 8vo. Cloth gilt, price 7s. 6d.

SYME (David).
Outlines of an Industrial Science. Second Edition. Crown 8vo. Cloth, price 6s.

SYME (David)—*continued.*
Representative Government in England. Its Faults and Failures. Large crown 8vo. Cloth, price 6s.

Tales from Ariosto. Retold for Children, by a Lady. With three illustrations. Crown 8vo. Cloth, price 4s. 6d.

TAYLOR (Algernon).
Guienne. Notes of an Autumn Tour. Crown 8vo. Cloth, price 4s. 6d.

TAYLOR (Sir H.).
Works Complete. Author's Edition, in 5 vols. Crown 8vo. Cloth, price 6s. each.
Vols. I. to III. containing the Poetical Works, Vols. IV. and V. the Prose Works.

TAYLOR (Col. Meadows), C.S.I., M.R.I.A.
A Noble Queen: a Romance of Indian History. New Edition. With Frontispiece. Crown 8vo. Cloth. Price 6s.
Seeta. New Edition with frontispiece. Crown 8vo. Cloth, price 6s.
Tippoo Sultaun: a Tale of the Mysore War. New Edition with Frontispiece. Crown 8vo. Cloth, price 6s.
Ralph Darnell. New Edition. With Frontispiece. Crown 8vo. Cloth, price 6s.
The Confessions of a Thug. New Edition. With Frontispiece. Crown 8vo. Cloth, price 6s.
Tara: a Mahratta Tale. New Edition. With Frontispiece. Crown 8vo. Cloth, price 6s.

TENNYSON (Alfred).
The Imperial Library Edition. Complete in 7 vols. Demy 8vo. Cloth, price £3 13s. 6d.; in Roxburgh binding, £4 7s. 6d.

Author's Edition. Complete in 7 Volumes. With Frontispieces. Crown 8vo. Cloth, price 43s. 6d.; Roxburgh half morocco, price 54s.

TENNYSON (Alfred)—*continued.*

Cabinet Edition, in 13 vols. with Frontispieces. Fcap. 8vo. Cloth, price 2s. 6d. each, or complete in cloth box, price 35s.

*** Each volume in the above editions may be had separately.

The Royal Edition. With 26 Illustrations and Portrait. Cloth extra, bevelled boards, gilt leaves. Price 21s.

The Guinea Edition. In 14 vols., neatly bound and enclosed in box. Cloth, price 21s. French morocco or parchment, price 31s. 6d.

The Shilling Edition of the Poetical and Dramatic Works, in 12 vols., pocket size. Price 1s. each.

The Crown Edition [the 118th thousand], strongly bound in cloth, price 6s. Cloth, extra gilt leaves, price 7s. 6d. Roxburgh, half morocco, price 8s. 6d.

*** Can also be had in a variety of other bindings.

Original Editions:

Ballads and other Poems. Fcap. 8vo. Cloth, price 5s.

The Lover's Tale. (Now for the first time published.) Fcap. 8vo. Cloth, 3s. 6d.

Poems. Small 8vo. Cloth, price 6s.

Maud, and other Poems. Small 8vo. Cloth, price 3s. 6d.

The Princess. Small 8vo. Cloth, price 3s. 6d.

Idylls of the King. Small 8vo. Cloth, price 5s.

Idylls of the King. Complete. Small 8vo. Cloth, price 6s.

The Holy Grail, and other Poems. Small 8vo. Cloth, price 4s. 6d.

Gareth and Lynette. Small 8vo. Cloth, price 3s.

Enoch Arden, &c. Small 8vo. Cloth, price 3s. 6d.

TENNYSON (Alfred)—*continued.*

In Memoriam. Small 8vo. Cloth, price 4s.

Queen Mary. A Drama. New Edition. Crown 8vo. Cloth, price 6s.

Harold. A Drama. Crown 8vo. Cloth, price 6s.

Selections from Tennyson's Works. Super royal 16mo. Cloth, price 3s. 6d. Cloth gilt extra, price 4s.

Songs from Tennyson's Works. Super royal 16mo. Cloth extra, price 3s. 6d.

Also a cheap edition. 16mo. Cloth, price 2s. 6d.

Idylls of the King, and other Poems. Illustrated by Julia Margaret Cameron. 2 vols. Folio. Half-bound morocco, cloth sides, price £6 6s. each.

Tennyson for the Young and for Recitation. Specially arranged. Fcap. 8vo. Price 1s. 6d.

Tennyson Birthday Book. Edited by Emily Shakespear. 32mo. Cloth limp, 2s.; cloth extra, 3s.

*** A superior edition, printed in red and black, on antique paper, specially prepared. Small crown 8vo. Cloth extra, gilt leaves, price 5s.; and in various calf and morocco bindings.

Songs Set to Music, by various Composers. Edited by W. G. Cusins. Dedicated by express permission to Her Majesty the Queen. Royal 4to. Cloth extra, gilt leaves, price 21s., or in half-morocco, price 25s.

An Index to "In Memoriam." Price 2s.

THOMAS (Moy).
A Fight for Life. With Frontispiece. Crown 8vo. Cloth, price 3s. 6d.

THOMPSON (Alice C.).
Preludes. A Volume of Poems. Illustrated by Elizabeth Thompson (Painter of "The Roll Call"). 8vo. Cloth, price 7s. 6d.

THOMSON (J. Turnbull).
Social Problems; or, an Inquiry into the Law of Influences. With Diagrams. Demy 8vo. Cloth, price 10s. 6d.

THRING (Rev. Godfrey), B.A.
Hymns and Sacred Lyrics. Fcap. 8vo. Cloth, price 3s. 6d.

TODHUNTER (Dr. J.)
Forest Songs. Small crown 8vo. Cloth, 3s. 6d.
The True Tragedy of Rienzi. A Drama.
A Study of Shelley. Crown 8vo. Cloth, price 7s.
Alcestis : A Dramatic Poem. Extra fcap. 8vo. Cloth, price 5s.
Laurella; and other Poems. Crown 8vo. Cloth, price 6s. 6d.
Translations from Dante, Petrarch, Michael Angelo, and Vittoria Colonna. Fcap. 8vo. Cloth, price 7s. 6d.

TURNER (Rev. C. Tennyson).
Sonnets, Lyrics, and Translations. Crown 8vo. Cloth, price 4s. 6d.
Collected Sonnets, Old and New. With Prefatory Poem by Alfred Tennyson; also some Marginal Notes by S. T. Coleridge, and a Critical Essay by James Spedding. Fcap. 8vo. Cloth, price 7s. 6d.

TWINING (Louisa).
Recollections of Workhouse Visiting and Management during twenty-five years. Small crown 8vo. Cloth, price 3s. 6d.

UPTON (Major R. D.).
Gleanings from the Desert of Arabia. Large post 8vo. Cloth, price 10s. 6d.

VAUGHAN (H. Halford).
New Readings and Renderings of Shakespeare's Tragedies. 2 vols. Demy 8vo. Cloth, price 25s.

VIATOR (Vacuus).
Flying South. Recollections of France and its Littoral. Small crown 8vo. Cloth, price 3s. 6d.

VILLARI (Prof.).
Niccolo Machiavelli and His Times. Translated by Linda Villari. 2 vols. Large post 8vo. Cloth, price 24s.

VINCENT (Capt. C. E. H.).
Elementary Military Geography, Reconnoitring, and Sketching. Square crown 8vo. Cloth, price 2s. 6d.

VYNER (Lady Mary).
Every day a Portion. Adapted from the Bible and the Prayer Book. Square crown 8vo. Cloth extra, price 5s.

WALDSTEIN (Charles), Ph. D.
The Balance of Emotion and Intellect: An Essay Introductory to the Study of Philosophy. Crown 8vo. Cloth, price 6s.

WALLER (Rev. C. B.)
The Apocalypse, Reviewed under the Light of the Doctrine of the Unfolding Ages and the Restitution of all Things. Demy 8vo. Cloth, price 12s.

WALSHE (Walter Hayle), M.D.
Dramatic Singing Physiologically Estimated. Crown 8vo. Cloth, price 3s. 6d.

WALTERS (Sophia Lydia).
The Brook: A Poem. Small crown 8vo. Cloth, price 3s. 6d.
A Dreamer's Sketch Book. With Twenty-one Illustrations. Fcap. 4to. Cloth, price 12s. 6d.

WATERFIELD, W.
Hymns for Holy Days and Seasons. 32mo. Cloth, price 1s. 6d.

WATSON (Sir Thomas), Bart., M.D.
The Abolition of Zymotic Diseases, and of other similar enemies of Mankind. Small crown 8vo. Cloth, price 3s. 6d.

WAY (A.), M.A.
The Odes of Horace Literally Translated in Metre. Fcap. 8vo. Cloth, price 2s.

WEBSTER (Augusta).
Disguises. A Drama. Small crown 8vo. Cloth, price 5s.

WEDMORE (Frederick).
The Masters of Genre Painting. With sixteen illustrations. Large crown 8vo. Cloth, price 7s. 6d.

32 A List of C. Kegan Paul & Co.'s Publications.

WHEWELL (William), D.D.
His Life and Selections from his Correspondence. By Mrs. Stair Douglas. With Portrait. Demy 8vo. Cloth, price 21s.

WHITAKER (Florence).
Christy's Inheritance. A London Story. Illustrated. Royal 16mo. Cloth, price 1s. 6d.

WHITE (A. D.), LL.D.
Warfare of Science. With Prefatory Note by Professor Tyndall. Second Edition. Crown 8vo. Cloth, price 3s. 6d.

WHITNEY (Prof. W. D.)
Essentials of English Grammar for the Use of Schools. Crown 8vo. Cloth, price 3s. 6d.

WICKSTEED (P. H.).
Dante: Six Sermons. Crown 8vo. Cloth, price 5s.

WILKINS (William).
Songs of Study. Crown 8vo. Cloth, price 6s.

WILLIAMS (Rowland), D.D.
Stray Thoughts from his Note-Books. Edited by his Widow. Crown 8vo. Cloth, price 3s. 6d.

Psalms, Litanies, Counsels and Collects for Devout Persons. Edited by his Widow. Crown 8vo. Cloth, price 3s. 6d.

WILLIS (R.), M.D.
Servetus and Calvin: a Study of an Important Epoch in the Early History of the Reformation. 8vo. Cloth, price 16s.

William Harvey. A History of the Discovery of the Circulation of the Blood. With a Portrait of Harvey, after Faithorne. Demy 8vo. Cloth, price 14s.

WILSON (Sir Erasmus).
Egypt of the Past. With Illustrations in the Text. Crown 8vo. Cloth, price 12s.

WILSON (H. Schütz).
The Tower and Scaffold. Large fcap. 8vo. Price 1s.

Within Sound of the Sea. By the Author of "Blue Roses," "Vera," &c. Fourth Edition in one vol. with frontispiece. Price 6s.

WOLLSTONECRAFT (Mary).
Letters to Imlay. With a Preparatory Memoir by C. Kegan Paul, and two Portraits in *eau forte* by Anna Lea Merritt. Crown 8vo. Cloth, price 6s.

WOLTMANN (Dr. Alfred), and WOERMANN (Dr. Karl).
History of Painting in Antiquity and the Middle Ages. Edited by Sidney Colvin. With numerous illustrations. Medium 8vo. Cloth, price 28s.; cloth, bevelled boards, gilt leaves, price 30s.

WOOD (Major-General J. Creighton).
Doubling the Consonant. Small crown 8vo. Cloth, price 1s. 6d.

Word was made Flesh. Short Family Readings on the Epistles for each Sunday of the Christian Year. Demy 8vo. Cloth, price 10s. 6d.

Wren (Sir Christopher); his Family and his Times. With Original Letters, and a Discourse on Architecture hitherto unpublished. By LUCY PHILLIMORE. Demy 8vo. With Portrait, price 14s.

WRIGHT (Rev. David), M.A.
Waiting for the Light, and other Sermons. Crown 8vo. Cloth, price 6s.

YOUMANS (Eliza A.).
An Essay on the Culture of the Observing Powers of Children. Crown 8vo. Cloth, price 2s. 6d.

First Book of Botany. With 300 Engravings. Crown 8vo. Cloth, price 2s. 6d.

YOUMANS (Edward L.), M.D.
A Class Book of Chemistry. With 200 Illustrations. Crown 8vo. Cloth, price 5s.

LONDON:—C. KEGAN PAUL & CO., 1, PATERNOSTER SQUARE.